Food of the Sun

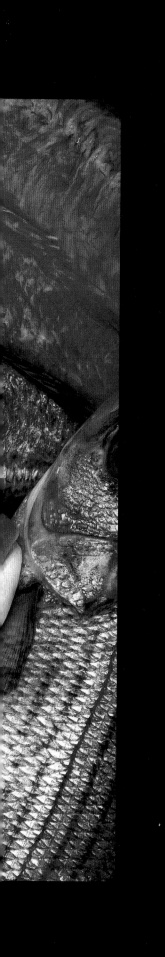

FOOD OF THE SUN

A Fresh Look at Mediterranean Cooking

by Alastair Little & Richard Whittington

Photographs by David Gill

Illustrations by Alison Barratt

Quadrille Publishing

Throughout the book recipes are for four people unless otherwise stated.
Both metric and imperial quantities are given. Use either all metric or all imperial, as the two are not necessarily interchangeable.

Editorial Director: Anne Furniss
Art Director: Mary Evans
Editor & Project Manager: Lewis Esson
Design: Paul Welti
Photography: David Gill
Styling: Hilary Guy
Food for Photography: Alastair Little and
    Richard Whittington with Jane Suthering
    assisted by Emma Patmore
Editorial Assistant: Penny David
Indexer: Hilary Bird

First published in 1995 by
Quadrille Publishing Limited
9 Irving Street
London WC2H 7AT
This edition printed 1996
Text © 1995 Richard Whittington and Alastair Little
Photography © 1995 David Gill
Design & Layout © 1995 Quadrille Publishing Limited

Cataloguing-in-Publication Data: a catalogue record for this book is available from the British Library.

ISBN 1 899988 05 X

Typeset by Peter Howard
Produced by Mandarin Offset Limited
Printed and bound in Hong Kong

CONTENTS

INTRODUCTION

Much of the charm of traditional Mediterranean food comes from its largely peasant origins, a simplicity that has been seized upon as an antidote to the complexity of *haute cuisine*. Ever since Elizabeth David excited austere post-war Britain with her alluring story 'of sea and sun and olive trees', the ingredients and cooking of the countries around The Middle Sea – as it was called in ancient times – have enthralled Northern Europeans. The food of the sun is vibrant, heat-tinged and forceful. It uses ingredients which are of a climate that both differentiates and defines them: the freshest grilled fish, intensely flavoured ripe tomatoes, warm basil, hot chillies, limpid green oil of first-pressed olives, elements of a diet now thought to be the healthiest in the world. Once these were foreign ingredients and difficult to obtain, but now year-round availability has moved them within the everyday reach of the supermarket shopper. This is cooking where marinated meats and fish are frequently plainly seared over charcoal. Salads are simple, redolent of the pungent herbs of unwatered and harsher landscapes. It is a world where the use of ovens is limited.

The topography of the countries that border the Mediterranean offers a convenient way of describing the food emanating from it. Being essentially local in character, on the one hand this reflects a highland inland culture and on the other a fish-based coastal resource. It is therefore of both the mountains and the sea. The internationalism of smart society at one end of the social scale and mass tourism on the other may impact on indigenous restaurant fare around the Mediterranean. However, we can still be entranced by its food traditions, which can be enjoyed – with subtle variations – little changed to this day, for these countries are still not great importers of global produce. Seasonal variation and proximity to source materials are more likely determinants of what people eat.

This is a book about a journey, not a literal passage around the Mediterranean but a deliberate culinary voyage inspired by the foods of the sun. It is about remaking recipes not to impose change for its own sake but for better taste, texture and appearance. It is about stripping away preconceptions and not cooking from habit. Then you can make a dish with the excitement of a novice but with the benefit of understanding the consequences of your actions. This is not invention but a conscious deconstruction and reconstruction of dishes that have stood still for a long time, unquestioned perhaps for hundreds of years. It does not mean our version is better, but it does mean a different slant, and sometimes you have to push things to the limit to be able to see the start point afresh. The idea of inventing dishes is nonsensical, for all recipes are in reality the product of a seamless development that is more historic than original. It is not about revolution but evolution, incremental improvements and modifications that are driven by a conception of food that is essentially simple, where flavour always comes first. The result is inevitably idiosyncratic for food is very personal in its interpretation.

Rolling away the rock of time and allowing the sun to shine anew on the ground this reveals carries risks as well as excitement. There are rules that have to be broken, but not before the reason for their existence is understood. This is strategic redefinition, a sympathetic procedure that allows us to celebrate the most exciting food fusions in the world. Hopefully, there are no surreal combinations, just harmonious marriages. Serendipity plays its part, too, since there are happy accidents as well as planned effects. What happens to be to hand will always influence a cook's thinking.

Rather than take the well-trodden Western path, our exploration emphasizes the Eastern road as we believe this aspect of Mediterranean food will exert the most profound influence on cooking in the next few years. Its influence is already being felt in California and Australia, is beginning to affect chefs here and will soon impact on domestic cooking internationally. Many of the dishes you will find in these pages reflect the historic cooking of Greece, Turkey, the Lebanon, Egypt and Morocco – countries whose culinary influences have cascaded throughout the Mediterranean. You do not have to look hard to find Middle-Eastern references in Italian, Spanish and Provençal food.

This book is essentially a practical work in which the emphasis is on what can realistically be achieved by the private cook working in a domestic kitchen. The reader will find specific national references, but our themes are most clearly expressed through naturally sympathetic groupings of dishes, allowing a menu to be eclectic without being dissonant. For example, Greek food has had a notoriously bad press, often for no better reason than prejudice, so all the more reason to look at it again. It was fun to return to basics, stripping out the mediocre, eschewing bad practice and emerging on occasions with something that pleased us by its refreshing difference. You might not find the dish in the country that inspired it, but frankly, so what?

Wherever the national start-point, clean tastes and fresh uncomplicated flavours rule. This food can be a picture on a plate – but only in the sense that what you see is what you taste, because no fripperies, frills or artifice get in the way. Mediterranean food imposes discipline in uncomplicated presentation, for its beauty is in natural austerity: a plate of fine plump beans dressed only with olive oil and salt; a skewer of marinated lamb grilled over wood, and flat bread which is to be eaten immediately it comes from the oven, still ballooned from the heat. A bowl of brilliant roasted peppers can be perfect, glistening with olive oil and sun splashed with basil. The idea of a garnish is alien: all that is on the plate is to be eaten.

People wonder about how two people write one cook book. Of course, only one of them actually writes the text but they both have to be sure they agree with what it says. In our case we started with talking about Mediterranean food for three months before arriving at a definition of what aspects would be most interesting to explore. Having arrived at the same vision we then worked separately; putting together dishes that fired us individually, before looking at what the other had done. At times there was an uncanny overlap, sometimes they were about as far apart as you could imagine. We cooked each other's recipes; were in turn rude, dismissive or enthused by what the other had been doing. Everything went into the melting pot and was changed in some way by the process. In the end we found we had each contributed half of the recipes. It was not planned that way, but that was what shook down.

The result? For better or worse, a fresh look at Mediterranean cooking.

1 SOUPS

A conundrum: when is a soup not a soup? Answer: when it is a Mediterranean meal. *Bouillabaisse* is a good example. It has soup elements, yes, but also the substance of a fish main course. Corn and Cumin Soup with Chicken and Roast Red Pepper? Change the amount of chicken and put some bread on the side and then ask whether you have a soup or a main course. In our European tradition, soup can be just as filling as any main course and it is interesting to consider when the idea of a soup as a distinct course at the beginning of a meal first became common practice. Almost certainly it was not until Victorian times and then only in grander houses. The word 'soup' comes from humbler origins and the use of bread to sop up broth is a distinction that recognized the food in the bowl was more liquid than solid. Before then soups were thicker affairs that would have contained pulses and grains, one-pot dishes indistinguishable from stews.

The separation and enjoyment of broth as an element in its own right was a sophistication and one that endures to this day in dishes like *bouillabaisse* and *pot-au-feu*. In our Mediterranean context we can find similar examples, of which classic *avgolemono* is typical. In Greece only the

broth, thickened with egg and flavoured with lemon, is drunk, perhaps with the inclusion of a little rice but never with the flesh of the chicken, which is eaten separately. We have decided to turn that on its head and eat the chicken with an *avgolemono* sauce – a heresy to traditionalists, but an example of the deconstructional thinking that is at the heart of this book, a case of look at what is there until your eyes hurt. Only then will you see it in a different light. (Sorry, Cézanne, you were talking about apples when you said that of painting a still life but it is equally true of food.) You will find that recipe in the chapter on poultry and game, not here in soups.

Among the soups that do follow you will find elements of sophistication and simplicity, say, in the Chilled Tomato and Couscous Soup; of peasant austerity in Garbanzo and Spring Greens Soup; and of absolute freshness in Iced Cucumber, Prawn and Yogurt Soup. Our *Bourride* may shock a Niçois restaurateur by its innovative reconstruction, but then they can continue to eat overcooked fish if they wish. You can try the difference for yourself before deciding whether the changes are justified. If you don't travel, how can you enjoy the pleasure of coming home?

BOUILLABAISSE, PEUT-ÊTRE?

The sea fish soups and stews of southern France, *bourride* and *bouillabaisse*, have a number of things in common: they share an intensely flavoured broth; are scented with saffron, garlic, fennel and orange peel; are often sweetened with tomato; and, of course, they both contain fish. But here is where the two begin to part company. *Bourride* most frequently contains John Dory, sea bream, sea bass, conger eel and monkfish, while *bouillabaisse* rather ostentatiously sports more in the way of spiny Mediterranean species, like *rascasse* (the red and spiny scorpion fish) and *rouget-grondin* (red gurnard) which, with deliberate orthodoxy, are served separately from the broth. This is eaten first, with toasts spread with *rouille*.

Marseilles and Nice separately lay claim to *bouillabaisse*, but then so does Toulon, where the addition of mussels and potatoes causes a *frisson* of disgust in Provence. Only in France could a society exist for the sole purpose of ensuring that *la vraie bouillabaisse* is not corrupted by revisionists, insisting that it must contain only Mediterranean fish and that these are served separately after the broth has been consumed.

This is all very well and quaintly Niçoise, but both *bouillabaisse* and *bourride* lend themselves readily to sympathetic interpretation and it could be argued that whatever we do in colder northern climes is merely imitation, that by definition it cannot be 'the real thing'. Spain and Portugal have similar stews in *zarzuela* and *caldeirada*, both of which combine different fish and shellfish, while Greece has its *kakkavia*. We think of these mixed fish stews as being rather grand, but they are all based on the elements of the catch fishermen could not sell and therefore ate as the family meal to save money.

Travesties occur in all seafood stews, most particularly when the fish have been overcooked, a heinous offence frequently compounded by leaving them to stand about while the broth is consumed. *Rascasse* and *étrilles* – the tiny crabs frequently used to boost the flavour of the fish stock – which make *bouillabaisse* unique are, anyway, not readily come by in this country and, alas, whatever you do in the way of emulation or imitation is unlikely to match the

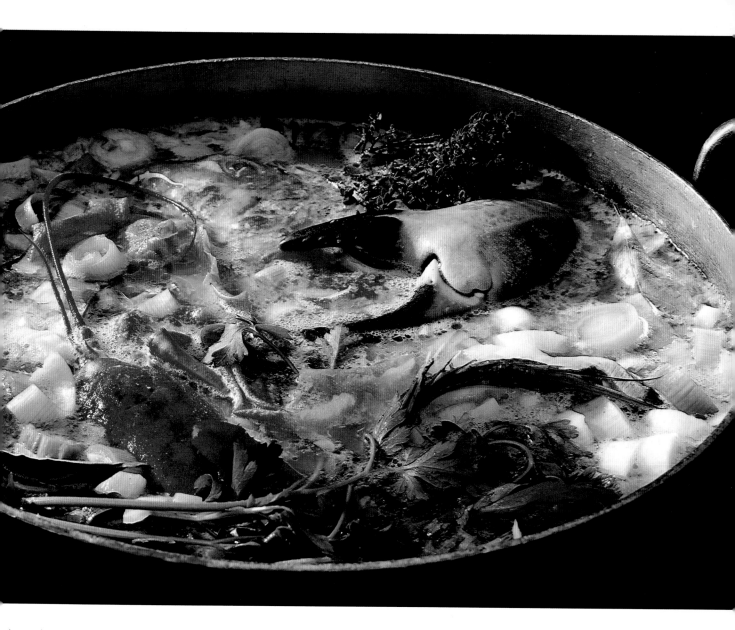

(ABOVE) Preparing the fish broth.

total experience of, say, a *bouillabaisse* consumed in one of those enchanting fish restaurants by the old harbour in Cannes or overlooking La Baie des Anges.

Without a magic carpet to whisk the reader there, we have danced somewhere between the two and since in the recipe overleaf the fish is filleted and served in the soup, we call the dish *bourride* – a fish stew. First an authentic broth is prepared, bursting with the flavours of fish and crab, glowing with tomato, pungent with garlic, fennel, saffron and olive oil. The fish is poached gently in this until only just cooked. *Rouille*, made potent by *harissa*, glosses the mayonnaise which is floated on the steaming surface of the soup on crisp olive oil croûtes. Peeping up through the broth are succulent chunks of red mullet and monkfish and tiger prawns, though cod, haddock, snapper and pretty well any sea fish could peep just as alluringly.

All the flavours of Provence and not a single bone to choke a queen's mother. La Croisette? Maybe not, but virtual Provençal reality to savour, *bien sûr* and who cares less whether it is authentic…

BOURRIDE, BIEN SÛR!

Keeping white fish heads and bones in the freezer, so that you have the wherewithal to make fumet or fish stock when required, is good kitchen practice. Always rinse the bones well and cut out the gills before freezing. Most fishmongers will be happy to give you heads and bones. Any white fish – like sole, turbot, brill, cod, conger eel, monkfish and whiting – are good for stock. Avoid oily fish, like mackerel, salmon or herring. Any shellfish heads and shells are excellent additions. A good time to make fish stock is when you have crab or lobster shells after another meal, otherwise buy a hen crab and bash it up with a mallet or rolling pin.

The amounts given are for 8–10 people, because this is a special dish that lends itself to sharing on a large scale. The addition of tiger prawns or langoustines (scampi) – say 3 per person – can add a nice luxurious touch. Ask your fishmonger to fillet the fish for you in order to give you the required 1.8kg/4lb fillets and ask for 1kg/2¼lb of white fish heads and bones for the broth. Apart from the fish mentioned, conger eel, cod and even coley are also fine.

Grated Gruyère is a common addition at the table, but it is strictly optional.

PREPARATION

First make the rouille: pour 2 tablespoons of boiling water over the saffron threads in a small bowl and leave to steep for 15 minutes. Put the egg yolks in a bowl and beat lightly. Start dribbling in the sunflower oil, a few drops at a time, until the mixture binds

1.8kg/4lb mixed white fish
fillets, including a
monkfish tail, sea bass or
sea bream and red mullet,
plus 1kg/2¼lb white fish
heads and bones

24–30 raw tiger prawns or
langoustines (optional)

8 ripe plum tomatoes

1tbsp Pastis, Pernod or Arak

16 saffron strands

FOR THE BROTH:

450g/1lb onions

6 garlic cloves

1 head of fennel

450g/1lb leeks

4 celery stalks

2 carrots

285g/10oz potatoes
(optional)

bunch of flat-leaf parsley

125ml/4fl oz olive oil

1 hen crab or shells of crabs
and lobsters

900g/2lb tinned chopped
tomatoes

2 sprigs of thyme

2 bay leaves

3 or 4 strips of dried orange
peel

1 bottle (750ml/27fl oz) of
cheap dry white wine

3 litres/5pt boiling water

FOR THE ROUILLE:

10 saffron strands

2 egg yolks

300ml/½pt sunflower oil

1tbsp Dijon mustard

1 lemon

300ml/½pt olive oil

salt and pepper

Harissa, to taste (see page
89)

TO SERVE:

1 thin baguette (ficelle), for
croûtes

olive oil, for greasing

115g/4oz Gruyère cheese
(optional)

together. When it thickens, add the mustard. Juice the lemon and
add to the mixture. Mix the remaining oils and add these at a
slightly faster rate, until you have a thick rich mayonnaise. Add the
saffron strands and their soaking liquid. Season and stir in just
enough harissa, a teaspoonful at a time, to achieve the heat intensity
you find most pleasing.

Meanwhile, prepare the croûtes: preheat the oven to 220°C/425°F/gas7.
Cut the baguette across into 1cm/½in slices. Brush them on both
sides with a little of the olive oil, arrange on a baking sheet and
toast in the oven until golden brown. Check every few minutes,
because they burn fast!

Prepare the vegetables for the broth: peel and chop the onion and garlic.
Dice the fennel. Trim, rinse and coarsely chop the leeks and celery.
Peel and coarsely chop the carrots. Peel the potatoes and cut them
into 2cm/¾in dice. Destalk and chop the parsley.

Prepare the other ingredients: skin the fish fillets, reserving the skins. Peel
the prawns or langoustines if using, reserving the shells.

COOKING

To make the broth: in a large heavy saucepan, fry the onion and garlic in
the olive oil until translucent, taking care not to let them brown as
this would ruin the flavour.

Bash the crab to small pieces (if it is live, aiming the first stroke
between the eyes is the recommended humane means of despatch) and
add to the pot or add the shells, together with fish heads and bones and
any skins. Add any prawn or langoustine shells.

Add all the vegetables, together with the canned tomatoes with
their liquid, the thyme, parsley (reserving a good handful for
garnish), bay leaves and orange peel. Pour in the wine and the
boiling water. Bring to the boil. Skim, lower the heat to a simmer
and cook gently for 30 minutes.

Strain into a clean saucepan through a sieve, pushing with a
wooden spoon to extract all the juices. Taste and season with salt and
pepper. With the addition of some puréed cooked fish this basic fish
stock becomes a soup in its own right.

Blanch the tomatoes for 60 seconds in boiling water, refresh in
cold water, then peel and dice. Add to the broth and bring to a
simmer. Add the saffron and the Pastis, Pernod or Arak. (Adding
these at this late stage delivers a much more emphatic taste – add saffron
too soon and much of its unique and expensive taste cooks out.)

Cut the fish fillets into large chunks and add to the broth. After 3
minutes, add the peeled deveined prawns or langoustines, if using.
Poach for a further 2 minutes (5 minutes in total), when the fish
flesh should be opaque and just cooked.

Transfer the cooked fish to a warmed serving dish. This makes it
easier to apportion.

SERVING

Place the fish in large soup bowls, ladle over broth and scatter on
some parsley. Offer the baguette croûtes and rouille at the table for
people to help themselves by spooning some rouille on the bread,
adding a spoonful of grated cheese on top if using, and then floating
the slices on their broth.

MINESTRONE DI FRUTTI DI MARE

In common with bourride, this is more a stew than a soup. It makes a satisfying seafood combination for a one-dish meal and if you want to enlarge it then no more than a plain green salad and some cheese are needed to round things off.

It is based on our basic fish soup stock (see the previous recipe) which you will have reduced and frozen for the day you decide to try this recipe. If you have to make the fumet first then use the cleaned bones and trimmings from the freezer. Fresh out of frozen fish bits? Then remember to ask your fishmonger for a kilo of white fish heads, bones and trimmings.

INGREDIENTS (FOR 8)

450g/1lb cod fillets
450g/1lb mussels
450g/1lb palourde clams
450g/1lb squid
1 carrot
1 onion
200g/7oz potatoes
1 head of fennel
1 celery stalk
1 courgette (optional)
1 hot red chilli
5tbsp olive oil
2 litres/3½pt fish stock
225g/8oz ditaloni (soup pasta)
salt and pepper
extra-virgin olive oil, for
    dressing
handful of flat-leaf parsley, to
    garnish

PREPARATION

About 4 hours before you intend to start to cook: put the cod fillets in a dish, sprinkle with a tablespoon of salt and chill.

About 30 minutes before cooking: wash and beard the mussels, discarding any which do not close when tapped. Scrub the clams. Clean the squid and cut into rings. Rinse and skin the cod and cut into bite-size chunks.

Peel and dice the carrot, onion and potatoes. Slice the fennel, celery and courgette, if using. Deseed and slice the chilli.

COOKING

In a heavy-based saucepan, sauté the vegetables in the olive oil until softened.

Pour in the stock, bring to the boil and then simmer for 10 minutes.

Holding point – you can hold the broth at this point for an hour or so.

Return the broth to the boil and add the pasta. Cover the pan and cook for 3 minutes.

Add the clams, cover and cook for 3 minutes. Now add the mussels, cover and cook for 2 minutes. Finally, add the cod and the squid. Taste and season with salt and pepper. Leave the lid off and lower the heat to a gentle simmer and cook until the cod is opaque and just cooked.

SERVING

Serve in large soup bowls, dressing each dish with 1 or 2 tablespoons of extra-virgin olive oil and with whole parsley leaves scattered over.

CORN & CUMIN SOUP WITH CHICKEN & ROAST RED PEPPER

Sweetcorn is now grown in many Mediterranean countries, though it is rarely eaten on the cob. Polenta — maize porridge and originally the food of the poor — is an obvious, if ancient, example of the way it is used. The widespread use of corn as animal feed has further helped project a rather downtrodden image.

This recipe uses fresh sweetcorn, cut from the cob and flavoured with roast cumin seeds, though you could use frozen corn instead. Chicken breasts and red peppers are pan-grilled separately and only cut into strips and added just before serving.

A pretty and appropriate garnish is blue corn chips, which come from the USA and can now be found in better delicatessens and some food shops.

INGREDIENTS

1 red sweet pepper
3 tsp cumin seeds
450g/1lb fresh corn (about 6 ears)
1 onion
1 garlic clove
2 tbsp olive oil
2 boneless skinless chicken breasts
1 kaffir lime leaf (optional)
1.1 litres/2pt light chicken stock
salt and pepper

TO GARNISH:
coriander leaves
few blue corn chips (optional)

PREPARATION

Blister the pepper on the end of a fork over a flame on the hob, on a preheated hot ridged grill pan or under a preheated hot grill. When cool enough to handle, peel, deseed and reserve.

Toast the cumin seeds in a dry heavy pan over the lowest flame for 3 minutes and then grind to a powder.

Cut away the corn from the cobs and reserve. Peel and dice the onion. Peel and thinly slice the garlic.

COOKING

Fry the onion in the olive oil until translucent. Stir in the garlic with the cumin.

Season chicken breasts and fry in a dry non-stick frying pan over a fairly low heat, turning occasionally. They take about 10–12 minutes and when done will feel quite firm when pressed with a finger. Let them rest in a warm place.

Add the corn and a lime leaf, if available, to the onions and cover with the chicken stock. Bring to the boil, lower the heat and simmer until the corn is just tender, which will take anything from 5 to 10 minutes depending on the type of corn.

Taste, and when the texture is to your liking, season with salt and pepper.

SERVING

Slice the chicken and peppers into strips and divide between 4 large soup bowls. Ladle on the corn broth and scatter with a few corn chips, if using, and some whole coriander leaves.

SPINACH SOUP WITH CHILLI GNOCCHI

Gnocchi can be light and, when spiced with hot chilli and fresh coriander, make a very Mediterranean addition to this deeply green fresh — yet satisfying — soup.

There is a view that if you include eggs in gnocchi they will go rubbery. However, the addition of just one size-3 egg does nothing but lighten the dumplings a fraction and ensures that the potato-and-flour base does not sog into the cooking water.

This is a recipe in which frozen spinach works if fresh is unobtainable. Onions can be substituted for shallots.

INGREDIENTS

675g/1½lb potatoes
4 hot fresh red chillies
handful of coriander leaves
¼ nutmeg
200g/7oz self-raising flour,
    plus more for dusting
1 size-3 egg
250g/8½oz shallots
450g/1lb spinach leaves or
    defrosted frozen leaf spinach
5tbsp olive oil
1.1 litres/2pt chicken stock
salt and pepper

PREPARATION

Peel the potatoes, cut them into large chunks and cook in a large pan of boiling salted water until just tender. Drain, return to the pan and shake over a low heat to dry off excess moisture.

Destalk, deseed and shred the chillies and add to the potatoes. Destalk and chop the coriander leaves and add these. Season with a little grated nutmeg, salt and pepper.

Mash with a potato masher or an electric whisk until free of lumps. Take out 2 heaped tablespoons and reserve these for thickening the soup. Add the flour and beat briefly to amalgamate. Add the egg and beat in.

Turn out on a floured surface, knead briefly and divide into 4. Roll each quarter into a cylinder with a diameter of about 2.5cm/1in. Shake more flour over, cover with a cloth and leave while you make the soup.

Peel and chop the shallots. If using fresh spinach, pick it over, discarding any blemished leaves and cutting out larger stalks.

COOKING

Heat a large pan of salted water to poach the dumplings.

Fry the shallots in the olive oil until translucent, grate in a little nutmeg to taste and add the stock. Bring to the boil and add the spinach. Lower the heat and simmer for 5 minutes.

Put in a liquidizer or food processor with the reserved potato and whizz to a creamy purée. Season with salt and pepper, return to the pan and keep hot over a very low heat.

Cut the gnocchi cylinders into individual dumplings. You decide how big you want to make them, but 2.5cm/1in lengths puff up nicely.

Poach in the simmering salted water for 5 minutes and remove with a spider or slotted spoon.

SERVING

Transfer the cooked gnocchi to warmed soup bowls and ladle over the spinach soup. A neat combination.

GARBANZO & SPRING GREENS SOUP

Garbanzos — as the Spanish call chickpeas — are greatly loved in that country, but not much eaten here. Most familiar here in hummus, the tahina-flavoured purée that has given supermarkets one of their most profitable ready-made offerings, whole chickpeas have failed to make the necessary leap into our collective food conscious to become other than an oddity on the domestic table. This is a pity, because they are cheap and have much to offer the cook, with their distinctly nutty taste and texture.

This soup is one which is quite dry and substantial, ideal for a one-dish supper. Good bread and olive oil are essential accompaniments.

INGREDIENTS

225g/8oz dried chickpeas
225g/8oz Spanish onion
2 bay leaves
4 garlic cloves
2 red chillies
450g/1lb spring or winter greens
300ml/½pt Quick Tomato Sauce (see page 60)
2tbsp sherry vinegar
12 saffron strands
225g/8oz red onions
100ml/3½fl oz extra-virgin olive oil, plus more to serve
salt and pepper

PREPARATION

The night before: put the chickpeas to soak overnight in plenty of cold water.

Bring to the boil in the same water, strain through a colander and return to the pan. Cover with fresh water.

Top and tail the Spanish onions, but leave whole and with the skin on. Add to the pan, together with the bay leaves, 2 peeled whole garlic cloves, the whole chillies and some pepper.

COOKING

Bring the contents of the pan to the boil, lower the heat and simmer for about 1½ hours, until the chickpeas are just tender. Drain through a colander, reserving the cooking liquid. Discard the Spanish onions and other aromatics.

Meanwhile, bring a large pan of salted water to the boil. Discard the outer leaves of the greens and cut out the stalks of the remaining leaves. Blanch the leaves for 3 minutes, refresh briefly in cold water and reserve.

Return the chickpeas to the pan. Add the tomato sauce, the vinegar and 850ml/1½pt of the reserved cooking liquid and season with salt. Stir and bring to a bare simmer. Add the saffron.

Peel and dice the red onions and the remaining garlic cloves and fry these in 3 tablespoons of the olive oil until translucent. Stir into the chickpeas and simmer for 5 more minutes.

Cut the greens into large strips and add to the pot. Stir all together and simmer for 2 minutes.

SERVING

Serve at once in 4 warmed deep soup bowls with parsley scattered over and the remaining olive oil dribbled on each portion.

Have more oil on the table for people to help themselves.

ICED CUCUMBER, PRAWN & YOGURT SOUP

Cacik is the Turkish word for a lovely salad made from diced cucumber, garlic and fresh mint leaves, seasoned and turned in yogurt. The same mixture is called tzatziki in Greek. If you thin it with a little iced water and add some prawns, you will have a delicate chilled soup which is as light and refreshing as it is quick and easy to make. Imported Greek yogurt is the nicest type to use for this dish.

INGREDIENTS

20 tiger prawns (or
  450g/1lb cooked Atlantic
  prawns in the shell)
2 tsp cumin seeds
1 cucumber, diced but not
  peeled
2 garlic cloves
575ml/1pt thick natural
  yogurt
about 150ml/¼pt iced water
20 mint leaves, to garnish
salt and pepper

PREPARATION

If using tiger prawns, shell and devein. Cover with salted water and swirl to clean, then rinse under cold running water and drain well. Cook in a preheated heavy frying pan for 1½–2 minutes over a medium heat, tossing until opaque. Remove from the pan and leave to cool. If using pre-cooked Atlantic prawns, shell and reserve.

Toast the cumin seeds in a dry heavy pan over a low heat for 2–3 minutes, stirring, and reserve.

Dice the cucumber small and put into a large bowl. Peel, smash and finely chop the garlic. Add to the cucumber, then pour over the yogurt and season with 1 teaspoon each of salt and black pepper.

Thin the soup with iced water until you have a pourable consistency. Taste and adjust the seasoning and chill for 1 hour.

SERVING

Ladle the soup into individual bowls. Arrange 5 tiger prawns on each or, if using the smaller prawns, divide them equally. Scatter mint leaves on top and strew over a few cumin seeds.

INGREDIENTS (FOR 6)

1 tbsp white wine vinegar
2 tsp sugar
4 large ripe plum tomatoes
1 litre/1¾pt passata
8–12 basil leaves
300 ml/½pt plain natural
  yogurt
salt and pepper
12 small basil leaves, to garnish

FOR THE LEMON COUSCOUS:
½ red onion
1 red sweet pepper
1 yellow or green sweet pepper
1 hot red chilli
small bunch of flat-leaf parsley
8 mint leaves
½ packet (225g/8oz) instant
  couscous
2 lemons
150ml/¼pt extra-virgin
  olive oil

CHILLED TOMATO & COUSCOUS SOUP

Two ingredients which have a natural affinity are combined to create a refreshing chilled soup that has heaps of flavour and a positively dramatic appearance.

PREPARATION

First make the couscous: peel and dice the onion. Deseed the sweet peppers and dice. Deseed the chilli and chop finely. Remove the stalks from the parsley and chop the leaves coarsely, reserving a few whole leaves for garnish. Shred the mint leaves.

Boil the amount of water specified on the couscous packet and pour it over the couscous. Stir for 2–3 minutes to stop lumps forming. Juice the lemon and stir in, together with the prepared vegetables and herbs. Stir in the olive oil and season. Chill.
Make the soup: heat the vinegar and dissolve the sugar in it, then allow to cool.

Meanwhile, blanch the tomatoes briefly in boiling water, then refresh in cold water. Peel, deseed and dice them.

Mix the passata and fresh tomato. Shred the basil and stir it in. Season. Now drip in the vinegar mix, a teaspoonful at a time, tasting after each addition until you like the balance. Chill.

SERVING

Put a heaped tablespoon of couscous in the centre of each soup bowl. Ladle the tomato soup around this, then pour irregular splashes of yogurt towards the edge. Dribble a little olive oil over. Tear basil leaves and the reserved parsley leaves and scatter over all.

OVEN-BAKED BRIAMI SOUP

The idea of cooking soup in the oven sounds positively surreal. Indeed, if overheard saying, 'I must just put the soup in the oven', expect somebody to reach for the jacket that does up at the back. The idea is Greek and has an interestingly different effect on both flavour and consistency. Emperor's new clothes? Check it out.

Briami can be served hot or at room temperature, with a choice of coriander pesto or zhug. Obviously, the soup can be made well in advance, though if it is refrigerated it should be brought out a good hour before serving, to take the chill out and allow the flavours to shine through.

INGREDIENTS
(FOR 6–8)

450g/1lb ripe plum tomatoes
450g/1lb potatoes
450g/1lb onions
2 yellow sweet peppers
350g/12oz courgettes
350g/12oz aubergines
55g/2oz flat-leaf parsley
4tbsp olive oil
salt and pepper

TO SERVE:
Coriander Pesto (see page 131)
Zhug (see page 91)

PREPARATION

Put to heat about 2 litres/3½pt of water. Preheat the oven to 150°C/300°F/gas2.

Blanch the tomatoes in the boiling water, refresh and peel.

Peel the potatoes and onions. Halve the peppers, deseed them and cut into strips. Cut all the other vegetables into bite-sized pieces. Destalk and chop the parsley.

COOKING

Put all the prepared vegetables in an ovenproof casserole into which they will fit comfortably. Season with salt and pepper and spoon over the olive oil.

Pour over enough of the boiling water nearly to cover, put on the lid and bake for 1 hour. Remove the lid and bake for a further 30 minutes. Remove and allow to cool.

SERVING

Once cooled to room temperature, stir in the parsley and serve from a tureen at the table in large soup bowls, allowing people to help themselves from the pot with a ladle. Serve the relishes in small dishes.

GARLIC SOUP

This is to be made when new-season's garlic is available, with its plump cloves still encased in soft damp skins and when the flavour, while indisputably powerful, is not yet demonic. Though the recipe calls for 30 cloves, they will cook to a subtle and gentle taste and the result will be surprisingly mellow. The combination of egg yolks and turmeric makes this a very colourful first course, the strong yellow of the soup contrasting prettily with the bright green chives.

INGREDIENTS
(FOR 4-6)

1/4 baguette
5 tbsp olive oil
900g/2lb onions
30 cloves of new-season's
   garlic
1 tbsp flour
1 tbsp turmeric
2 litres/3 1/2 pt chicken stock
yolks of 3 eggs
2 tbsp white wine vinegar
salt and pepper
16–24 chive stalks, to
   garnish

PREPARATION

Preheat the oven to 200°C/400°F/gas6. Cut 4–6 slices of baguette, brush them with some of the olive oil and crisp on a baking tray in the oven until golden brown. Check every few minutes as they burn easily. When done transfer to a tray and reserve.

Peel and slice the onions. Peel and chop the garlic.

COOKING

Fry the onions in the remaining oil in a large heavy saucepan over a low heat until translucent, taking care not to let them brown as this would spoil both the colour and the flavour.

Add the garlic to the pan and continue cooking gently for 3 minutes, stirring.

Sprinkle over the flour and turmeric, stir these in and cook for a minute before adding the chicken stock. Season with salt and pepper and bring to the boil over a high heat. Reduce the heat and simmer for 20 minutes.

Liquidize in a blender or food processor, return to the saucepan and bring back to a simmer.

Beat the egg yolks with the vinegar. Continuing to beat, add about half a ladle of the broth in a thin stream and, when well combined, pour this liaison back into the soup, stirring vigorously. The soup must not boil now or the eggs will cook and separate from the liquid, so remove from the heat before tasting and adding more salt and pepper if it needs it.

SERVING

Put a croûte in each bowl, ladle over the soup and garnish with 4 chives per bowl, cut into 2.5cm/1in lengths. They somehow look more dramatic against the bright yellow of the soup when not snipped too small.

2 MEZZE & FIRST COURSES

A chapter about *mezze* and starters begs the questions why and what is the difference? When asked about their impressions of what is typical Eastern Mediterranean food, most people will invariably identify *mezze* as a key determinant – a defining factor, if you like, which says this is something different from what you will find anywhere else. It is food that reflects a way of life and a culture of hospitality. When you pause for liquid refreshment you are offered something to eat with your drink. This can be so small it is almost symbolic, or it can be a *grande bouffe*, the sort of elegant overload that shouts out 'party time, eat until you drop'. Much more, it describes a food style and one that has an ancient heritage but is also, on consideration, about as modern as you can get. For better or worse, we live today in a food culture where people eat as whim or hunger dictates. Restaurants, increasingly, are no longer formal centres for ritual dining, but places to use when the customer dictates. It is a world where we – and not the restaurateurs – decide when and what to eat. Two first courses and no pudding? A plate of oysters and a glass of wine? Why not? The French have done it for years in the *brasserie*, and in the Mediterranean it is an eating style so taken for granted that to comment on it is frankly bizarre.

This section does not try to be all-embracing. Entire books have been written on the subject of *mezze* and there are people who would say that if you do not include them all then you are only scratching the surface. Our selection of dishes is small, but within it are all the keys you need to unlock a treasure-house of entertaining ideas – for *mezze* are building blocks in conception and ingredients, rarely in technical skill. You are the architect: make of them what you will.

The lessons of the past are not exclusively defined in terms of *cuisine grandmère*, the farmhouse of our imagination where dishes bubble gently all day long and the cooking is the product of constant and loving attention. We should be able to step back from such images and see them for what they are, essentially folk memories not absolute or objective truths. In *mezze*, by comparison, we have snacks or starters: a mouthful or a feast; food for every mood and any occasion. Here you will find dishes that can be turned into main courses by simply changing the proportion or amount of ingredients, for many *mezze* can be dishes in their own right. Conversely, as you go through this book you will start seeing how many things can be redefined in *mezze* terms. Then *mezze* becomes an attitude and a framework of opportunity, a place free from convention. It is an exciting point of departure and a fine place to begin our Mediterranean journey around the foods of the sun.

TIGER PRAWN
CHERMOULA SAUTÉ

*Chermoula is the heady spice mix that is one of the signal flavours of Morocco.
The dominant elements are garlic, cumin, hot and sweet red peppers, saffron and
coriander leaves. It lifts any fish or chicken dish and here, tossed quickly in a hot
pan with large prawns, makes them into a great first course. Fresh chilli is used for
heat and paprika for colour, but you could omit the chilli if you hate hot things.
Don't omit the ginger, though, as it makes this variation special.*

*This dish works just as well as a main course, which you might like to eat
with rice or maybe a rocket salad. Chermoula can also be used as a marinade for
meat or fish prior to grilling but, if so, leave out the saffron and stock.*

INGREDIENTS

4 ripe plum tomatoes
450g / 1lb raw tiger prawns in
    the shell
2tsp light plain white flour
2tsp ground cumin
1tsp paprika
1 glass (150 ml / ¼ pt) of
    dry white wine
1 kaffir lime leaf
10 whole black peppercorns
12 saffron strands
bunch of flat-leaf parsley
bunch of coriander leaves
1 hot chilli
8 spring onions
2 garlic cloves
4cm / 1½ in piece of root
    ginger
6tbsp extra-virgin olive oil
½ lemon
salt and pepper

PREPARATION

Plunge the tomatoes into a small
pan of boiling water for 30
seconds, refresh in ice-cold water
and peel. Cut the peeled tomatoes
into halves, scoop out the seeds
and pulp and reserve. Dice the
flesh and reserve.

Behead and shell the prawns,
leaving the tail on. Reserve the
trimmings. Devein the prawns and
put them in a bag with the flour, 1
teaspoon each of salt and pepper,
the cumin and the paprika. Toss
well to coat. Reserve.

Put the reserved prawn heads
and shells in a small saucepan with
the white wine, tomato pulp, lime
leaf and peppercorns. Bring to the
boil, lower the temperature and
bubble gently for 15 minutes.
Strain into another pan and reduce
over a high heat to about 4
tablespoons. Remove from the heat
and put the saffron threads in it to
infuse.

Destalk the parsley and
coriander and chop coarsely,
reserving some whole coriander
leaves for garnish. Destalk, split
and deseed the chilli. Cut it into
thin strips. Trim and cut the spring
onions into 2cm / ¾ in pieces. Peel,
smash and chop the garlic. Peel the
ginger and cut it into julienne
strips.

COOKING

Put a large heavy frying pan over a
medium heat and add the olive oil.

When the olive oil is hot but not smoking, tip in the pieces of spring onion, garlic, diced tomato, the ginger and chilli strips and stir-fry for 1 minute.

Add the saffron stock and the juice from the lemon. Stir vigorously and immediately throw in the prawns and toss for about 2 minutes, when they will be pink and just cooked.

Turn off the heat and stir in the chopped parsley and coriander. Taste and season with a little more salt, if necessary.

SERVING

Serve in warmed soup plates, scattered with the reserved coriander leaves.

SEAFOOD MOUSSELINE BÖREK

Börek – deep-fried filo pastry parcels – are a universal part of eating out in the Middle East and Turkey. In their usual minced meat or cheese versions they can be quite heavy and unsubtle, but these are altogether lighter and – with their luxurious filling of crab, prawn and whiting – have elegance as well as substance. They are baked in the oven rather than deep-fried.

The mousseline is a construction of classic French cuisine, where it forms the basis for quenelles – feather-light fish dumplings – but, since the filling does not have to expand in the same way, it uses fewer egg whites than usual. Puréeing the crab and half the prawns gives body to the filling and helps hold it together.

The traditional method of making a mousseline by hand involves lengthy preparation, and temperature is critical – if the mixture is not to separate it must be beaten over ice. The food processor is entirely more forgiving and makes the whole procedure quick and easy.

Whiting makes an ideal base, but you could also use hake, sole or monkfish. Everything should be as cold as possible. Try chilling the processor bowl in the freezer or put all the ingredients except the cream into the bowl and put it in the refrigerator for an hour before making the mousseline. Only take the cream from the refrigerator when you are ready to begin.

INGREDIENTS
(MAKES ABOUT 40)

225g/8oz raw prawns
2 shallots
8 pistachio nuts
handful of coriander leaves
1tsp cumin seeds
1tsp coriander seeds
$1/2$tsp black peppercorns
225g/8oz skinned whiting
  fillets
225g/8oz white crab meat
whites of 2 size-2 eggs
1tsp fresh oregano leaves
  (optional)
1tsp salt
500ml/16fl oz double cream
450g/1lb filo pastry
55g/2oz butter
lemons, to serve

PREPARATION

Peel the prawns and devein them, then rinse in cold water. Peel the shallots and cut into small dice. Shell and finely chop the pistachios. Destalk the coriander leaves.

Toast the cumin, coriander seeds and peppercorns in a dry heavy pan over a low heat for 2–3 minutes, stirring. Remove from the heat, cool and grind to a powder.

To make the stuffing: chop the whiting into pieces and put in the food processor. Chop the prawns and put half of them in with the whiting. Add the crab meat, shallots, spices, egg whites, coriander, oregano leaves if using, and salt. Process to a smooth paste.

With the machine working at full speed, pour the cream in through the feeder tube in a thin stream until incorporated. Scrape out into a glass bowl and stir in the remaining pieces of prawn and the chopped pistachios. Pack down, cover with film and chill for up to 4 hours, or until you are ready to make the börek.

To make the börek: remove the filo from its box and cover with a slightly damp cloth. Taking one sheet at a time, cut it across in half and put a dessertspoon of mousseline on each half and fold and wrap as described on page 39. Do not overfill or the package may leak.

COOKING

Preheat the oven to 190°C/375°F/gas5.

Melt the butter and brush the böreks with it. Place them on a baking sheet, not touching each other. Bake for 20–25 minutes, until the parcels are crisp and golden brown.

SERVING

Serve hot with wedges of lemon. They are also nice warm or at room temperature.

VARIATIONS:

This is rather a grand and expensive mixture, but you can dispense with either the crab meat or the prawns, increasing the percentage of white fish, and still end up with a very good result. Alternatively, you could move the dish even further up market by incorporating lobster meat into the mix.

TARAMA WITH
SHREDDED LOBSTER

The inclusion of a recipe for this — the most ubiquitous of dips — may seem unnecessary, until you do a little research and find how few people ever make it for themselves. For the majority it seems that taramasalata is a pink substance produced in small plastic pots and seemingly made from rancid fish oils, food dye and unpleasant chemical substances. This revolting glop is sold at a premium price, presumably to much laughter from the managements involved in its production and marketing — who doubtless find the idea of people paying for it nothing less than incredible.

The original taramasalata of the Eastern Mediterranean was made from the salted roes of grey mullet but today it is more commonly made from cod's roe. Even working with a blindfold and with one hand tied behind your back, leaving the other free to turn the food processor on and off, real tarama takes no more than five minutes to make and is delicious. It is pale golden in colour, a light and fragrant mixture of smoked cod's roe, bread, lemon juice and olive oil, all beaten to a creamy purée. The precise percentages of the ingredients are not fixed; for example, you can use more bread for a less intense — and cheaper — result. The texture should be thick enough to scoop up with bread, but how stiff you make it is up to you. This depends ultimately on the amount of olive oil you use. For a lighter finish, the purée can be thinned with a little water after the oil has been beaten in.

For a luxurious variation on this simple theme, shredded boiled lobster is scattered over each serving. If this sounds outrageous, settle for a little more parsley and some olives.

INGREDIENTS

4 slices of white bread, crusts
   removed
2–3tbsp milk
350g/12oz smoked cod's roe,
   skin on
$^1/_2$ red onion
4 spring onions
1–1$^1/_2$ lemons
about 100ml/3$^1/_2$fl oz extra-
   virgin olive oil, plus more
   for serving
black pepper
1 cooked lobster, weighing
   about 900g/2lb, or about
   20 stoned black olives
handful of flat-leaf parsley

PREPARATION

Dice the bread and put it into a bowl with the milk to soften.

Cut open the thick skin of the roe and scrape the eggs into the food processor (the skin is of no culinary use). You will have 115–170g/4–6oz of eggs.

Peel and dice the red onion. Trim the spring onions and slice across thinly. Add with the diced red onion to the roe. Juice one lemon and pour over the lemon juice, season with pepper and process at full speed.

With the machine still running, add the olive oil in a thin stream through the feeder tube. Switch off and scrape down the sides.

Taste and add more lemon juice if you want a sharper finish, then whizz again. If too thick, dribble in a little cold water with the machine running.

Holding point – the taramasalata will keep covered in the refrigerator for 3–4 days, but is best eaten within 48 hours.

SERVING

Spoon some tarama into the centre of each of 4 flat serving plates. With the spoon, spread the tarama in a spiral to fill the plate. Scatter over pieces of lobster meat or olives. Dribble over some olive oil and scatter over parsley leaves.

MEZZE

Gentle reader, on sight of the word 'mezze' do not grit your teeth and turn the page, your heart in the freeze-dried grip of reactive boredom. On the broad conceptual sweep we all seem to love the idea of mezze, but when addressing the subject in detail we yawn and say, 'Oh please, give me a break,' and close our ears and look for another story, a subject more likely to tease our culinary imagination and stimulate the palate.

The problem is that we have been sold the whole mezze thing so hard by writers like Claudia Roden who use words like 'ecstasy', 'sensual' and 'mystical' to describe the pleasures of savouring the mezze experience, making it sound like a cross between a seriously hedonistic drug and a religious trip. Mezze can be marvellous, but let's not over-sell with unnecessary hyperbole. As the woman watching Meg Ryan simulate orgasm over her food in the famous deli scene from the movie When Harry Met Sally tells the waitress, 'I'll have what she's having.'

Setting exaggeration to one side, let us return to basics and the real world where sensual and mystical feelings are not so readily conjured up, drink notwithstanding. And the drink is important because mezze are what the Americans call appetizers, food to go with drinks. They can be dead basic – a couple of greasy potatoes roasted in dubious oil consumed with an ouzo at an Athens pavement café table in a swirl of exhaust fumes are mezze – or they can be a frighteningly sophisticated buffet washed down with champagne at a smart party. They can be a bowl of salted nuts or a saucer of olives. Salads, too, can be mezze. So can little savoury pastries, like deep-fried börek, squid in batter, sautéed spiced liver and meatballs. But they can be much simpler: hard-boiled eggs or radishes dressed with lemon and sea salt are honourable examples. Purées of chickpeas, beans or fish roe, served with pocket breads, are very definitely mezze material. You can dress them up or down. Indeed, just about anything can be mezze, with the proviso that this is essentially food to be eaten with the fingers. Soup is therefore out and lamb casserole is not a candidate, but skewered grilled lamb most definitely is. Make things bite-size and that won't drip gunk all over people when they pick them up and you have functional mezze.

Of course one can err too far on the side of debunking the myth. Our aim is to emulate the best and eschew those greasy potatoes, though small crisp potatoes roasted in olive oil make a terrific mezze. What you have in the totality of the mezze experience is a great basis for party food

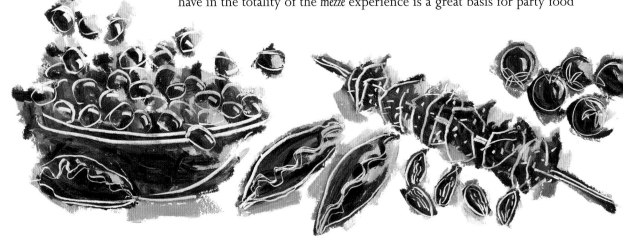

or a summer lunch, a good way to create something refreshingly different for your guests without being too self-conscious about the exercise. The concept has a freshness to it and an excitement if you really embrace the spirit of the thing. A carefully planned *mezze* will always satisfy all your guests because they can pick and choose the things they like. This is a meal for the pickiest eater, for omnivore and vegetarian alike. There will be protein in meat and fish and cheese, but there will also be protein in pulses and egg dishes. There will be raw things and cooked things; hot food and cold. Every individual component is delicious, but the whole is greater than the sum of its parts. A mouthful of sour here, of salt there... the ripe sweetness of a tomato can be followed by the richness of a spicy lamb tartlet. If there was ever food on which to graze then this is it. A spread of *mezze* also looks entrancing, full of colour and different tastes and textures. You don't like octopus? Fine, you don't have to eat it – try the coriander pesto chicken instead.

One word of warning, if you serve *mezze* then that is all you serve. Do not make the mistake of thinking they can be an *amuse-gueule* before dinner – if you do, people will burst somewhere around the main course. Do it right and your *mezze* are the main event.

Because some of the elements will be bought-in ready to eat or will only involve the simplest preparations, *mezze* offer great practical benefits to the cook who can spend as much or as little time and effort as expediency and love dictate. Your choice will also depend on whether you are serving food at a drinks party – where people will be standing up – or at a table, obviously an opportunity for food which demands plates and even knives and forks.

How many dishes you serve is up to you. It is not ultimately the range of choice which will make the meal memorable, but the balance you strike. You want to offer contrasting flavours and textures, and these days as many vegetarian dishes as meat and fish.

Simply by way of example, a big *mezze* could include, as hot dishes, skewers of grilled marinated chicken, deep-fried vegetables in a light batter with an anchovy and garlic dip, salt cod and moussaka tartlets, grilled cheese and *pizzette*. *Hummus* and *taramasalata* may be old-hat, but let us not forget how delicious they are when made properly, particularly when served with flat breads you have baked yourself. Then there should be dishes of salted nuts, olives, radishes, hard-boiled eggs and pickled cucumbers, and perhaps a salad like *horiatiki*.

You will find the recipes for almost all these things in this book. Otherwise, the idea of always offering a little something to eat when you offer a drink is plain civilized.

BRANDADE TARTLETS

These could be served in conjunction with Moussaka Tartlets (see opposite) at a drinks party or as part of a buffet. Both use filo — well, they would, wouldn't they? — but have pleasantly contrasting flavours.

A good use for home-salted cod (see page 109), though this is one occasion when you might like to try using shop-bought salt cod instead. If you do, remember you have about three days of desalination ahead of you before it is edible.

When you have a black truffle going begging, grate a little on top of each tart just before it goes into the oven for a sumptuously different twist.

INGREDIENTS
(MAKES ABOUT 24)

350g/12oz floury potatoes
450g/1lb desalinated salt cod
  (see page 109)
575ml/1pt milk
1 bay leaf
3 garlic cloves
1 lemon
small bunch of flat-leaf
  parsley
450g/1lb filo pastry
about 250ml/8fl oz extra-
  virgin olive oil
salt and pepper

PREPARATION

Put the potatoes in their skins in a large pan of boiling salted water and cook until tender. Drain and leave until cool enough to peel.

Poach the cod in the milk with the bay leaf for 5 minutes. Drain through a colander, reserving the milk. Pull off the skin from the fish and discard with any bones.

Peel, smash and chop the garlic. Juice the lemon. Destalk and chop the parsley.

COOKING

Preheat the oven to 250°C/475°F/gas9. If the filo is in the freezer, take it out when you turn on the oven. Brush a couple of bun tins with a little olive oil.

Put the fish and peeled potatoes into a food processor. Add the garlic, parsley, lemon juice and about 1 teaspoon of ground pepper. Turn on at full speed and slowly pour about 150 ml/$\frac{1}{4}$pt of the reserved milk in through the feeder tube. Now add just enough oil in a thin stream to give a thick, scoopable consistency. Taste and adjust the seasoning, if necessary.

Keep the filo under a damp tea towel and working with 2 or 3 sheets at a time, cut the pastry sheets into squares slightly larger than the bun depressions and lay 2 squares in each, arranging the second at an angle to the first so you have 8 points around the outside. Brush with a little oil.

Fill each with a spoonful of brandade and put to bake for 10 minutes on a tray in the oven. When done the filo will be crisp and the brandade browned and bubbling hot.

SERVING

Serve hot or warm.

MOUSSAKA TARTLETS

Serve these as an alternative to Brandade Tartlets (opposite) — or serve both when having a party — or serve them as a dish in their own right. The lamb meat sauce is that used in a classic moussaka, a Greek shepherd's pie, enlivened with aubergines and topped with a cheese béchamel. In this case, the mixture is the same but miniaturized — it can, of course, be used in as large a moussaka as you like.

A general word of warning when thinking Greek food after a holiday there: never use retsina when dry white wine is specified. The culinary consequences are too horrid to contemplate.

INGREDIENTS
(MAKES ABOUT 24)

450g/1lb aubergines
450g/1lb filo pastry
olive oil, for greasing
salt and pepper

FOR THE LAMB SAUCE:
450g/1lb minced lamb
4tbsp olive oil
450g/1lb onions
2 garlic cloves
300ml/$^1/_2$pt dry white wine
450g/1lb tinned chopped
    tomatoes
3tbsp white wine
    Worcestershire sauce or
    2tbsp ordinary
    Worcestershire sauce
    (optional)
2tsp oregano
1 bay leaf
1 tsp ground cumin seeds
4tbsp chopped flat-leaf parsley

FOR THE CHEESE BÉCHAMEL:
55g/2oz butter
55g/2oz flour
575ml/1pt milk
1 cinnamon stick
1 bay leaf
yolks of 3 eggs
55g/2oz grated Parmesan
    cheese

PREPARATION

First make the meat sauce: brown the lamb in 1 tablespoon of olive oil in a frying pan over a high heat, stirring, and transfer to a saucepan.

Peel and slice the onions and garlic. Sweat them in the remaining olive oil until translucent and add to the meat. Deglaze the pan with the wine and scrape into the saucepan.

Add the canned tomatoes with their liquid, Worcestershire sauce — that old Athenian standby — if using, the oregano, bay and cumin. Season with salt and pepper and simmer uncovered for 1 hour, topping up with a little water if it shows signs of drying out. Stir in the parsley for the last 10 minutes of cooking. Reserve.

Make the béchamel: melt the butter in a saucepan over a low heat. Stir in the flour and cook for about 3 minutes. Whisk in the milk. Add the cinnamon and bay. Simmer for 20 minutes, stirring from time to time. Pass through a sieve, discarding the bay leaf and cinnamon. Beat in the eggs and then the cheese. Season to taste and reserve.

Cut the aubergines across in 1cm/$^1/_2$in slices and dry-fry them in a non-stick pan until golden with darker blisters. Reserve.

Holding point — the two sauces can be held overnight in the refrigerator.

COOKING

Preheat the oven to 250°C/475°F/gas9 and lightly oil 2 bun tins.

Keeping the filo under a damp tea towel and working with 2 or 3 sheets at a time, cut the sheets into squares slightly larger than the depressions in the bun tins. Lay 2 pieces in each depression, the second piece at an angle to the first so you have 8 points around the edge.

Dice the cooked aubergine and put a spoonful into the bottom of each. Cover with meat sauce followed by a spoonful of béchamel.

Put the tin on a baking tray and cook in the oven for 10–15 minutes, until the top is golden and the filo crisp and brown.

SERVING

Serve straight from the oven, bubbling hot, or allow to cool to room temperature.

ANCHOVY & POTATO PANCAKE

The Italian name for this dish is tortino di alici e patate, somehow less prosaic than the English translation and closer in feeling to its subtle tastes and melting textures.

This is to be cooked when you can lay your hands on fresh anchovies. The next best alternative is to use the lightly brined Spanish anchovy fillets called bochorones. Salted and tinned anchovy fillets in oil may be substituted, but the character of the dish is then profoundly changed and you will need to use less salt when seasoning.

Boning fresh anchovies is not difficult and you use the same technique as for a herring. Indeed, you could use sprats — baby herring — as an alternative. Having gutted and rinsed them, press the back with your thumb along the length of the backbone to detach it from the flesh. Cut through at the head and tail and gently pull the fillets away from the backbone. If your fishmonger loves you, get him to do it.

INGREDIENTS

550g / 1¼ lb large double
   anchovy fillets
2 garlic cloves
2 tbsp chopped flat-leaf parsley
55g / 2oz fresh white
   breadcrumbs
2 heaped tsp fresh oregano or
   1 level tsp dry
450g / 1lb potatoes
2 tbsp olive oil
salt and pepper
1 lemon, to serve

PREPARATION

Preheat the oven to 200°C/400°F/gas6. If using brined anchovies, rinse them and then pat dry.

Chop the garlic and mix with the parsley, breadcrumbs and oregano. Peel the potatoes and slice paper-thin on a mandoline grater.

Brush a non-stick ovenproof frying pan with a little olive oil and lay the potatoes overlapping to line the pan.

Arrange the anchovies on top radially, like the spokes of a wheel. Season with salt and pepper, then cover with the breadcrumb mixture and moisten with the remaining olive oil. If using tinned anchovy fillets, then use less salt.

COOKING

Start the potatoes cooking on the hob over a medium heat for about 2 minutes, then transfer to the oven and bake for 20–30 minutes, until the surface is brown and the potato base has shrunk away from the sides.

SERVING

Slide the pancake out of the pan and on to a cutting board. Cut in wedges and serve warm, with a lemon wedge on the side.

MERGUEZ DATES

Bizarre? It would be if you used the sort of dates which people of a certain age remember as an early Proustian whiff of Christmas past, squeezed into a box the size and shape of a rodent's coffin, sticky with sugar and clustered around a plastic fork. But here we use fresh dates that are not sweet at all. The dates are stoned and the merguez mixture, traditional in North African sausages, is spooned into the cavities before they are egged, crumbed and deep-fried. They make great mezze and are a whole new spin on Scotch eggs.

INGREDIENTS
(MAKES 30)

30 fresh dates
225g/¹/₂lb merguez mixture
    (see page 161)
seasoned flour, to coat
2 eggs
55g/2oz fresh white
    breadcrumbs
vegetable oil, for deep-frying

PREPARATION

Slit open the dates down one side and pop out the stones. Fill each date with a teaspoonful of merguez sausage mix.

Dredge with seasoned flour, roll in beaten egg and then in breadcrumbs to coat. Put on a tray until all are done.

COOKING

Heat the oil to 180°C/350°F (a small cube of dry bread will brown in 60 seconds) and deep-fry the stuffed dates in 2 or 3 batches, for 5 minutes each until well browned.

Drain on paper towels.

SERVING

They are fine at room temperature, but nicest when really hot.

FILO-WRAPPED ASPARAGUS & PROSCIUTTO

Seventeenth-century artist and food-writer Giacomo Castelvetro, whose beautiful and extraordinary fruit and vegetable paintings would not look remotely anachronistic in the glossiest contemporary food magazine, was appalled on visiting this country in 1614 to find that asparagus was both expensive and a rarity in London's markets. If he time-travelled to see us today he would be a little comforted by its year-round availability, thanks to the miracle of jumbo-jet supply, but might still wonder at how few people still take advantage of its joys.

As recently as 20 years ago, the only asparagus most people ever saw at a party came out of a tin. This was pre-cooked to an odd and slippery consistency and smelt and tasted peculiar. Do not laugh, it is true, and if you doubt it, tinned asparagus is still sold side by side with fresh in every supermarket. In those distant days when we thought tinned was the real thing, it invariably came wrapped in thinly sliced and heavily buttered brown bread.

Fortunately a few culinary leagues have been marched since then and with the new-found availability of decent asparagus we can enjoy it in as many different ways as our imagination suggests. During the first month of its early summer season, to give it more than the simplest treatment would be a sacrilege.

The asparagus to use here is the fat Californian type that is available all year round, and two spears per person are sufficient for a first course. This is a lovely combination of textures and flavours, the crispy garlic pastry contrasting with the rich salty Parma ham and the fresh clean finish of the asparagus.

INGREDIENTS

2 garlic cloves
55g/2oz butter
8 asparagus spears
55g/2oz Parmesan cheese
8 sheets of filo pastry
8 thin slices of Parma ham
1 lemon, to serve

PREPARATION

Crush and finely chop the garlic and put with the butter in a small pan over a low heat. Remove after 10 minutes and leave for a further 10 minutes off the heat to allow the flavour to infuse. Pass through a fine sieve into a bowl. (You are going to use this butter to brush the filo and if you leave the garlic in it will burn and go bitter on the outside of the pastry when exposed to the high heat at which it is cooked.)

Peel and trim the bases of the asparagus stalks. Grate the Parmesan.

COOKING

Preheat the oven to 230°C/450°F/gas8.

Working one sheet at a time and keeping the sheets not in use under a damp tea towel, spread out each sheet of filo, brush with the flavoured butter and double over. Sprinkle with Parmesan and pepper but no salt (remember that the ham is salty).

Lay a slice of the ham on top, then place an asparagus spear across and roll up. Brush the roll with more butter, then cut it into 5cm/2 in lengths and put on a non-stick baking tray. Repeat with the remaining ingredients.

Bake for 10 minutes until nicely golden.

SERVING

Serve hot or at room temperature, with a lemon quarter on the side.

GOATS' CHEESE

Goats' cheese is produced all over the Mediterranean, although we tend to think of it as being French. The most superior *chèvre* is said to come from Poitou and the Vendée, where goats – known as *les vaches des pauvres* ('poor men's cows') – are kept for their milk. Goats are raised and milked in every Mediterranean country, even though they produce only 4 litres of milk a day at best, for goats are notoriously temperamental (the word capricious comes from the Latin for goat). They do, however, have the benefit of being able to thrive in the most arid and inhospitable conditions.

Goats' cheese is always made from unpasteurized milk, which is why the character of the cheese changes so quickly. When newly made, a goats' cheese is mild. As each day goes by, and the bacteria work, it grows more forceful; the longer it is kept the more pungent it becomes. Day-old goats' cheese dredged with sugar and sprinkled with rose water is served as a pudding in Provence.

Goats' cheese comes in many guises: round young cheeses, cylindrical and conical cheeses, cheeses wrapped in vine, chestnut or savoury leaves, bound with straw or rolled in charcoal. These cheeses also reflect the seasons, being fragrant in the spring when the goats eat young grass and herbs and more acidic as autumn approaches and the grazing coarsens.

Marinated *chèvre* is easy to make at home and the process enhances both flavour and texture. Buy young firm round cheeses that weigh between 55–75g/2–2$^{1}/_{2}$oz each. Put them on a cake rack overnight in the refrigerator to allow excess moisture to drain off. Next day, put them in a jar with 2 bay leaves, a sprig of thyme, 4 small dried hot red chillies and 12 black peppercorns. Cover with olive oil and put on a lid. Leave for a week in the refrigerator before eating, but do not keep for more than six weeks – or they will disintegrate. Serve grilled on toast with a salad of sharp leaves.

GRILLED & FRIED CHEESE

The sour salt cheeses of the Middle East are particularly good grilled or fried and are delicious in filo pastry tarts. In Greece, sharp and salt Kephalotyri is cooked with butter in small heavy pans in a ratio of four parts cheese to one of butter. The butter is first melted and the cheese then cut in strips and added to it. As the two amalgamate and start to bubble – but before the mixture browns – pepper is added liberally, followed by a squeeze of lemon. The bubbling cheese is taken to the table still in the pan and eaten scooped up with bread while still very hot and before it stiffens and becomes tough – an obvious precursor to fondue with a lot more charm. You can treat any high-fat hard cheese the same way. If you can't find Kephalotyri or Halumi, then equal amounts of Cheddar and Parmesan or Cheddar and Wensleydale or Red Leicester all work well. Feta, with its high water content, is unsuitable.

The simplest treatment of all is often the best. Halumi, a hard leathery cheese when cold, takes on a different quality altogether

(*ABOVE*) *Pan-grilled Halumi*

when pan-grilled or briefly barbecued. Heat a heavy ridged grill pan over a medium heat until very hot. Next to it put a non-stick frying pan over a low heat to get hot slowly. Brush a handful of trimmed spring onions with olive oil and toss into the grill pan, then turn with tongs to wilt and sear them. This takes no more than a minute. Put on a warmed plate and keep warm. Cut the Halumi lengthwise into 2.5cm/1in slices and lay these in the pan at a 45 degree angle to the ridges for a few seconds to mark. Turn over and repeat at the same angle, then turn for a third and last time, laying in the opposite direction to complete a neat cross-hatch on one side. Before the slices stick and start to melt, transfer to the hot non-stick pan, cross-hatch side up, and leave for a minute or until they start to soften around the edges. Transfer to the warmed plate, season with pepper, arrange the spring onions around the cheese and serve immediately.

Goats' cheeses can also be fried, but first need to be coated in an egg-and-crumb coating. The best for the job are the log-shaped cheeses, which you cook while still fresh. You don't want them to have matured too far, or they will be horribly powerful when hot. Cut across in slices about 2cm/³/₄in thick. Roll in seasoned flour, dip in beaten egg then roll in fresh breadcrumbs. Shallow-fry in olive oil, drain and serve on a salad of sharp-tasting leaves.

Tiganites tiropites, fried egg-and-cheese triangles, are another Greek speciality. To fill 450g/1lb filo sheets you will need 100g/3¹/₂oz each hard cheese, such as Kephalotyri or Parmesan, and Feta (its water content is actually beneficial here). Grate your hard cheese and put in a processor with 4 eggs, the Feta, ¹/₄ nutmeg grated, 1 tablespoon each coarsely chopped parsley and coriander, 1 tablespoon chopped chives and 1 teaspoon of pepper. Whizz briefly to bind.

Take the first sheet of filo, keeping the rest covered with a damp cloth, and cut into 3 strips lengthwise. Brush the first strip with olive oil. Put a heaped teaspoon of the cheese paste in the middle of the strip about 2.5cm/1in from one end and fold the filo back over it. Take the top corner of the fold and bring it across to make a triangle at the base line. Fold again in the opposite direction to make another triangle and again to the end of the strip for a final time to complete the triangle. Put on a tray, cover with a damp cloth and repeat until you have used up all the filling.

Heat sunflower oil for deep-frying to 180°C/350°F and fry in batches for 4–5 minutes until golden, turning once. Drain on paper towels and keep warm until all are cooked.

SPAGHETTI AGLIO OLIO PEPERONCINI

This is one of the simplest and purest pasta dishes. It was originally a poor man's meal, for the ingredients are literally spaghetti, olive oil, garlic and chilli. Like all brilliant flavour and texture combinations, however, it is now enjoying popularity in a market where cost is not the most significant factor. How spicy-hot you make it is entirely up to you and the chillies you use.

INGREDIENTS

4 small dried red chillies
4 garlic cloves
6tbsp olive oil
400g/14oz spaghetti
salt and pepper

PREPARATION

About half an hour ahead, put the chillies to soak in warm water.

When ready to start cooking, put a large pan of salted water to heat.

Slice open the chillies, scrape out the seeds and cut the flesh across into thin strips. Peel, smash and chop the garlic.

COOKING

Put the olive oil in a frying pan over a low heat. Add the garlic and chilli strips. You want to infuse the flavours in the oil, but not brown the garlic too much or you will get a bitter result.

When the water in the pan reaches a fast boil, cook the pasta for 8–10 minutes until just al dente (that is, tender but still retaining residual bite).

Drain in a colander, reserving some of the cooking liquor, and return immediately to the hot pan. (In any case, never drain pasta until all the water has evaporated – it should go back into the pan still with a coating of water as this contributes to the sauce.)

Immediately pour over the hot oil, with the garlic and chillies. Toss to mix and coat the spaghetti. If too dry, add a few spoonfuls of the reserved cooking water. Season with salt and pepper and toss again.

SERVING

Serve heaped in hot bowls. This dish is so good it is addictive.

FRITTATA

When it was called a Spanish omelette or tortilla people showed a reluctance to cook it. The tortilla most frequently served in Spain as tapas in bars is 90 per cent potato, so this lukewarm response is understandable. Since restaurants have taken to serving its Italian cousin, frittata, which usually comes without potatoes and is altogether less substantial, it is now much more fashionable and sought after. The Spaniards lean heavily towards the potato, pushing the eggs into second place; while the Italians, although favouring a thinner variant, have a tendency to overcook.

Perhaps this should be called a 'fritilla', because it is substantial but has a high egg-to-filling ratio and, being only just cooked through, produces a moist and creamy result. Whatever you name them, they are large filled omelettes which are allowed to cool to room temperature and served cut into portion-size wedges.

Our main version of the theme is flavoured with basil, Parmesan and spring onions and differs in execution from the classic frittata — in which all the ingredients are thrown into the pan at the same time — by being cooked in two stages. Cooking the eggs in two layers has the effect of holding the filling in the middle, while the protective egg base prevents it sticking or breaking up.

New potatoes are preferred, but old potatoes — peeled, boiled and diced — are also fine. The inclusion of Parmesan and basil push this omelette firmly into the Italian camp. Finishing the cooking under the grill produces a slight soufflé effect and delivers a nicely browned finish.

INGREDIENTS

450g/1lb potatoes
8 spring onions
8 basil leaves
55g/2oz Parmesan cheese
10 eggs
2tbsp olive oil
salt and pepper

PREPARATION

First cook the potatoes until just tender in a large pan of boiling salted water. Refresh in cold water and, if they have a full skin, peel while still warm. If using large potatoes, dice into 1cm/½in cubes; otherwise cut them into quarters.

Trim the spring onions and slice thinly. Tear the basil leaves into strips. Grate the Parmesan.

Beat 4 eggs in one bowl and 6 in another. Season both with salt and pepper. Into the bowl with 6 eggs, stir 2 tablespoons of the cheese and the basil.

COOKING

Preheat a moderate-to-hot grill.

Put a 22cm/8¾in non-stick frying pan over a low heat (this helps extend the life of the non-stick surface). When hot, turn up the heat to moderate and add the olive oil.

Pour in the 4-egg mixture and swirl to cover the base of the pan.

When just set, cover with potatoes and spring onions, then pour over the remaining egg mixture. Lower the heat and cook for 4 minutes.

Transfer the pan to the grill and continue to cook until done. It is impossible to be precise about how long this will take and the omelette should be cooked all the way through, but only just. During the grilling, reposition the pan 2 or 3 times to ensure even cooking.

Slide out of the pan and on a board. Leave to cool, but do not refrigerate

SERVING

Serve at room temperature as a first course.

VARIATIONS:
Once you have mastered the technique, variations on the theme instantly spring to mind. For example, instead of spring onions and cheese, substitute 2 red peppers which have been roasted in the oven with olive oil and garlic. Leave them to cool, peel and then cut into strips before adding to the second batch of eggs.

Other possibilities include lardons of cooked bacon or ham, masses of different fresh herbs, cubes of Feta cheese, diced cooked chicken breast and so on and so forth. Oven-dried tomatoes are good in this context, but not fresh or tinned tomatoes, which exude water.

EASY OLIVE OIL BREAD

Ask people which bread typifies the Mediterranean and they may answer focaccia or, on reflection and looking east, pitta. Perhaps the oldest known yeast-raised bread was baked in Egypt 1,500 years ago. A similar flat wheat bread, aish, is still a staple there today and is produced using the same primitive wood-fired brick ovens that make real pizza such a treat in Italy.

Baking is one of those things most of us prefer to leave to professionals and, in many cases, we are right to do so. Domestic ovens will not bake perfect baguettes, but this should not preclude making focaccia and pizza yourself – if you have a food mixer with a dough hook, they are really easy to produce at home. You can also make this dough with a food processor, though the results will not be as light. If you do, then put all the dry ingredients into the processor bowl and, while working at full speed, add the olive oil through the feeder tube followed by the warm water until the dough balls. Knead by hand for 5 minutes after processing, then proceed in the same way.

The kind of flour you use will materially affect the quality of your bread. You want a flour with a high protein and gluten content; both of which contribute to the texture of the bread, delivering a crisper crust and making it lighter by assisting even distribution of air throughout the loaf. High-protein flours need less kneading and, usually, less liquid when making the dough, and are closer to the durum wheat used in making pasta. Some of the best wheat for bread comes from Canada, where it contains an average 14 per cent protein content compared to home-grown wheat, which is closer to 10 per cent. Britain used to import a lot of Canadian flour, but restrictive EC tariffs have unfortunately put a stop to this on any significant scale and, as a consequence, white flour produced here is much softer than it used to be. This is true even of flours which are described on the packet as 'strong for bread baking'. Health-food shops are the kind of place you may find Canadian flour, or they might listen to your request and find a supplier. Summon the manager in your local supermarket and make your feelings known on the subject. Write to his or her head office. Come to think of it, have you ever seen a female manager of a supermarket?

This recipe makes an incredibly versatile bread dough which can be stretched and pulled for pizza or focaccia, put to rise in loaf tins for a light airy bread, or rolled for wheat flour tortillas or Arab-style pocket breads. It is also very forgiving when baking and can be cooked successfully at 220°C/425°F/gas7, though best results are achieved at 250°C/475°F/gas9. When baking bread, spray a little water into the preheated oven to give a steam lift and help produce a crisper crust – but be quick... the temperature of a preheated domestic oven drops very rapidly when the door is opened.

The recipe specifies 900g/2lb flour, though you may make it with half the amount. If you do, it is vital to halve the quantities of yeast and oil as well as flour. However, the dough does work better when made in larger amounts. Two pounds of flour is not expensive and in any case does not go all that far. Once made, the dough will keep in a zip-lock bag in the refrigerator for two to three days, but needs to be returned to room temperature before it is pulled or rolled out.

PREPARATION

Put 550ml/18fl oz of the warm water in the mixing bowl, together with the yeast, salt, sugar and oil.

Using the dough hook and starting at a low speed, pour the flour into the liquid and work for 6 minutes. If the dough is not holding and is pulling apart in strands, add more water and increase to a higher speed, working for a further 2 minutes until elastic.

Turn off and push the dough with your fingers. It should be quite springy and a little sticky. If too resistant to the touch, turn on again, add a last tablespoon of water and work for a minute.

Turn out on a floured surface and knock into a ball. Put this into a bowl large enough to allow it to treble in size and brush it with olive oil. Cover the top loosely with cling film and put to rise in a cool but draught-free place. Excessive heat should be avoided as this will force the dough and deliver a heavier result.

After 90 minutes to 2 hours, when the dough has risen fully, transfer to a heavily floured surface and knock down. It will be very moist, sticky and elastic when you take it from the bowl. Knead by hand for a minute. It is now ready to shape for whatever type of bread you want to make.

For focaccia (this amount will make 2 focaccia the size of Swiss-roll tins): divide the dough into 2 and fill the tins, pushing and stretching it to cover the surface to a depth of about 1cm/½in. Brush the surface generously with olive oil, cover with cloths and leave to prove for an hour before baking.

You can flavour the bread with rosemary or garlic by pressing them into the dough while stretching and pushing it into the baking tins. Alternatively, give the focaccia an Eastern flavour by scattering the top with chopped raw red onions, cumin, coriander and mint.

For pitta (pocket bread): cut the dough into 12 equal parts and shape into balls. Flatten with the heel of your hand, then roll on a floured surface into discs about 5mm/¼in thick. Dust lightly with flour and cover with a cloth. Leave to stand for an hour in a cool place to rise. Fold each disc in half and again roll to a round about 5mm/¼ in thick.

You can make an interesting variation by adding 1 tablespoon of honey to the mix before starting to knead the dough.

For pizza (this amount will make 3 Swiss-roll-tin-sized pizzas, enough to feed 12 comfortably): divide the dough into 3 and push the dough thinner; working from the centre, press the dough outwards until you have an even layer about 1cm/½in thick.

After its second proving in the tins, cover the tops with, say, chopped Oven-dried Tomatoes (see page 61), anchovies, olives and a scattering of finely diced buffalo Mozzarella. Keep this topping quite sparse – the aim is a base with a crisp bottom crust, not a leaden pie smothered with too many things.

While the dough is proving, preheat the oven (see below).

INGREDIENTS

575ml/1pt hand-warm water

1 sachet (11g/1tbsp) of instant yeast (we use Sainsbury's)

2 tsp sea salt

1 tsp caster sugar

1tbsp olive oil, plus more for brushing

900g/2lb strong white wheat bread flour, plus more for dusting

For focaccia: bake in a preheated oven at 240°C/465°F/gas8–9 for 8–10 minutes.

For pitta (pocket bread): bake in a preheated 240–250°C/465–475°F/gas8-9 oven for 5–6 minutes, until puffed and tinged golden.

For pan-grilled bread: proceed as for pitta, but cook in a hot dry frying pan for 1–2 minutes a side, pressing down with a spatula as it cooks. This encourages the bread to balloon. This type of bread can also be cooked on a barbecue or grill, but a heavy pan delivers the best results.

For pizza: dribble olive oil generously over the surface and bake in a preheated oven at 250°C/475°F/gas9 for 8–10 minutes.

CAPONATA DI MELANZANE

This cold sweet-and-sour aubergine relish from Sicily goes well with all cold meats, as well as eggs or grilled aubergines, and makes a nice starter with bruschetta. It is unusual in using green olives, where most sauces and relishes – like tapenade – use black. Caponata can also be the main feature of a dish, for example as a topping for crostini or bruschetta, or you can use it to fill börek which can then be baked in the oven or deep-fried. The amounts given can be halved but, as preparation time is quite lengthy and since it keeps well filmed with oil in jars stored in the refrigerator, there are sound reasons for making the larger amount.

INGREDIENTS (FOR 8)

450g/1lb onions
1 celery stalk
225g/½lb stoned green olives
4tbsp salt capers
100ml/3½fl oz olive oil
450g/1lb tinned chopped tomatoes
55g/2oz caster sugar
100ml/3½fl oz white wine vinegar
900g/2lb small aubergines
pepper
handful of coriander leaves or flat-leaf parsley

PREPARATION

Peel and dice the onions. Destring and thinly slice the celery, chop the olives and rinse and drain the capers.

COOKING

Fry the onions gently in 4 tablespoons of olive oil, until soft and translucent. Add the chopped tomatoes with their liquid and bubble over a high heat, stirring, until reduced to a thick paste.

Add the celery, olives and capers to the paste, together with the sugar and vinegar and simmer gently over a low heat for 20 minutes, stirring from time to time. Transfer to a bowl to cool.

Peel the aubergines, cut into cubes and fry over a medium heat in the remaining olive oil in a non-stick pan until lightly browned. Stir the cubes into the sauce and leave to cool. Taste and add pepper and a little salt, if necessary.

SERVING

Scatter with some chopped coriander or parsley just before you serve it. The addition of coriander is not Sicilian, but very good just the same.

AUBERGINE DIP

Aubergines like being turned into dips. It is one of the things for which God created them and they look happy when you tell them how they are going to end up. The purée is fine on its own, but one way to serve it is with Muhammara Purée (see page 50) and a bean purée, with all three on the same plate and some warm pitta bread to scoop them up.

The aubergines are roasted before they are puréed and, cooked this way, make a nice vegetable in their own right.

INGREDIENTS

100ml/3¹/₂fl oz extra-virgin
   olive oil, plus more for
   brushing and serving
450g/1lb aubergine(s)
1tbsp sesame seeds
2 garlic cloves
handful of flat-leaf parsley
1 lemon
salt and pepper

PREPARATION

Preheat the oven to 250°C/475°F/gas9 and brush a baking tray with a little olive oil.

Cut the aubergine(s) in half lengthwise and season the cut surfaces with salt and pepper. Lay the aubergine halves cut side down on the baking tray and bake for 20 minutes, when the aubergines will have collapsed and gone dark brown on the cut face. Remove and leave to cool, turning them cut side up.

While the aubergines are cooking, toast the sesame seeds in a dry heavy pan over a low heat. Reserve.

With a metal spoon, scoop out the aubergine flesh into a food processor.

Peel, smash and finely chop the garlic. Destalk the parsley and juice the lemon. Add these to the aubergine, reserving some parsley for garnish. Season generously with salt and pepper and whizz to a purée. Continuing to process, pour in the olive oil through the feeder tube. You want a scoopable consistency, so add more oil if you think it needs it. Taste, adding more lemon juice and more salt and pepper if you think it needs them.

SERVING

Spoon some purée into the centres of 4 flat serving plates. With the spoon, spread the purée in a spiral to fill the plate. Scatter over the toasted sesame seeds. Dribble over some olive oil and scatter over the reserved parsley.

GARLIC PURÉE WITH AUBERGINE CRISPS

Eat enough garlic and you will smell like a Marseilles cab driver. This is inescapable and fortunately no longer ensures social death in modern life-style-magazine-reading households. In this dip, the garlic is new-season's for preference, which is much milder in flavour and less halitotic in impact, while repeated boiling of the cloves further reduces the pungency level. New-season's garlic is available in Britain during May and June. Eat our purée and smell like the uniformed chauffeur of the mayor of Marseilles.

INGREDIENTS

4 heads of new-season's garlic
2 tbsp extra-virgin olive oil
150ml/¼pt thick plain
    Greek yogurt
1 aubergine, weighing about
    225g/8oz
sunflower oil, for deep-frying
salt and pepper

PREPARATION

Put the unpeeled heads of garlic in a pan and cover with cold water. Bring to the boil, strain through a colander and refresh briefly in cold water. Repeat the process, this time peeling the cloves after refreshing them. Repeat the process yet again with the peeled cloves. (If you are very keen on alternative medicine, drink the water in which the garlic has been boiled. Like all things which taste foul, this is supposed to be good for you.)

Put the garlic cloves into a food processor with the olive oil and a ½ teaspoon each of salt and pepper. Process to a purée, add the yogurt and process again briefly to mix.

Cut the aubergine across into thin slices.

COOKING

Heat the oil to 180°C/350°F (a small cube of dry bread will brown in 60 seconds) and deep-fry the aubergine slices in batches until crisp. This takes up to 10 minutes and sometimes longer per batch. If they are not crisp, remove and increase the oil temperature to 190°C/375°F and plunge the crisps back in for about 30 seconds.. Drain on paper towels and sprinkle with salt.

SERVING

The resulting crisps are horrifyingly calorific but, when dipped into the garlic purée, make the drinks you have with them taste very special indeed.

PULSING GREAT BEANS

Adzuki, borlotti, coco, cannellini, flageolet, black-eyed, mung, pinto, butter and kidney – the list is long and as rich in opportunity as it is in choice. Beans of every sort and variety, long scorned as the poorest sort of food, are now seen in a much more flattering light. They can be dressed up with sauces or enjoyed in their utmost simplicity, with nothing more than good olive oil, salt and pepper. They are one of the cook's greatest resources and, being in the main dried, are always to hand in the store cupboard. They are mostly inexpensive and endlessly forgiving. Overcook them and all you need do is purée them for a delicious alternative to potatoes or polenta; or spike with garlic and chilli and spread on *bruschetta*. Beans can enter a meal quietly as a first course or play a starring role as its main feature.

The people of Mediterranean countries have always respected and enjoyed their bounty and we, at last, are realizing just how much we have been missing out. Just why this country has only recently started to wake up to the wider culinary opportunities provided by pulses is unclear, for our food traditions have always included them. Northern fish and chips would not be complete without mushy peas, and split pea soup has always been a splendid way of making the most of a piece of bacon or a ham bone.

Today supermarkets offer us a bewildering choice, though there is nothing to be afraid of. They do have slightly different characteristics, but the flavour difference is not enormous and they all cook in pretty much the same way. Dried beans play a more central role in other food cultures, like Spain, where it is widely understood that they are at their best some two to three months after the initial drying process and where people are happy to pay a premium for them in the spring. French farmhouse cooking honours dried beans perhaps most famously in the *cassoulets* of the South-west (see page 164), while Mexican food would be unthinkable without its ubiquitous *frijoles*. The brown butter bean of Egypt's *ful medames* is that country's national dish.

Black-eyed peas with spinach, garlic and olive oil are a delicious way to start a Greek meal. Bean purées, fragrant with garlic and parsley and dressed generously with good olive oil, are delicious with lamb or as a first course in their own right served with warm pitta breads.

Lentils, too, are greatly favoured. The French *lentilles du Puy*, for example, have a beautiful green colour and a pronounced nutty flavour, while Middle Eastern cooking without lentils would be unthinkable.

About 450g/1lb of dried beans when rehydrated will make 6–8 servings. If you have bought them in plastic packets from a supermarket then they will already have been cleaned. If buying by weight from a sack in a shop, however, you will need to pick over the beans, discarding any discoloured ones and throwing away the odd stone which may have been included.

Now put them to soak overnight in lots of cold water – at least 3 times the volume of water to beans. In the morning, drain and rinse them. Then put them in a pan and cover with fresh water. During the soaking process many of the indigestible elements are drawn out of the beans into the water which is why we throw it away. Bring to the boil and bubble vigorously for 10 minutes, then drain the beans in a colander and rinse with cold running water before again covering them in the pot with more water. This has the double effect of removing the scum which will have been thrown by the first boiling and also makes the finished product less flatulent. In the case of red and black kidney beans, it also removes the poisons which are present in their raw state.

There is a quicker way to rehydrate beans. Cover them with masses of cold water and bring to the boil. Turn off the heat and leave to stand for an hour. Bring back to the boil, drain in a colander and rinse. Cover with fresh water and proceed as before. Unless the beans are ancient relics, this streamlined treatment always works, though cooking time may be extended a little.

Whichever method you have used, return the beans to the boil and skim. Then lower the heat and simmer, adding 4 whole garlic cloves, 1 hot chilli split lengthwise and 2 bay leaves, and cook until just done. Season with salt only towards the end of cooking. How long the beans will take to cook will depend on how old they are, but in most cases it will take between 50 minutes and 1$^{1}/_{2}$ hours.

Chickpeas take the longest time to cook, up to three hours; Puy lentils the least, often no more than 15 minutes. Small Oriental round black beans also take about 20 minutes, but large black beans can take up to 2 hours. With the majority of beans, taste at 50 minutes, then every 10 minutes until they are fully tender but not disintegrating. If overcooked, the best thing to do is to whizz them briefly to a purée in a food processor with some olive oil, herbs and a little of the cooking liquid. Whatever the kind of beans, if you do not want to serve them immediately, remove them from the heat when done and leave to cool in their cooking liquor, reheating gently.

After draining, discard the chilli, garlic and bay leaves. You can now choose how sophisticated you want to make them. One of the nicest ways to serve any beans is with *gremolata* (see page 92). Stir in the *gremolata*, tossing to coat the beans, squeeze over some lemon juice, then season with salt and pepper. Finally dress liberally with extra-virgin olive oil. The dish has fresh flavours, looks lovely and has a good balance. It can be served hot or at room temperature, as a salad on its own, or as part of a *mezze*. Leftover beans can be gently reheated next day and then puréed if desired.

MUHAMMARA PURÉE

Dishes like this are so easy and quick to make you almost feel you have cheated. Muhammara looks entrancing with its bright glossy red colour, spread on a large plain plate, scattered with snipped chives and dressed with more olive oil just before coming to the table. The seasoning, however, is all important. If it looks pretty and tastes of nothing, forget it. Muhammara is an object lesson in seasoning. With the right salt balance it is memorable; insufficient salt and it becomes red wallpaper paste.

You can do other things with this purée. Try it as a pasta sauce or on bruschetta.

INGREDIENTS

4 large red sweet peppers
6 garlic cloves
about 250ml/8fl oz extra-
    virgin olive oil, plus more
    to dress
75g/2$^{1}/_{2}$oz walnuts
75g/2$^{1}/_{2}$oz white
    breadcrumbs
2tsp sugar
2tsp ground cumin
1tsp hot dried chilli flakes
1tsp salt
2 lemons
pepper
1tbsp chives to garnish
pitta bread (see recipe on page
    42, or allow 2 ready-made
    pitta per person), to serve

PREPARATION

Preheat the oven to 250°C/475°F/gas9.

Halve and deseed the peppers. Peel and finely chop the garlic cloves. Strew two-thirds of these inside the peppers. Put $^{1}/_{2}$ tablespoon of oil in each pepper half, then use a brush dipped in this to give them a coating inside and out.

Roast the peppers on a tray for 15 minutes, then turn them over. Continue to roast until they start to crumple and the edges just begin to blacken, which will take another 5–10 minutes depending on your oven. When done, remove and leave until cool enough to handle, then peel. Alternatively, blacken and cook on a barbecue or directly over a flame.

Roast the walnuts in a dry pan over a low heat, then finely chop them. Put the pitta to warm in a low oven.

Put the remaining garlic in a food processor. Remove the stems from the peppers, cut the flesh into strips and put these with the cooked garlic, the breadcrumbs, walnuts, sugar, cumin, chilli flakes, salt, the juice from the lemons and pepper to taste. Whizz at full speed until you have a smooth purée.

Continuing to process, pour in the remaining oil, working until you have a consistency thick enough to scoop up with pieces of bread. If too thick, add a little more oil and a spoonful of water. Taste and add more salt and pepper if it is too bland.

SERVING

Spread the purée on a serving dish, pour over a little more oil and scatter over some snipped chives. Serve with warmed pitta.

CHILLI CHICKPEAS WITH LIME

Chickpeas have a distinctly nutty flavour and a much firmer texture than beans, but are cooked in exactly the same way (see page 48). Lime juice helps give the dressing a different flavour and is added to the chickpeas while they are still hot. Spanish chickpeas, garbanzos (see page 17), are particularly good if you can find them.

INGREDIENTS

2 hot red chillies
4cm/1½in piece of root
　ginger
1 red onion
2 garlic cloves
bunch of coriander
2 limes
about 100ml/3½fl oz
　extra-virgin olive oil
450g/1lb cooked chickpeas
salt and pepper

PREPARATION

Stem and deseed the chillies and cut into fine strips. Peel the ginger and cut it into julienne strips. Peel and dice the onion. Peel, smash and chop the garlic. Destalk and chop the coriander. Grate the zest from the limes and juice them.

COOKING

In a large frying pan, sweat the vegetables in 2 tablespoons of the olive oil until soft and translucent.

Add the chickpeas and lime zest and continue to fry gently, turning the peas to coat them and warm through. Add the lime juice and bubble until absorbed and evaporated.

Transfer to a warmed serving bowl. Dress with the remaining olive oil. Taste and season with salt and pepper.

SERVING

Stir in the coriander just before serving.

BUTTER BEAN BRUSCHETTA

*Call grilled bread 'bruschetta' and people feel excited about it, as if it was
something sexy and fashionable, a Naomi Campbell among toasts. 'You're going to
love this dish, it's so Italian, so honest somehow. Shepherds adore to snack on it
under the shadow of olive trees. Sit and eat with us.' Pause. 'Share.'*

*The crusty wheat flour peasant bread is held under one arm and sliced with a
blade that unfolds from a bone handle, and then toasted over an open fire of vine
trimmings. A clove of garlic is peeled with a deft movement of the fingers and
rubbed against the toast, which is then drizzled generously with limpid extra-virgin
oil. Plump butter beans are mounded on top with some shredded arugula. A bottle
of ancient balsamic vinegar is upended over the bread, part stoppered by a work-
calloused thumb which allows a few intensely flavoured drops to burnish the leaves,
followed by a final fine spray of shining drops of the deep-green oil. Pure flake sea
salt is sprinkled on top. Fine curls of Parmigiano Reggiano are scattered over. All
that is needed is a glass of garnet-dark Barolo on the side to complement its simple
integrity. There: bruschetta.*

*'Hey, let's eat. You want some toast with butter beans?' The answer is not
recorded.*

INGREDIENTS

225g/8oz cooked dried butter
    beans (see pages 48–49)
2tbsp Gremolata (see page 92)
4 thick slices of good white
    bread (Wonderloaf will not
    hack it)
1 garlic clove
4tbsp extra-virgin olive oil
12 arugula (rocket) leaves
4tsp balsamic vinegar
55–85g/2–3oz Parmesan
    cheese (to be cut from a
    whole piece)
16 black olives
salt and pepper

PREPARATION

Warm the cooked beans in a pan, add the gremolata and toss to coat
evenly.

Toast the bread and rub with a peeled garlic clove. Put on
individual plates and drizzle with half the oil.

Dress the rocket with the remaining oil and the vinegar. Season.

Spoon some beans over one half of each toast and arrange
dressed rocket leaves on the other.

Use a potato peeler to shave curls from the Parmesan and scatter
these over all. Place the olives fetchingly where you can.

SERVING

Serve at once with a steady hand, so the topping does not fall off.

SPINACH SOUFFLÉ FILO TART

*One of the most famous Greek dishes is spanakotyropitta, the spinach-and-Feta
filo pastry pie of a thousand Aegean island holidays, 2,000 Cypriot restaurants
and 3,000,000 attempts globally to cook it at home. The combination of spinach
and cheese has always made sublime culinary magic; for some of us, however, its
more obvious manifestations have been leaden and prosaic.*

*We must all be thankful that filo — or fyllo or phyllo — the wafer-thin pastry
of the Middle East, is now winking from every supermarket freezer cabinet. If you
had to make it yourself then forget it... far too difficult... but you can use
commercial filo, just like the best ethnic restaurants.*

*This recipe is the result of having enjoyed the classic Greek pie, but never being
besotted by it. Here the classic ingredients meet a French soufflé and are
transformed to create a perfect first course.*

*Obviously it makes a great main course if sliced larger, or a wonderful supper
to eat while listening to bazouki music. And it makes a seriously different breakfast
with a bottle of Saint-Véran. The tart can be eaten warm or cold. It inevitably
settles as it cools but, even so, stays lighter than any quiche.*

INGREDIENTS
(FOR 6)

115g/4oz cottage
  cheese
55g/2oz Parmesan
  cheese
450g/1lb spinach
  leaves
55g/2oz butter
225g/8oz filo pastry
55g/2oz flour
300ml/$\frac{1}{2}$pt milk
$\frac{1}{2}$ nutmeg
6 eggs
salt and pepper

PREPARATION

Put the cottage cheese to drain in a sieve. Grate the Parmesan.

Pull off any big stalks from the spinach and blanch the leaves in
lots of fast-boiling salted water for 30–60 seconds. Drain
immediately and refresh in ice-cold water. Drain again and squeeze
gently to remove as much moisture as possible. Chop and reserve.

Melt half the butter. Working 2 sheets at a time and keeping the
other sheets under a damp tea towel, brush each sheet of filo with
the melted butter and use them to line a 23cm/9in tart tin,
overlaying the sheets 3 deep to cover the bottom and overlapping
them at angles to each other to create an even base. Allow them to
hang over the edges a little. All this does not have to be too uniform.
Make a thick béchamel: melt the remaining butter in a small saucepan,
stir in the flour and then whisk in the milk. Bring to the boil, lower
to a simmer and grate in nutmeg to taste. Whisk from time to time

and continue to simmer for 10 minutes. It will be very thick. Season with salt and pepper and remove from the heat. Stir in the drained cottage cheese and the Parmesan.

Preheat the oven to 180°C/350°F/gas4.

Separate the eggs and whisk the whites until stiff.

Beat 5 of the egg yolks into the béchamel (keep the other in the refrigerator to enrich another sauce), then put the sauce into a large bowl. Take a scoop of the egg whites, throw it into this mixture and cut and stir it in with a spatula. Rotate the mix vigorously and then add the remaining egg whites. Gently but firmly cut them in until you have a light and airy mixture.

Spoon the soufflé mixture into the lined tart tin.

COOKING

Pull up any edges of pastry to sit against the filling and put on a rack in the centre of the oven.

Cook for 15 minutes and then test with your finger: it should be risen, brown on the surface and resilient to the touch. If it is still liquid in the centre, return to the oven for another 5 minutes or so. Transfer to a cutting board and leave for 3 minutes.

SERVING

Cut into portion-size wedges and serve immediately, or leave to cool and serve at room temperature.

BROAD BEAN FALAFEL WITH CHILLI & CORIANDER

A broad bean rissole sounds a pretty grim prospect and not one guaranteed to have your trencher-persons fighting for first place at the trough. Falafel – for our bean rissoles are the very same thing – has a more appealing sound and, when sufficiently spiced, makes a very good vegetarian dish which you eat with warm pitta breads, mixed salad and hot sauce just like doneri kebab. They have the added advantage of being capable of domestic interpretation, whereas your typical lamb doneri – weighing in at 100kg/220lb or thereabouts – presents an unusually daunting challenge to the private cook.

Properly, they are made from dried white broad beans or chickpeas, depending on where you happen to be in the Middle East. Here, for a change, they are based on frozen fresh broad beans. You can also buy a reasonable falafel mix from Lebanese and Greek delicatessens and it is a good idea to use this the first time you make them, because then you know precisely the consistency you are looking for before deep-frying. As you enliven instant polenta and couscous with judicious applications of herbs and spices, so shop-bought falafel can be easily improved in the same way.

The inclusion of eggs is an inauthentic touch, but one that adds lightness, prevents excessive oil absorption and stops the falafel from falling apart during frying.

INGREDIENTS

2tsp cumin *seeds*
2tsp coriander *seeds*
2tsp sesame *seeds*
2 garlic *cloves*
1 red *onion*
large bunch of *coriander*
bunch of *parsley*
2 large red *chillies*
450g/1lb frozen broad *beans*
4 *eggs*
salt and *pepper*
flour, *for dusting*
sunflower oil, *for deep-frying*

FOR THE MIXED SALAD:
12 spring *onions*
1 *cucumber*
4 ripe plum *tomatoes*
1 *lemon*
4tbsp extra-virgin olive *oil*

TO SERVE:
Pitta Breads *(see page 42)*
Harissa *(see page 89)*

PREPARATION

Dice all the salad vegetables and put them in a bowl.

Toast the cumin, coriander and sesame seeds in a dry heavy pan over a low heat for 2–3 minutes. Grind to a powder and put into a food processor with 2 teaspoons of salt and 1 teaspoon of pepper.

Peel and chop the garlic. Peel and dice the onion. Destalk the herbs. Destalk and deseed the chilli and dice. Add to the processor.

COOKING

Cook the broad beans in water following the packet instructions. They need to be well cooked in order to purée properly. Drain and add to the contents of the food processor.

Whizz, dropping in the eggs one at a time through the feeder tube. Take a tablespoon of the mixture and shallow-fry it in a little oil. Taste and adjust the seasoning, if necessary. You should have a very smooth paste that you can shape with floured hands. If it is too sticky, turn out on to a heavily floured surface and work until it achieves a malleable texture. Leave to rest, covered with a damp cloth, for 30–45 minutes.

Preheat the oil to 180°C/350°F.

With floured hands, take tablespoons of the falafel mix and shape them into balls, then flatten them into a round. Deep-fry in batches until browned and crisp outside, turning them in the oil during cooking. Drain on paper towels and keep warm until all are cooked.

SERVING

Serve hot with warm bread and harissa, accompanied by the salad tossed at the last minute in the lemon juice, the oil and seasonings.

SPINACH & PINE NUT FELUCCA TART

The original Neapolitan pizza, with its thin crisp base and restrained topping of tomato, Mozzarella, olive oil and basil, charms us with its integrity. The dough is just right, the seasoning balanced and the goods are delivered – consistently. We know precisely what is on offer and rely on adherence to the known formula. This is an important part of the pleasure, for we all know what horrors can happen when it is ineptly reworked... pineapple and peperoni on a deep-dish crust... one shudders in disbelief. This is a case, however, where having understood the essentially simple nature of pizza we can go on to experiment to good effect.

The following has vaguely Turkish qualities, with its spinach and pine nuts, while the goats' cheese produces a much sharper finish than Mozzarella. Is it a pizza? No. With the edges crimped, it looks more like a boat, perhaps a felucca, the Middle Eastern working sail-boat. Well, it does if you squint a bit after a couple of bottles of Buzbag, that attractively named Turkish red wine.

PREPARATION

Divide the risen dough into 4, knock the pieces down, flour lightly and leave to prove again covered with a cloth.

INGREDIENTS

450g/1lb pizza dough (see page 42)
450g/1lb spinach
16 stoned black olives
2 garlic cloves
1 red onion
1tbsp pine nuts
5–6tbsp olive oil
2 small round goats' cheeses
$^1/_4$ nutmeg
salt and pepper

Trim and wash the spinach, dry and reserve. Chop the olives. Peel and chop the garlic finely. Peel and slice the onion thinly. Toast the pine nuts in a dry pan over a low heat, stirring, for 2 minutes.

Preheat the oven to 250°C/450°F/gas9 – even more if you can, as hot as you can get it. Do this at least 30 minutes before cooking.

COOKING

Over a low heat, soften the onion rings until translucent in a little olive oil and reserve.

Heat the remaining olive oil in a pan over a moderate heat. Add the garlic, stir briefly, throw in the spinach and toss to wilt.

Roll out the dough into 4 long ovals about 30x20cm/12x8in.

Distribute the spinach between them and spread out, leaving a clear rim about 4cm/1$^1/_2$in wide all around the edge. Crumble the cheese over the spinach and scatter over the nuts and olives.

Pull the sides up and over towards the middle. Lay the onions in the exposed centre. Season with salt, pepper and grated nutmeg. Bake for 10 minutes.

SERVING

Serve hot, warm or room temperature.

3 VEGETABLES, SALADS & RELISHES

Trekking north, away from the sun, something happened that made vegetables of colder climates dance attendance upon meat. One could argue that choosing to eat vegetables in their own right is a contemporary luxury, since southern climes produced fruit and vegetables in colourful abundance in conditions where arable farming was and is impossible. People eat what they eat for historic, social, climatic and topographic reasons – determinants more significant than any conscious decision on the part of the consumer.

Whatever the reason, when it comes to vegetables the British have drawn the short culinary straw. Our food heritage brings plates overloaded with inappropriate combinations of meat and vegetables, jostling discordantly together, demonstrating a basic misconception and a failure to understand balance. There is, to this day, a popular restaurant in South London, famous for its huge serving plates of overcooked vegetables that, irrespective of season, always include roast potatoes, mashed potatoes, cabbage, cauliflower, carrots and peas. These are served automatically with giant grey roast meats – an invariable menu that, bizarrely, has many devotees. In doing so, it promulgates the ancient perception of vegetables as bulk, the supporting act forever eclipsed by meat in the starring role.

In the Middle Ages, vegetables were the food of the

poor. Rich people ate meat, dairy products, sugar and salt. With hindsight, it would be hard to imagine a more poisonous diet. Root vegetables were for pigs and the poor, while pulses were the last resorts of desperation. Oats – as Dr Johnson acidly remarked – were for horses, but in Scotland were eaten by the people. Yet, throughout the Mediterranean, fruit, vegetables, pulses and grains have always taken centre stage. Coastal regions have naturally featured fish rather than meat and where meat is eaten it is almost always in small quantities – except for those rare occasions, such as weddings and feast days, when meat consumption on a larger scale has symbolic importance, like the whole sheep served to honour guests in Arab countries.

Today, in the Mediterranean's harmonious balance of fish and occasional free-ranging poultry, lightly cooked or raw vegetables and unrefined natural produce, we recognize a diet among the healthiest in the world. It is high in polyunsaturates and vitamins and low in saturated fats. The contemporary Western industrial scourges of heart disease and cancer do not visit these sun-drenched lands on the murderous scale with which they prematurely terminate the lives of Britons, Germans and, to a lesser extent, North Americans (who have in increasing numbers taken the healthy diet message on board and are now being rewarded by a reduction in heart disease).

VEGETABLES GALORE

One of the greatest joys of the food of the sun is in the raising of vegetable dishes to a high culinary art. It is a process which always starts with the freshest ingredients, for Mediterranean cooks do not need sell-by dates to know when a vegetable is past its best. Watch somebody shopping for food in a Southern Italian market, how they feel and sniff and weigh the produce in their hands before choosing. No cling wrap or expanded polystyrene here to stand between the consumer and the consumable.

We are not, however, excluded from quality. One can find excellent fresh produce in our shops and once you have good ingredients then the only things needed to create taste sensations that can easily push meat into the background are a perception of what a dish should be followed by sympathetic treatment.

QUICK TOMATO SAUCE

Once upon a time there were tinned tomatoes and, lo, they were an common sort of food eaten in transport cafés with bacon and a fried slice. And Elizabeth David did visit the Mediterranean and discovered sweet luscious red plum tomatoes and was mightily wrought by them and did market the idea of them in her gastroporn works of the lean post-war years when Britons did eat Spam and other abominations. And we did read her words and agreed with them, but for many moons no such tomatoes existed in this land save in the imagination. But what of the lowly tinned tomatoes? Did they not come in the main from those same exotic lands of which Mrs David did write with such joy? Indeed they did and indeed they do; and without much work they can be converted into a very passable sauce that shouts, 'Food of the sun!' A teensy bit of sugar helps them shout louder.

In recent times we have seen the introduction of jars and packets of passata, which is simply peeled and sieved tomatoes. Passata consequently does not have an intense flavour and needs to be cooked down before it can be used to good effect in a sauce. After reduction, however, you will end up with a similar result to that achieved using tinned tomatoes. You cannot, however, create pieces of tomato by cooking passata, so tinned tomatoes give you greater flexibility of use. If you put the contents of a tin of tomatoes in the blender or processor and whizz them up you will have passata plus pips. Put this mulch through a sieve and you have passata.

Once you get in the habit of making this sauce regularly you can forget about tomato purée. Try dispensing with the caster sugar in the recipe and substituting 2 tablespoons of good-quality tomato ketchup to give it an extra flavour boost.

INGREDIENTS

900g/2lb tinned chopped
   tomatoes
4 basil leaves, shredded
1 bay leaf
2tbsp olive oil
1tbsp caster sugar
1tsp oregano
2tsp salt
1tsp pepper

PREPARATION

Empty the tin's contents into a heavy saucepan, add all the other ingredients and bring to the boil. Then lower the heat and simmer gently for 20 minutes, or until thick and syrupy. Remove the bay leaf.

Without any need to sieve or purée, here is a basic pasta sauce, a topping for pizzas and the magic ingredient for innumerable dishes. You can make as much as you like at a time by increasing quantities proportionally and, since the sauce keeps for ages in jars in the refrigerator, this is good time-saving practice.

OVEN-DRIED TOMATOES

Home-dried tomatoes are fabulous in salads, as a relish with cold meats or cheese, or on pizzas or open tarts.

To home-dry tomatoes, first preheat the oven to 150°C/300°F/gas2. Cut the tomatoes in half and scoop out their pulp and seeds. Sit them, cut side up, on baking trays, sprinkle with a little salt and caster sugar, then drizzle with olive oil and roast until most of the moisture has evaporated from them. Depending on how many you are drying at a time, this can take anything from an hour upwards. All domestic ovens have hot spots, so reposition the tomatoes from time to time to avoid burning any of them. Remove from the oven and, when cool, pack tightly in jars and cover with olive oil.

For both the home-dried tomatoes and the Roast Tomato Sauce below, if you ensure your jars and lids are sterile and that the contents are not exposed to air, the contents should keep for months – only they won't, because they never get the chance to enjoy such longevity.

Roast Tomato Sauce

Preheat the oven to 190°C/375°F/gas5 and lightly oil a roasting tin. Fill this with halved tomatoes, cut side up and tightly packed, then sprinkle them with salt, pepper and a little sugar. Dress them with olive oil and roast for 20 minutes.

Dice 225g/8oz onion, 4 garlic cloves and 1 hot red chilli and scatter these over the tomatoes. Dress with more oil and return to the oven for 20–30 minutes more, until the tomatoes have shrunk and the onions browned. During this second roasting period, check at regular intervals to ensure that the tomatoes are not burning. If you allow them to burn you will make the sauce bitter and unpleasant.

Remove from the oven and, when cool, purée and sieve. Then pack in jars and film the surface with oil before storing. You can ring all kinds of changes to your sauce at the puréeing stage. Try adding anchovies or stoned black olives or basil.

PEPPERS

Mediterranean food is defined by so many things. It is indisputably of the sun, and vegetables have always played a central role. Olive oil is an absolute in the mix and, for all who live around the coast, fish takes pre-eminence over meat. Garlic is a prevalent flavouring agent and herbs, like parsley and coriander, feature almost in the sense of vegetables and certainly as salad elements in their own right. We know at once what is being implied in culinary terms when somebody uses the word Mediterranean as an adjective, but it is a suggestion of something rather than an absolute definition – a generalization rather than a specification. Thus, with the possible exception of the truly ubiquitous olive, you cannot isolate a single ingredient and ascribe to it uniquely Mediterranean properties. For a start, many natural foods like tomatoes did not originate from this part of the world, yet the idea of Mediterranean food without them would be unthinkable.

In this context, and from among a long list of candidates, the sweet red pepper takes pride of place. Rich in vitamins A and C, this pepper is called a 'bell pepper' in the USA, a *poivron* in France and a *pimiento* in Spain. They are all the same *Capsicum annuum*, produced by annual shrubs and, like tomatoes, technically a fruit but used as a vegetable.

Red sweet peppers start their life as seeds which grow first into green peppers before ripening to red or yellow. Once picked, they have a relatively long shelf-life, which can be further extended by refrigeration. Green peppers will continue to ripen after picking and may start to streak with red if left long enough. Eventually they wither, as moisture is lost, and if kept too long will go bad. Rotting can be prevented by sun- or oven-drying and, in Spain, sweet peppers are often peeled and canned. This book contains only one recipe – Chilled Tomato and Couscous Soup (see page 18) – which uses green peppers and, even then, only in the tiniest amount because they are literally unripe and in large quantities generally very indigestible. On that occasion, their minimal inclusion had as much to do with appearance as taste.

When cooked, the green pepper takes on an unpalatable brown and dirty look, has neither joy nor sweetness in its make-up and, in its immaturity, what passes for flavour lacks definition or force, being merely insipid and watery. The yellow pepper is quite sweet and in certain combinations, like the Roast Yellow Pepper and Chilli Salad (see page 80), its colour is a determinant in its selection.

In order to enjoy peppers at their best they must first be charred or grilled until the skins have blackened and blistered. While a grill or ridged grill pan can do the job adequately, it is actually better to put the peppers in direct contact with a flame. You can do them one at a time on a skewer, but the most efficient device is to squeeze the whole peppers into one of those hinged metal frames like the ones for doing toast on an Aga. Let them really blacken. They look hideous and the first time you do it you will think you have taken them too far, but do not worry. Next, to make them virtually self-peeling, put them while still

hot from the flame into a bowl and cover it with cling film and leave
for 10 minutes. Scrape and pull off the crusty exterior to reveal the
pristine red beneath.

Cut a piece off and eat it still warm and you will be blown away
by the taste and colour and texture of it. This is a moment of truth
and you feel chastened, because you could so easily have stopped at
the point of sneering disbelief, and at the same time grateful that
you went through the motions. Peppers treated this way are magic:
sweet, intense, smoky without the slightest bitter edge from the
charring. They look beautiful and once you have tried them you are
unlikely ever to eat a raw unskinned pepper again. Use skin charring
and peeling as an automatic preliminary *mise en place* for peppers
before adding them to cooked dishes for an equally startling
improvement in the end result.

GRILLED VEGETABLES

The most prosaic titles can conceal the most extraordinary culinary revelations. Grilled vegetables are sensational fare and so easy to do that they should not be left to restaurants to profit from. Where food-writers, too frequently, gild their lilies with purple prose to sell an idea, here is one that readily sells itself without hyperbole.

Grilled vegetables? It is a functional and accurate description, but one that conceals a rich and fertile ground of opportunity, a simple technique which delivers the goods every time. It is not haute cuisine, just great food. All you need is a ridged grill pan or a barbecue. For dressing, nothing more than lemon juice, a little garlic and some good olive oil. A large plate covered in grilled vegetables makes a splendid summer lunch.

INGREDIENTS

2 garlic cloves
150ml/$\frac{1}{4}$pt extra-virgin olive oil, plus more for brushing and serving
2 red sweet peppers
2 yellow sweet peppers
4 small aubergines
4 courgettes
4 large field mushrooms
2 large onions
16 halves of Oven-dried Tomatoes (see page 61)
2 lemons
salt and pepper
12 large basil leaves, to garnish

PREPARATION

Peel, and chop the garlic and put into a bowl. Pour olive oil over the garlic and stir. Leave to infuse. Preheat a ridged grilling pan or barbecue.

Grill the peppers whole over a flame or on a very hot ridged grill pan, turning frequently, till charred and blistered. Put them in a bowl, cover with cling film or a lid and leave for 20 minutes until the steam they generate loosens the blackened and blistered skins.

Pull out the stem, which will come away neatly with the seeds. Cut the flesh into bite-sized rectangles and use to cover the centre of a serving dish, alternating yellow with red.

Slice the aubergine lengthwise. Grill these slices dry until soft, brown and blistered. Arrange around the peppers.

Top and tail the courgettes and, if small, cut in half lengthwise. If large, cut into 4 slices. Grill dry, starting on the cut surfaces and turning at intervals until done.

Peel and remove the stems from the mushrooms. Grill dry, cap side down, until the beads of moisture start to exude into the stem point. Turn and cook the underside for 1 minute. Then transfer to paper towels, cap upwards, to drain.

Slice the onion across into solid discs, discarding the ends. Turn the heat right down, brush the onion discs with oil and grill them slowly, otherwise they will burn on the outside before they are cooked through. Arrange them overlapping down the centre of the plate.

Conclude by butterflying the home-dried tomatoes by cutting them almost all the way through their middles and grill briefly, turning once.

Season the vegetables with salt and pepper, dress with the juice of one of the lemons, then dribble the garlic-infused olive oil over all of them. Pour over more oil if you think this amount looks weedy.

SERVING

Scatter basil over and serve at room temperature with a wedge of lemon for everybody.

THE PRIEST FAINTS AGAIN

The literal translation of Imam bayildi, the name for this Turkish platter of cold tomato-stuffed aubergines, is 'the priest fainted' – not overcome with flatulence as a misreading might suggest. And how many times have you heard that before and thought what a sheltered life the Imam must have led? It is odd how many cultures have dishes called things to do with clerics and their fondness for the table. The Italians, for example, have a dish of spinach and ricotta dumplings called 'priest throttlers'.

In this case the Imam was so taken with how delicious the aubergines were he swooned, presumably after eating rather too many of them. Turkish readers may question the authenticity of this recipe. This is because, like so many dishes in the book, we have deconstructed the myth and remade it afresh. Now you have something which is both special and pretty to look at. Any priest eating it is entitled to faint, if not fart.

INGREDIENTS

6 small aubergines
450g/1lb onions
4 garlic cloves
6 large ripe plum tomatoes
bunch of flat-leaf parsley
100ml/3$^{1}/_{2}$fl oz extra-
   virgin olive oil
1tsp sugar
2 lemons
salt and pepper

PREPARATION

Choose small purple-black, smooth-skinned and plump aubergines and cut off both ends. Forget about all this salting nonsense: if the aubergines are old and bitter, no amount of salting is going to improve them. Peel 1cm/$^{1}/_{2}$in wide strips lengthwise to produce a striped effect. Cut a deep slit along one side of each aubergine to make a pocket, being careful not to cut all the way through.

Peel and thinly slice the onions and peel, smash and chop the garlic. Blanch, peel and chop the tomatoes. Destalk and chop the parsley.

COOKING

Preheat the oven to 200°C/400°F/gas6.

Fry the onions and garlic gently in 4 tablespoons of the olive oil, until soft and translucent.

Add the peeled and chopped tomatoes, season with salt, pepper and the sugar and continue to cook, stirring, until the water in the tomatoes has evaporated. Stir in the parsley, reserving some for garnish. Add the juice from one of the lemons and leave to cool.

Put the remaining olive oil in another pan and fry the aubergines over a moderate heat to seal, turning to brown lightly all over. Remove and drain.

When the aubergines are cool enough to handle, carefully open each along the cut and spoon in as much stuffing as you can.

Arrange them, cut side up, in an ovenproof dish just large enough for them to sit snugly without falling over. Spread any remaining stuffing over the top, pour over 300ml/$^{1}/_{2}$pt of cold water, cover loosely with foil and bake for about 45 minutes, when they should be tender but not collapsing. Check from time to time that they have not dried out, adding a little more water if necessary.

Take out and leave to cool.

SERVING

Garnish with some of the reserved chopped flat-leaf parsley and serve at room temperature as a first course, with the other lemon cut into wedges and with warm pitta bread or toasted ciabatta.

BLACK-EYED PEAS & SPINACH

This is a particularly good combination, which is as nice cold as it is hot. If accompanying a rich meat dish, like the Herb-braised Rabbit on page 138, then do not use more oil than is specified here.

If serving only 4, you could make half the amount given below, but since the dish will keep happily in the refrigerator for 2 days it is as well to make this large quantity to eat first hot, and then later cold as a salad or as part of a mezze. It can also be reheated and puréed with excellent results. If eating cold or as a purée, add more olive oil.

INGREDIENTS (FOR 8)

450g/1lb black-eyed peas
450g/1lb spinach
1 red onion
2 garlic cloves
5tbsp olive oil
salt and pepper
2 lemons, to serve

PREPARATION

The day before: put the peas to soak in cold water overnight.
The next day: destalk the spinach. Peel and dice the onion and garlic.

COOKING

Bring the peas to the boil in plenty of water, strain immediately in a colander. Rinse, return to the pan and cover with fresh cold water. Bring to the boil again, lower to a simmer and cook, tasting after 20–30 minutes when they may be done. If not, continue to simmer until they are, but checking every 5 minutes as black-eyed peas generally do not need such long cooking as other beans.

Blanch the spinach for 30 seconds in a large pan of rapidly boiling salted water, then refresh in cold water. Drain in a colander.

Fry the onion and garlic in the olive oil until translucent. Add to the beans and stir in the spinach. Season with salt and pepper and allow the spinach to warm through for a minute or so.

SERVING

Serve in bowls with lemon wedges as a first course.

CASTRATI OR BABY ARTICHOKES

Artichokes are Mediterranean in origin and, while they are now common enough in supermarkets and available all year round, baby artichokes – which are quaintly called *castrati* in Italy and picked before a choke has formed – are harder to come by. Their European season is from April to early June and they make a delicious simple first course. They are available brined in tins and jars, which are actually quite good but expensive.

To prepare baby artichokes, first pull off and discard the outer leaves to reveal the pale inner leaves. Cut off the top half of the globe and all but about 2cm/³⁄₄ in of stalk, peeling what is left. To prevent discoloration, put them into a bowl of water acidulated with lemon juice or vinegar until ready to cook.

In an enamelled or stainless steel saucepan, put a glass of dry white wine with 1 quartered lemon, 1 diced onion, 1 diced carrot and 1 diced celery stalk. Put in 2 or 3 bay leaves, about 12 mint leaves, a sprig of rosemary and some salt and pepper. Add the trimmed artichokes and barely cover with cold water, then film the surface with a little olive oil.

Put a suitably sized plate on top to push the artichokes beneath the surface and bring to the boil. Lower the temperature and simmer gently for 10 minutes.

Put on a lid, turn off the heat and leave the cooked baby artichokes to cool in the liquor. When cool, take out the artichokes and put into a plastic container. Strain the cooking liquid over. The baby artichokes will now keep covered in the refrigerator for up to a week or longer.

SPICED CAULIFLOWER STIR-FRY

Among vegetables, cauliflower is one of the most sensitive to overcooking. Take it a few seconds too far and it can be vile. In this more caring treatment, with a warm spicing which echoes the flavours of southern India, the florets are cooked just to the point where they retain some crunch. They are good hot and equally palatable when allowed to cool to room temperature.

INGREDIENTS

450g/1lb cauliflower
4 spring onions
2cm/$^3/_4$in piece of root
    ginger
4tbsp olive oil
3tsp mustard seeds
1tsp turmeric
$^1/_2$lemon
1 tsp salt
handful of coriander leaves, to
    garnish

PREPARATION

Separate the cauliflower into florets. Trim and cut the spring onions into 1cm/$^1/_2$in lengths. Peel and grate the ginger.

COOKING

Heat the oil in a heavy saucepan, then add the spices and ginger. Stir until the mustard seeds start to pop and jump.

Throw in the cauliflower and spring onions. Stir, add 2 tablespoons of water and cover. Cook, shaking every 30 seconds, for 4 minutes, adding another tablespoon of water if it dries out at any time.

SERVING

Squeeze over the lemon juice, season and scatter with coriander.

DOUBLE PEPPER BEAN POT

Chillies and sweet peppers are from the same Capsicum family and have natural flavour affinities, for chilli is about not only heat but taste. This dish can be served as part of a mezze, as a vegetable with a main course – it is particularly good with grilled fish – or as a vegetarian main course with rice.

INGREDIENTS (FOR 8)

450g/1lb red kidney beans
2 bay leaves
2 celery stalks
sprig of thyme
4 red sweet peppers (about
    450g/1lb)
4 hot red chillies
450g/1lb red onions
3 garlic cloves
4tbsp olive oil
1tbsp paprika
Quick Tomato Sauce (see page
    60)
salt and pepper
few chives, to garnish

PREPARATION

Soak the beans overnight in cold water. Boil hard for 10 minutes, then change the water. Add the tied bouquet garni of bay leaves, celery and thyme. Then cook for about 1 hour, until just done. Drain and discard the bouquet garni, but reserve the cooking liquid.

Preheat the oven to 150°C/300°F/gas2.

Blister and blacken the peppers over an open flame or on a ridged grill pan. Cover for 10 minutes, then peel. Destem and deseed the peppers and the chilli peppers. Cut the sweet peppers into 1cm/$^1/_2$in strips. Peel and dice the onions and the garlic.

COOKING

Put all the vegetables in a heavy casserole and sweat for 5 minutes in the olive oil. Add the beans, the paprika and tomato sauce. Turn with a spoon to mix evenly and pour over just enough of the cooking liquid barely to cover. Season with salt and pepper.

Put on the lid and bake in the oven for 1$^1/_2$hours. During the baking, remove the lid from time to time and give the pot a stir.

SERVING

Just before serving, snip the chives over.

DEEP-FRIED VEGETABLES WITH GARLIC & ANCHOVY DIP

A selection of brightly coloured vegetables coated in the lightest of batters and fried briefly at a high temperature combines perfectly with a robustly flavoured garlic-and-anchovy sauce to produce an original first course that offers a satisfying range of tastes and textures.

The key to success is to fry as many different vegetables as you can find in lots of clean sunflower oil at 190°C/375°F. Take care not to overcrowd the pan, or the temperature will drop too low and the batter will absorb oil and become greasy. The batter, which is essentially a Japanese tempura coating, may also be used with pieces of fish fillet, calamari or tiger prawns.

Ideally the sauce should be presented at the table in a bagna cauda, or glazed pot set over a candle to keep the contents warm.

INGREDIENTS

about 900g/2lb of assorted
    vegetables, such as
    asparagus, yellow peppers,
    red peppers, green peppers,
    courgettes, small
    aubergines, onions, spring
    onions etc

FOR THE SAUCE:
6 garlic cloves
6tbsp olive oil
115g/4oz anchovy fillets
125ml/4fl oz thick plain
    yogurt

FOR THE BATTER:
1 size-2 egg
250ml/8fl oz ice-cold lager
pinch of bicarbonate of soda
pinch of salt
115g/4oz fine plain flour,
    sifted

PREPARATION

Trim the vegetables. Deseed peppers and cut them into strips. Cut courgettes lengthwise into 4 and then into neat batons. Slice onions into rings. Cut aubergines into discs. Trim the spring onions.

Make the sauce: peel, smash and chop the garlic and put in a pan with the olive oil over a low heat together with the anchovies. Stir from time to time until the anchovies break down to form a thick paste.

Remove from the heat and when just warm, stir in the yogurt and transfer to a bagna cauda over a flame or to a suitable bowl.

Heat the sunflower oil to 190°C/375°F and preheat the oven to 130°C/275°F/gas1.

Make the batter: beat the egg in a bowl. Continue to beat, adding the lager in a thin stream. Add the bicarbonate and salt to the flour, then dump this in one go into the liquid and stir a few times barely to mix. There should be lumps! Stir until smooth and you will end up with a heavy coating when fried. Let stand for 10 minutes.

COOKING

Dip the vegetables in the batter and fry a few at a time, transferring them to a dish lined with paper towels and keeping them in the low oven until all are done.

SERVING

If using a bagna cauda, place in the centre of a large serving dish surrounded by fried vegetable pieces for people to help themselves and dip into the warm sauce. Alternatively, put a spoonful or two of the sauce into the middle of each plate and arrange the battered vegetables around, giving everybody a selection.

OVEN-ROAST VEGETABLES

These days we have learned to like our vegetables underdone. Just when you thought that was settled, here is a recipe which calls for them to be cooked till they literally keel over. But first they are sliced and topped with crunchy olive oil breadcrumbs before being slow-baked to the point of collapse. The vegetables may be cooked and served individually; but a mixture of onions, aubergines, tomatoes and peppers, each topped with a differently flavoured crumb, provides contrasting flavours, textures and colours in a dish that is perfect for a summer lunch with a basket of flat breads (page 42). This is for 8 or even 10 people and should be presented on a large serving dish.

INGREDIENTS (FOR 8–10)

8–10 slices from a stale
    crusty white loaf
about 150ml/¼pt extra-
    virgin olive oil, plus more
    for serving
4 large red sweet peppers
2 garlic cloves
450g/1lb white onions
450g/1lb purple onions
handful of thyme leaves
handful of fresh oregano (if
    available)
450g/1lb aubergines or
    courgettes
1tbsp Tapenade (see page 91)
1tbsp Pesto (see page 91)
900g/2lb plum tomatoes,
    home-dried (see page 61)
1 hot red chilli
salt and pepper

PREPARATION

The day before: make the breadcrumbs. Preheat the oven to 200°C/400°F/gas6. Trim any dark crust off the bread and arrange the slices on a baking tray. Brush lightly on both sides with olive oil, sprinkle over a little salt and pepper, then bake until golden brown. It will take no more than 10 minutes but start checking after 5, because they have a tendency to burn the instant you turn your back. Remove from the oven, leaving it on, and allow to cool until you can handle them. Put into a food processor and chop until you have coarse crumbs. Do not over-process. Put into a screw-top jar and chill.

Cut the sweet peppers lengthwise in half, carefully cutting though the stalk so both halves have an elegant tail, then deseed. Brush inside and out with olive oil. Chop the garlic cloves and distribute equally between the peppers, then bake for 20 minutes. Lower the oven setting to 140°C/285°F/gas1½ and continue to cook until the peppers are collapsed (about another 40 minutes). Cling-wrap overnight (you can refrigerate for up to 5 days).

On the day you plan to serve the vegetables: preheat the oven to 140°C/285°F/gas1½.

Peel and trim the tops of all the onions, but leave the root ends intact. Cut the onions lengthwise into slices about 1cm/½in thick. Brush a baking tray with olive oil and arrange the slices in it in a single layer. Mix 2 heaped tablespoons of the crumbs with the chopped thyme leaves and the chopped fresh oregano, if using. Sprinkle over the onions.

Cut the aubergines lengthwise into 1cm/½in slices. Brush both sides of each slice with olive oil and arrange in an oiled baking tray. Mix 2 heaped tablespoons of crumbs with the tapenade and scatter over the top. Do the same for courgettes.

COOKING

Put both trays to bake for about 1 hour, until the vegetable slices have shrunk by half and the onions are golden brown.

Mix 2 heaped tablespoons of crumbs with the pesto and sprinkle over the tomatoes.

Mix 2 heaped tablespoons of crumbs with the deseeded and diced chilli and sprinkle over the sweet peppers.

Put the tray of tomatoes in the oven to heat through for the last 10 minutes, as the aubergines and onions finish cooking. Preheat the grill.

Just before serving, finish the peppers under the grill for 2-3 minutes, keeping a close watch on the crumbs to prevent them burning.

SERVING

Transfer all to a serving dish, dress with more oil and serve with warm bread.

SEVERAL SEXY SALADS

We are all creatures of habit and, as cooks, nowhere is this more evident than in the matter of salads. People get into a particular mind-set and often serve the same leaf salads again and again. This book has dwelt at length on the subject of beans, which provide an obvious opportunity to make salads with a difference. The following examples can all be made quickly and offer refreshing different ideas to play around with and, thankfully, there is hardly a worthy pulse to be seen or heard. There is nothing remotely sexy about any of them, but the title is alliterative.

MARINATED SALT COD & ROCKET

This is a brave dish to get into because it sounds so basic. Think of all the food writing which promises the world and then, when you follow it, delivers very little. This is the contrary example. It sounds too obvious, but delivers much more.

The recipe specifies borlotti beans, but you could use a different variety and still have a good result. Fresh beans are best and rehydrated dried beans are fine, but even tinned are acceptable, if drained and rinsed well.

INGREDIENTS

350g/12oz Home-salted Cod
  Fillets (see page 109)
2 lemons
225g/8oz cooked borlotti
  beans
1tbsp Gremolata (see page
  92)
4tbsp extra-virgin olive oil
115g/4oz rocket
salt and pepper
chopped chives, to garnish

PREPARATION

Rinse the fish and pat dry. Cling-wrap and refrigerate until ready to make the salad. Use the same day.
Half an hour before serving: slice the cod thinly like smoked salmon and arrange on a porcelain dish, dress with the juice from the lemons and leave to marinate.
5 minutes before serving: in a salad bowl, dress the beans with the gremolata and half the olive oil and toss to coat evenly. Taste and season with salt and pepper if you think it needs it.

SERVING

Mound the rocket on individual plates and arrange 2 or 3 slices of cod around it. Divide the beans equally, mounding them on top of the rocket. Dribble a little of the lemon juice marinade over each serving, pouring the remaining olive oil on top. Scatter with chives and serve.

INSALATA DI PEPERONI E CAPPERI

A good dish to make with capers is a salad of sweet peppers and tomatoes, in which the piquancy of the capers balances the other flavours. The rich sweetness of the balsamic vinegar strikes just the right sweet-sour note.

INGREDIENTS

3 red sweet peppers
3 yellow sweet peppers
4 ripe plum tomatoes
1 garlic clove
1 tbsp balsamic vinegar
4 tbsp extra-virgin olive oil
2 tbsp salted capers
10 basil leaves
10 mint leaves
salt and pepper

PREPARATION

Blister the skins of the peppers over a flame or under the grill. Put in a covered bowl for 10 minutes then peel, deseed, cut into strips and put on a serving plate.

Blanch, refresh and peel the tomatoes. Purée in a blender or liquidizer and push through a sieve into a bowl.

Peel, smash and chop the garlic and add it to the bowl. Stir in the vinegar and oil and season with salt and pepper to taste. Spoon the tomato vinaigrette purée over the peppers.

Rinse the capers, dry them and scatter them over.

SERVING

Finish the dish with whole mint and basil leaves.

RUNNER BEAN SALAD WITH CHILLI & GARLIC

Runner beans have tended to play second fiddle to fine French beans, but they can be very good. Easy to grow and prolific, they tend to be damned by too frequent appearance on the tables of those with vegetable gardens. When you have grown bored with runner beans plain boiled and tossed with butter, try this rather more aggressive treatment, where they are finished in a frying pan with hot chilli and garlic. However you cook them, runner beans are always better while the beans are still quite small. Those old ones, the size of cucumbers and with skin like a green tarantula, should go straight on the compost.

INGREDIENTS

1 hot red chilli
2 garlic cloves
1 1/2 tsp salt
450 g / 1 lb young runner beans
4 tbsp olive oil
1 tbsp Kikkoman soy sauce, to dress
1 lemon, to serve

PREPARATION

Split and deseed the chilli, cut it into thin strips then across into small dice. Finely chop the garlic and mix with the chilli and salt.

String the beans and slice into strips, cutting at an angle into pieces about 3 cm / 1 1/4 in long.

COOKING

Blanch the beans in a pan of rapidly boiling water for 5–6 minutes. Refresh in ice-cold water and drain.

Put a large frying pan over a high heat. Add the oil and, as it starts to smoke, throw in the beans – standing back as the beans spit viciously. Toss once, then add the chilli garlic paste. Toss and stir for 1 minute, then transfer to a serving dish.

SERVING

Dress with the soy sauce and serve hot or at room temperature, with lemon wedges.

OLIO SANTO

Throughout the Mediterranean, olive oil is so much a part of culinary life its absence from the daily diet would be unthinkable. Two thousand years ago olive oil was held in such esteem by the Romans that they called it olio santo, 'sacred oil', and to this day Italy is widely regarded as the place where the finest olive oil is produced — something that we all now rather take as read. However, a substantial percentage of olive oil exported from Italy is in fact sourced by the Italians from Spain and Greece, so an Italian label may not be everything it suggests.

The large-scale importation of olive oil into this country means we are able to buy a selection of good oils in any supermarket. Not that long ago, however, olive oil was something you only bought in Boots the Chemist, to treat earache or to rub into sore muscles. Indeed, as recently as 20 years ago the majority of us had never tasted olive oil and found the idea of its widespread use in cooking little short of repugnant — as package-holidaymakers returning from the Mediterranean made clear.

Flavoured olive oils are now growing in popularity, though some additions work better than others. There are good arguments not to make garlic oil, for example, since the principal joy of garlic is the pungency of its fresh, just-peeled state. When old, it develops a rancid, stale taste. The best flavoured oil is undoubtedly that infused with white truffles; the nastiest with lemons, which taste — oddly in this context — of soap. It is still fun to experiment with flavouring oils at home. However, when adding raw organic solids to oil you will find that while the process of decomposition is slowed by the absence of oxygen it is not stopped completely.

One flavoured oil that is worth making is still referred to as olio santo in Tuscany, the home of much of Italy's finest olive oil production. This can be used for frying to add spice to your cooking or simply added by the spoonful to chicken broth at the table, as is done there.

INGREDIENTS

10 whole dried hot chilli
 peppers
10 fresh basil leaves
575ml/1pt extra-virgin
 olive oil

PREPARATION

Make the olio santo in a screw-top glass jar. Hygiene is vital: the jar should first be sterilized and your hands scrubbed clean before handling the peppers and basil.

In a large bowl, pour boiling water over the chillies and leave for 20 minutes. Strain through a sieve, dry on paper towels, then put them into the jar with the basil leaves.

Fill the jar with oil. It is important to fill the jar right to the top to allow as little exposure to the air as possible. Close the jar tightly and put it somewhere cool and dark, but not the refrigerator as the oil solidifies at low temperature and the flavours and heat will not pass into the oil. Leave for 2 weeks. Then pass through a fine sieve into another clean jar or bottle, discarding the basil leaves which will have turned black and slimy. The chillies may be returned to the oil if you want it to get hotter.

VARIATION:
A more rustic southern variant is made using rosemary rather than basil.

HORIATIKI

This is indisputably one of the prettiest and nicest salad combinations ever to feature on the same plate. The sweet succulence of the tomatoes, the sour saltiness of the cheese, the clean peppery taste of the parsley, the sharp bite of the raw onion and the dark complexity of the olives all come together to make a perfect lunch dish that needs only warm pitta breads as an accompaniment.

The tomatoes are cut into chunks and the onion into bite-sized pieces, for this is essentially a peasant dish and should not have anything effete about it, like neat slices or tiny dice. When dressed simply with lemon juice and olive oil, it will sing to you about holidays in Greece. Indeed, it may be the only thing you ate in Greece that you could conceivably imagine wanting to hear sing, but that is just carping.

At the risk of stating the obvious, it is very important to have perfect ripe tomatoes. Your average domestic salad tomato is not for inclusion in any of these recipes. The quality of Feta is a variable thing too; if you have a Greek delicatessen near to you, buy the cheese and parsley there. They will probably have been imported from Cyprus and will be delicious.

This is one of the few dishes in the book which emulates and does not redefine. If it is not broken, do not fix it — and there is nothing you can do to add to its charms.

INGREDIENTS

12 ripe plum tomatoes
225g/½lb Feta cheese
1 red onion
12 Kalamata black olives
20–30 leaves of flat-leaf
    parsley
1 lemon
5tbsp extra-virgin olive oil
salt and pepper

PREPARATION

Cut the tomatoes in half lengthwise, then across into 3, giving you 6 chunks from each tomato.

Cut the Feta into 2cm/½in cubes and distribute evenly on top.

Peel the onion and cut in half, then across into half circles. Cut these into 2.5cm/1in strips and scatter over.

Strew the olives on top. Push the parsley leaves in between the tomatoes, so they stick up.

Dress first with the juice from the lemon, then the olive oil. Season liberally with sea salt and black pepper.

SERVING

Eat at as soon as possible with warm pitta. Play bazouki music and put on your tape of cicada scratching. If feeling masochistic, drink a glass of retsina. If determined to be authentic, then a white Demestica will hit the Aegean spot. If you are like most people, drink whatever is to hand.

ROAST YELLOW PEPPER & CHILLI SALAD

Yellow peppers are frankly indistinguishable in taste from the red variety, but they present nicely with the chillies. These are large fresh hot chillies, which you can find in Asian markets and increasingly in supermarkets. They are not the fiendishly hot variety, unless you want to torture your guests. Roasting them cools their ardour a little, but the idea is for them to be pointedly spicy.

INGREDIENTS

4 large yellow sweet peppers
8 large red chillies
2 garlic cloves
$^{1}/_{2}$ tbsp lemon juice
4 tbsp olive oil, plus more for brushing
salt and pepper
12 small mint leaves

PREPARATION

Preheat the oven to 250°C/475°F/gas9.

Cut the sweet peppers in half lengthwise and remove the seeds, stalks and pith. Brush the pepper halves inside and out with olive oil and arrange on a metal baking tray, cut side downwards.

COOKING

Cook the peppers in the oven for 30 minutes.

Cutting from just below the stem, halve the chillies lengthwise and scrape out the seeds and membranes. The main body of the chilli is now halved but still attached at the stem. Brush inside and out with oil. Peel and chop the garlic.

Remove the sweet peppers from the oven and turn them cut side up. Position the chillies around them, strew with the chopped garlic and return to the oven for a further 20 minutes.

Remove from the oven, put the peppers in a bowl and cover with cling film. After 15 minutes, peel the peppers and cut them into strips.

Put the pepper strips with the chillies in a salad bowl and dress with lemon juice and olive oil and season with salt and pepper.

SERVING

Toss and serve at room temperature, scattered with mint leaves.

SALATIT FIJL

Radishes go best of all with, well, radishes. Throughout history they have been eaten in glorious isolation — usually with nothing more than a little sea salt — and they make a deliciously peppery nibble to enjoy with an aperitif. The French eat them with unsalted butter, salt and baguette, a splendid combination. They are equally good with thin toasted slices of sourdough bread. Radishes really do not combine with any of the usual leaves or vegetables of the European salad tradition, being altogether too forceful and dominant. In Morocco, however, they are successfully paired with oranges: the radishes cut in thin slices and the oranges in small segments, which are then tossed together with lemon juice and a little salt. The Lebanese salatit fijl is properly made from the giant white winter radish and raw diced onion, but is nicer — we think — with an English radish, like White Icicle, mixed with spring onions.

INGREDIENTS

3 bunches of radishes
8 spring onions
$1/2$ lemon
1 garlic clove
4tbsp olive oil
salt
handful of coriander leaves, to
    garnish

PREPARATION

Top and tail the radishes and cut them across into thin slices. Trim the spring onions and cut across at an angle into 2cm/$3/4$in lengths.

In a salad bowl, put 1 tablespoon of juice from the lemon and 1 teaspoon of salt. Stir to dissolve the salt.

Smash and chop the garlic and add to the juice. Stir in 4 tablespoons of olive oil, then add the radish slices and spring onions and toss to coat.

SERVING

Scatter over a handful of coriander leaves and serve immediately as a palate cleanser after a meat main course or as part of a mezze.

BEETROOT SALAD WITH HORSERADISH YOGURT

For those who think beetroot only comes pickled in ferociously strong vinegar, the following treatment will be a revelation.

INGREDIENTS

450g/1lb small beetroots
6 spring onions
handful of coriander leaves
1 lemon
2.5cm/1in piece of
    horseradish
about 300ml/½pt thick
    plain yogurt
salt and pepper

PREPARATION

If not already cooked, boil the beetroots for about 20 minutes, until tender. Refresh in cold water and skin. Cut into small, bite-sized chunks and put into a serving bowl.

Trim the spring onions and cut across into thin slices. Add to the beets with the coriander, the juice from the lemon and salt and pepper.

Peel the horseradish and grate into the yogurt, then taste for heat. If you have overdone it, calm the mix down with more yogurt; or, if it needs more pep, grate in extra horseradish. Spoon this over the beets and turn to coat evenly.

TARATOR FRENCH BEANS

The beans are cooked just sufficiently to lose crude rawness but not enough to lose their snap before being coated — while still warm — with a garlic and walnut dressing. For more on Tarator sauce see page 94.

INGREDIENTS

450g/1lb fine green beans
115g/4oz walnuts, skinned
55g/2oz fresh white
    breadcrumbs
3 garlic cloves
2tbsp lemon juice
150ml/¼pt olive oil
salt and pepper
parsley leaves, to garnish

PREPARATION

Blanch the beans for 4 minutes in a large pan of rapidly boiling salted water, refresh in cold water and drain.

Put the nuts, breadcrumbs, garlic, lemon juice, salt and pepper into a food processor and whizz to a paste. Then add the olive oil in a thin stream through the feeder tube until you have a smooth purée.

Spoon this over the beans and toss to coat.

SERVING

Scatter over some parsley leaves to serve.

CAULIFLOWER, CARROT & GINGER SALAD

We usually eat cauliflowers, carrots and root ginger cooked, but raw and combined they make a fresh and crunchy salad. Those who hate cauliflower because they were served it overcooked as children may love it like this.

INGREDIENTS

1 small cauliflower
4 small carrots
5cm/2in piece of root ginger
1 small red chilli
4tbsp olive oil
1tsp ground cumin
1tsp paprika
1 lemon
2tsp orange flower water
salt and pepper
handful of coriander leaves, to
    garnish

PREPARATION

Separate and trim the cauliflower into florets and put into a salad bowl. Trim, peel and cut the carrots and ginger into julienne strips. Deseed the chilli and cut into fine julienne strips. Add these to the bowl.

Put the olive oil in a small saucepan over a low heat. Stir in the cumin and paprika. Add the juice from the lemon and the orange flower water, together with 1 teaspoon salt and $1/2$ teaspoon of pepper and warm through. Pour this dressing over the salad and toss to coat. Leave for 30 minutes.

SERVING

Serve at room temperature, scattered with coriander leaves.

TABBOULEH

Bulghar, a type of cracked wheat, is an alternative to couscous and can be substituted for it in most recipes. If you cannot find instant-style bulghar you will need to cook 'coarse bulghar', which takes about 20–25 minutes. The phrase 'you coarse bulghar' may be used to encourage kitchen assistants if they slacken over an assigned task.

INGREDIENTS

175g/6oz bulghar
4 ripe plum tomatoes
1 red sweet pepper
1 cucumber
bunch of parsley
16 mint leaves
6 spring onions
1 garlic clove
2 lemons
4tbsp olive oil
salt and pepper

PREPARATION

Soak the cracked wheat in cold water for 10 minutes.

Drain it and put in a pan with 350ml/12fl oz cold water. Season with 1 teaspoon of salt and bring to the boil. Lower the heat, cover the pan and simmer gently until the wheat has absorbed all the water and swelled up. This will take about 20–25 minutes. Alternatively, cook in a rice steamer with $1^1/2$ times the volume of water to cracked wheat.

Blanch, refresh and peel the tomatoes and cut into small dice. Deseed the pepper and dice it and the cucumber as small as sanity and time allow. Destalk and chop the parsley and shred the mint. Trim the spring onions and cut at an angle into 2cm/$3/4$in lengths. Peel, smash and chop the garlic. Zest and juice the lemons.

Stir the diced vegetables, chopped parsley, garlic, mint and lemon zest into the wheat and refrigerate.

SERVING

Just before serving, dress with juice from the lemons and the olive oil. Taste and adjust seasoning, if necessary.

BABY BROAD BEAN & PECORINO SALAD

In Italy this salad is eaten in May, when the beans are barely formed in the pod. They are served raw, tossed only in extra-virgin olive oil and seasoned with salt and pepper. The Pecorino is cubed from a young cheese and mixed in. 'Faites simple', as somebody once remarked. You can get baby broad beans here now, though you need to talk to a greengrocer about this. Once they have formed a thick skin, they first need to be briefly parboiled and peeled. The result will not be as splendid, but will still be very good. Frozen beans do not work.

While mild Pecorino is the authentic and preferred choice for this dish, a Swiss Gruyère is also appropriate. Gruyère in France is a generic description for similar cheeses with holes and these include Comté, Beaufort and Emmental, which all make acceptable alternatives. Small cubes of Cheddar, if not too mature and strong-tasting, also combine well.

2kg/4½lb young broad
    beans in the pod
225g/8oz Pecorino cheese
3½ tbsp extra-virgin olive oil
salt and pepper

PREPARATION

Pod the beans and cut the cheese into 1cm/½in dice. Put the beans into a bowl and season with salt and pepper. Add the oil and toss until every bean has a thin coating. Add more oil if it is too dry, but do not swamp the dish with too much. Scatter over the cheese and serve at once.

If the beans are older and have a skin, parboil in lots of boiling salted water for 1–2 minutes, refresh briefly in cold water and peel before proceeding as above.

SPICY CROTTIN FATTOUSH

Fattoush, the omnipresent salad throughout the Middle East which uses up day-old bread, can be pretty grim. Encouraged towards mediocrity by beastly fashion, its worst misconceptions can look and taste like garbage, rather like those horrid thin soups bulked with stale lumps of baguette you used to get in low-grade French pensions.

This version of fattoush has moved a few miles on down the salad road and is altogether more elegant, the bread present only as crunchy spiced crumbs to give a textural counterpoint to the strongly flavoured goats' cheeses. These are crottins, the small discs matured in olive oil.

INGREDIENTS

6 stale slices of baguette
5 tbsp olive oil, plus more for
    brushing
1 tsp cayenne pepper
1 cos lettuce
1 small cucumber
4 ripe plum tomatoes
1 red onion
handful of flat-leaf parsley
handful of mint leaves
2 crottins (see above)
2 lemons
24 stoned black olives
salt and pepper

PREPARATION

Preheat the oven to 220°C/425°F/gas7. Brush the slices of bread on both sides with olive oil, put them on a baking tray and crisp in the oven for 8–10 minutes.

Remove and whizz to coarse crumbs in a food processor. Put the crumbs back on the tray and sprinkle with 1 teaspoon each of cayenne pepper and salt.

Return to the oven and bake for 5 minutes, stirring to redistribute them on the tray a couple of times, until golden and very crisp. Put back in the food processor, whizz again and reserve.

Wash, dry and tear the cos lettuce into large, bite-sized pieces. Dice the cucumber and tomatoes and slice the onion across into discs, then into 1cm/½in pieces. Coarsely chop the parsley and mint leaves.

Put all these into a salad bowl. Cut the crottins into pieces and scatter them over.

Juice the lemons into a jug or bowl and add salt and pepper to taste, then whisk in the 5 tablespoons of olive oil. Pour over the salad and toss.

SERVING

Mound on plates and scatter the olives and toasted crumbs over all. Serve at once.

PARSLEY & GRILLED VEGETABLE SALAD

We are used to thinking of parsley as a herb to flavour dishes and, too often, as an automatic garnish. This is certainly the principal application for curly parsley, which otherwise mainly features in white sauces or is deep-fried as a classic accompaniment to whitebait. Jane Grigson's Vegetable Book, published in 1978, makes no reference at all to flat-leaf parsley — which is also known as Continental, Cyprus or Italian parsley — an indication of how recent a culinary phenomenon this vastly superior version of the herb is in our lives. In Mediterranean countries, flat-leaf parsley has always been eaten as a salad in its own right, its sharp yet subtle flavour providing a perfect counterpoint to so many dishes. Here it balances the blander tastes of aubergines, courgettes and peppers; its distinctive pepperiness and astringency giving definition and coherence to the other flavours.

The best way to grill the vegetables is on a barbecue, which adds its inimitable smokiness to the finished dish. However, a ridged grill pan also works adequately; an overhead grill does not. Take care not to over-oil the vegetables. A variation on the theme can be achieved by substituting grated Parmesan cheese for the breadcrumbs — say 55g/2oz.

INGREDIENTS

large bunch of flat-leaf parsley
2 garlic cloves
4tbsp olive oil
2 medium-sized aubergines
225g/8oz courgettes (2 large ones are best)
1 red sweet pepper
1 yellow sweet pepper
8 spring onions
4 thick slices of country-style bread
salt and pepper

FOR THE DRESSING:
15 salt-packed capers
16 salt-cured black olives
$^1/_2$ red onion
1 garlic clove
4 Oven-dried Tomatoes (see page 61)
150ml/$^1/_4$pt extra-virgin olive oil
1tbsp red wine vinegar
salt and pepper

PREPARATION

If using the barbecue, light this before doing anything else. Preheat the oven to 220°C/425°F/gas7.

Pick over the parsley, remove and discard the stalks. Wash, spin-dry and reserve the leaves.

Smash and finely chop the garlic. Put to infuse in 4 tablespoons of the olive oil with some salt and pepper.

Cut the aubergines across into 5mm/$^1/_4$in slices. Slice the courgettes lengthwise into 5mm/$^1/_4$in strips. Halve and deseed the peppers. Trim the spring onions.

Brush the slices of bread on both sides with the garlic oil and toast on a baking tray in the oven until crisp and golden brown. Remove and, when cool enough, process to a fine crumb and reserve.

Make the dressing: rinse the capers and olives. Stone the olives and chop them and the capers, onion, garlic and tomatoes with a large-bladed knife. Do not use a processor, which will smash the ingredients to a mulch. Adjust the seasoning, if necessary. Put into a salad bowl with the olive oil and vinegar and stir.

Brush the vegetables with garlic oil and grill sequentially, starting with the aubergines, then doing the courgettes, followed by the peppers and last of all the spring onions, transferring them to a tray as they are done. Cut the pepper halves into strips.

SERVING

Mix all the vegetables together in a large serving bowl. Add the parsley to the dressing and toss, then add to the vegetables and mix thoroughly. Scatter the crumbs on top.

As the aim is only to cover the dish with a thin crunchy topping; you may not use all of the crumbs. Any left over can be kept in a screw-top jar in the refrigerator.

AROMATIC MUSHROOM SALAD

Even cultivated mushrooms can be given flavour and substance by marinating them. That being said, cultivated button mushrooms really have no discernible flavour unless – with eyes closed and great concentration – you may discern the faintest whiff of damp cellars. This recipe uses the large, flat-cap field mushrooms which are grilled to remove excess water before being marinated. This enhances the flavour and gives them a more substantial taste.

INGREDIENTS

450g / 1lb field mushrooms
2 lemons
4 garlic cloves
150ml / $^1/_4$pt extra-virgin
   olive oil
2 bay leaves
sprig of thyme
4 hot red chillies
10 black peppercorns
large handful of flat-leaf
   parsley
salt

PREPARATION

Start the day before you plan to serve: preheat the grill to high.

Wipe the mushrooms clean with a damp cloth, remove the stems and peel the caps. (Use the stalks and peelings in a stock or soup.) Zest and juice one of the lemons. Finely chop 3 of the garlic cloves.

COOKING

Grill the mushrooms, caps down, until water exudes from the surface and fills the depression where the stalk joined the cap, about 5–6 minutes. Turn over and grill for a further minute. Remove, pat dry with paper towels and put on a glass or china serving dish.

Put the olive oil in a saucepan with the garlic, the zest and juice of 1 lemon, the bay leaves, thyme, chillies and peppercorns. Heat gently for 5 minutes at a bare simmer.

While still very hot, strain through a fine sieve over the mushrooms, discarding the aromatics. When cool, refrigerate overnight.

SERVING

Just before serving: turn the mushrooms in the marinade and sprinkle with salt.

Zest the second lemon. Smash and chop the remaining garlic clove. Remove the stems from the parsley and chop the leaves. Mix with the garlic and lemon zest. Scatter over the mushroom salad.

If you do not wish to serve the day after making, the salad will keep in the refrigerator for up to 4 days, but will then start to become rather slippery.

ROAST BEETROOT & OLIVE SALAD WITH AÏOLI

Usually boiled, these baby beetroots are here roasted with chunks of red onion and tossed in a garlic mayonnaise. Raw onions and a garlic sauce? The combination sounds strident, but these are sweet mild onions and the garlic is cooked before being puréed and incorporated into the mayonnaise. The result is a successful balance of firm chunks of beet and crunchy onion, the aïoli giving a moist rich gloss to the dish. This is a salad to serve when the new-season's garlic is available.

INGREDIENTS

900g/2lb (2 bunches) small
   raw beetroots
3tbsp olive oil
1 head of new-season's garlic
1 red onion
24 kalamata olives

FOR THE HERBED AÏOLI:
yolks of 2 eggs
300ml/$\frac{1}{2}$pt sunflower oil
1tbsp fresh oregano
2tbsp flat-leaf parsley
salt and pepper

PREPARATION

Preheat the oven to 190°C/375°F/gas5.

Wash and trim the beetroots, brush them with olive oil and put on a roasting tray. Season with salt and pepper. Separate the garlic into cloves, toss with a little of the oil and reserve.

COOKING

Roast the beetroots for 20 minutes. Add the garlic to the tray and continue cooking for 15–20 minutes more, until the beetroots and garlic are just done (push a skewer into a beetroot to check it is tender and continue cooking until they all are). Remove and leave to cool.

While they are cooling, make the herbed aïoli: peel the roasted garlic cloves and mash to a pulp. Whisk in the egg yolks, season with 1 teaspoon of salt and $\frac{1}{2}$ teaspoon of pepper. Then add the sunflower oil, a few drops at a time to begin with, building to a thin stream as the sauce thickens.

Chop the oregano leaves and half the parsley and stir into the sauce.

Peel the beetroots, cut them into quarters and put in a bowl. Peel the onion and cut it into wedges. Add 4–5 tablespoons of the herbed aïoli and toss to coat.

SERVING

Transfer the salad to a serving dish, scatter over the olives and strew with the remaining parsley.

RAVISHING RELISHES

Chilli-hot sauces like *harissa* and *zhug*, lemon-sharp piquant *gremolata*, soothing yogurt with chives, astringent brined limes and unctuous walnut-rich *tarator*. The choices available in Mediterranean condiments are startlingly different and flooded with powerful flavours. They make you stop and reconsider as you see intriguing opportunities, your mind as stimulated as your palate by the strong yet subtle tastes, the bright colours and the pleasingly complex textures.

HARISSA

Harissa is the fiercely hot chilli paste of Morocco, zhug its slightly more aromatic Israeli equivalent. They are used in small amounts to lift dishes and the more you eat, the better you like the fire they engender. If you eat harissa or zhug injudiciously and burn yourself, then treat the pain with spoonfuls of yogurt. Sugar also helps — one reason why desserts in countries where a lot of chillies are eaten are so often tooth-achingly sweet.

Harissa keeps well in a jar in the refrigerator though, given its ferocity, it is surprisingly not impervious to bacterial contamination. This is perhaps caused by children licking their fingers and dipping them into the harissa for a treat when bored with chocolate bars.

INGREDIENTS

115g/4oz dried hot chillies
10 garlic cloves
1 tbsp coriander seeds
$\frac{1}{2}$ tbsp caraway seeds
1 tbsp black peppercorns
$\frac{1}{2}$ tbsp salt
3 tbsp olive oil
3 tbsp vinegar

PREPARATION

Pour boiling water over the chillies and leave to soak for 20–30 minutes. Don't throw away this water.

Destem the peppers, then scrape out the seeds and discard them. Put the flesh into a food processor. Peel and chop the garlic and put with the chillies.

Toast the coriander, caraway and black peppercorns in a dry pan over a low flame. Grind and add to the processor, with the salt, olive oil and vinegar. Whizz to a thick paste. If too thick, add a couple of tablespoons of the pepper soaking water.

CHILLIES

The chilli on which so many relishes are based came originally from South America and was brought back to the Mediterranean in the sixteenth century by Spaniards and, in due course, exported on to the Middle East, then India and Southeast Asia.

Used fresh, the larger milder chilli is a vegetable like a hot sweet pepper. When dried, it is used as you would a spice and people in the countries where they are grown value the chilli in its dried form just as much as when it is fresh. The heat-producing element in chillies is called capsaicin and the heat itself is measured in 'Scoville units', which range from zero for a sweet pepper to 300,000 for the *habanero* – also called the Scotch bonnet – and the hottest chilli in the world (rated 10 on a simplified scale of 1 to 10).

When cooking with dried chillies, soak them first in just-boiled water for 20 minutes, then purée them in a food processor with some of the soaking liquid and add them by the spoonful to whatever you are cooking, tasting after each addition to control the amount of heat. Larger, meaty dried chillies, like the *ancho*, can be stuffed after a preliminary soaking. Dried chillies can also be soaked, then cut into thin strips to add to stir-fries, or marinated in olive oil and vinegar for salads.

When handling hot chillies – fresh and dried – try to remember to wash your hands carefully before touching eyes, nostrils or other sensitive parts. If you forget to take this precaution, you will remember why it was a good precept for some time afterwards. Like years.

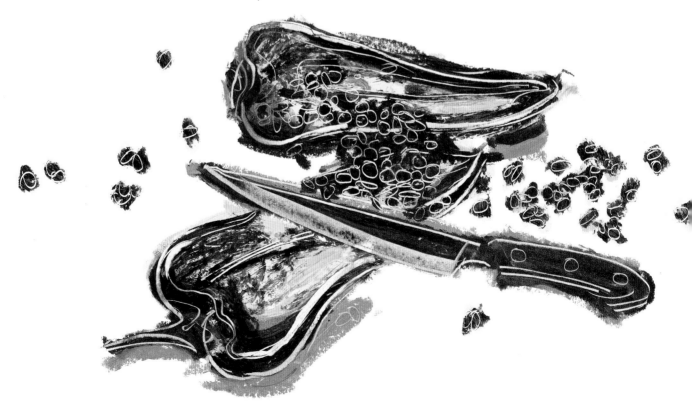

ZHUG

Originally a Yemeni relish, zhug is now thought of as being as Israeli as El Al. It can be sweetened a little with tomato purée or even ketchup if liked.

INGREDIENTS

115g/4oz hot red chillies
10 garlic cloves
1/2 tbsp black peppercorns
1 tsp cardamom seeds
handful of coriander leaves
1 tbsp salt
4 tbsp olive oil
1 tbsp tomato purée (optional)

PREPARATION

Pour boiling water over the chillies and leave to soak for 20–30 minutes. Don't throw away this water.

Destem the chillies, then scrape out the seeds and discard them. Peel and chop the garlic.

Toast the spices in a dry pan over a low flame and grind.

Put all the ingredients into a food processor and work to a thick paste. Add a little of the soaking water if too thick. Store as you would harissa.

TAPENADE

There is no one absolute recipe for tapenade, the Provençal olive spread, and the ratio of one ingredient to another varies according to taste. The capers are usual but not obligatory. The best olives for this relish are the black Greek ones you can buy salted in jars. Cover these with extra-virgin olive oil and leave at room temperature for one month. After this time, much of the salt will have been extracted, while the olives absorb the oil and plump up to a delightful succulence.

INGREDIENTS

350g/12oz black olives
2 garlic cloves
6 anchovy fillets
2 tbsp salt capers (optional)
1 tsp pepper
175ml/6fl oz extra-virgin
   olive oil

PREPARATION

Stone the olives. Peel and chop the garlic. If using, rinse and drain the capers.

Put all the dry ingredients into a food processor. With the machine at full speed, pour in the olive oil through the feeder tube to produce a thick coarse paste.

Pack in a jar, film with more oil and refrigerate until needed. It keeps well.

PESTO

The classic Italian pasta sauce also works wonders as a relish for many vegetable, poultry and fish dishes. It will keep for a week in the refrigerator, filmed with oil in a tightly sealed jar.

INGREDIENTS

2 large bunches of basil leaves
   (sufficient to fill the bowl of a
   processor after the stems have been
   removed andwhen loosely packed)
2 large garlic cloves
150g/5 1/4 oz Reggiano
   Parmesan cheese
85g/3 oz pine nuts
about 300ml/ 1/2 pt extra-virgin
   olive oil

PREPARATION

Destalk the basil leaves. Peel and chop the garlic. Break the cheese into pieces small enough to push down the feeder tube of the food processor.

Turn on the processor at full speed and work the cheese until it has the texture of coarse breadcrumbs. Do not over-process. Add the garlic and pine nuts and whizz briefly to incorporate. Stop the processor between each ingredient addition. Now add the basil and work again briefly until all the ingredients are evenly mixed.

With the processor working continuously, pour in the oil in a thin stream to achieve a thick oily paste. Taste and add salt and pepper as you like. Process again briefly to incorporate the seasoning and taste.

GREMOLATA

Gremolata is most often the garnish that finishes osso buco, the Milanese stew of shin of veal usually served with a rich risotto. In this context, its last-minute addition of gremolata — a mixture of lemon zest, parsley and garlic — makes a lot of sense, for a richer combination than osso buco is difficult to imagine. Many Italians do not approve of a gremolata garnish here, finding it too obvious a counterpoint for such an unctuous and subtle dish. Perhaps they are right and in our redefined Mediterranean sensibility its application is broader-based, bringing bean and salad dishes alive with vigorous and assertive flavours in a way that should please both those who find it too strident in its traditional use as well as those who have never thought of using it at all.

The precise proportions of lemon to garlic to parsley are not absolute, but the garlic should never dominate. Experiment with increasingly higher percentages of lemon and parsley until you hit upon the formula that pleases you most.

INGREDIENTS

1 garlic clove
1 scrubbed or uncoated lemon
    (see below)
bunch of flat-leaf parsley

PREPARATION

Peel, smash and chop the garlic and put into a bowl. Zest the lemon and add this to the garlic. Destalk the parsley and chop the leaves. Add these to the bowl and stir and toss to ensure an even distribution of all the elements.

Always make it fresh as close as possible to the moment you want to add it to the finished dish.

CITRONS CONFITS

We tend to think of salt-preserved lemons as being Moroccan, though they are popular throughout North Africa. They are offered as a side dish straight from the pickle jar or are cut up and added to stews to give them a sharp, astringent edge. In this context, a little goes a long way and a heavy hand will result in an inedibly salty dish. They are easy to make and go particularly well with lamb. Always use ripe lemons — or limes, which can be salt-pickled in exactly the same way.

The majority of lemons sold in this country are coated with a chemically treated wax to lengthen their shelf-life. For any dish in which they are used whole or their zest is used, this coating needs to be removed by vigorous scrubbing in hot soapy water, followed by a thorough rinse. However, many supermarkets now sell organic uncoated fruit, which is preferable — if more expensive.

INGREDIENTS

1.35kg/3lb scrubbed or
    uncoated lemons or limes
    (see introduction, right)
170g/6oz sea salt

PREPARATION

On a board, hold a lemon or lime upright with the stem downwards and cut in half, stopping just before the stem. Cut down at right angles to the first cut, again almost to the base. You now have 4 quarters attached at the stem.

Open them up and spoon salt on the cut surfaces. Close the quarters back together and repeat with the remaining fruit.

Pack into a large kilner jar, or similar, and sprinkle the remaining salt over. Refrigerate for a minimum of 4 weeks, by which time the

juice of the fruit will have made a brine with the salt and the peel
will be fully pickled.

It is the skin, cut into strips, that you want to serve. Discard the
pulp or liquidize it and add sparingly to marinades or stews.

TARATOR

It sounds like one of those futuristic robot heroes of Japanese animation announced in basso profundo voice-over: TAR-A-TOR! In fact, it is the walnut-and-garlic sauce which you will find dressing runner beans in the salad section.

The fresher the walnuts the better, so make your children shell some as a Christmas penance. If using packet walnuts, then open them exclusively for the sauce. After being left to sit and fester in the cupboard for a few weeks your tarator will scare more than the children. It makes an unusual pasta sauce, but is extraordinarily rich so you need only swabbing amounts to make the point. Check with your guests that they can eat walnuts; it is surprising how many people they upset.

INGREDIENTS

2 slices of white bread (plastic
    sliced is fine)
3 tbsp milk
170g/6oz shelled fresh
    walnuts
1 lemon
3 garlic cloves
150ml/¼pt olive oil
salt and pepper

PREPARATION

Trim the crusts off the bread. Tear the slices into pieces, moisten with the milk and put in the processor with the walnuts and juice from the lemon.

Peel, smash and chop the garlic and add. Season with salt and pepper.

Whizz to a paste and, while continuing to process, pour in the olive oil through the feeder tube until you have a smooth purée.

Eat the same day.

CHILLI CUCUMBER PICKLE

Small cucumbers for pickling are now sold by supermarkets. This is a spicy cure which has a chilli tingle to the tongue. The coriander and cumin seeds in the pickle give it further depth.

INGREDIENTS

1 tbsp cumin seeds
1 tbsp coriander seeds
1 tbsp black peppercorns
300ml/½pt white wine
    vinegar
150ml/¼pt malt vinegar
3 tbsp salt
1 tbsp sugar
900g/2lb baby cucumbers
6 hot red chillies
4 garlic cloves

PREPARATION

Toast the cumin, coriander and peppercorns in a dry heavy pan for 2–3 minutes over a low heat.

Put into a saucepan with the vinegars, salt, sugar and 300ml/½pt of water. Bring to a boil, then leave to cool.

Pack the cucumbers upright into 2 kilner jars or similar and pour over the pickling liquid, distributing the chillies equally between the jars. Peel the garlic cloves and put 2 into each jar.

Keep in a cool dark place for 2–3 weeks. Refrigerate after opening.

TURNIP & BEET PICKLE

The beetroot colours the turnip a delicate rose-pink during pickling. The flavour is quite mild and the texture pleasantly crunchy. The pickle may be eaten after 2 weeks and is best not left more than 3 weeks, or it becomes too salty and the vegetables too soft.

INGREDIENTS

675g/1½lb small turnips
225g/8oz beetroots
4 hot red chillies
2 garlic cloves
2 bay leaves

FOR THE PICKLING LIQUID:
300ml/½pt red wine
   vinegar
1 level tbsp caster sugar
3 level tbsp salt
20 black peppercorns
4 cloves

PREPARATION

First make the pickling liquid: bring the vinegar and 300 ml/½pt water slowly to a boil with the sugar, salt, peppercorns and cloves. Remove from the heat and allow to cool and the flavours to infuse.

Top and tail the turnips and beetroots and parboil for 5 minutes in boiling salted water. Refresh in cold water and peel. Cut into 5cm/2in by 1cm/½in batons.

Pack into two 450g/1lb screw-top jars, alternating layers of turnip with beet, with 2 chillies, 1 garlic clove, 1 bay leaf and 10 peppercorns in each jar. Pour over the pickling liquid with its aromatics to cover and close tightly.

Leave in a cool dark cupboard to mature for 2–3 weeks. Refrigerate once opened.

4 FISH & SEAFOOD

We increasingly have adopted the barbecue as the cooking icon of summer but, in doing so, have tended to embrace the American rather than Mediterranean ethos – with an emphasis on meat rather than fish. The smell which hangs like a pall over a sunny evening in suburbia is of charred animal flesh, interwoven with the whiff of kerosene. It is rarely of fish and herbs, is more crematorium than *taverna*.

The reasons for this carnivorous bias are not hard to work out and are largely historic. Meat was always considered better fare than fish, a food downgraded by its association with fasting. Indeed, fish on Fridays is an enduring habit based on its designation as a meat-free day in the Catholic calendar and a penance by definition. Oysters, herring and salmon were for hundreds of years the food of the poor; a role that low-grade quality farmed salmon can now ironically play again, with prices plummeting below that of broiler turkeys. Fish was something you fed invalids. With multiple unpleasant connotations, it is not surprising that so many of our countrymen stand with their backs to the sea.

This contempt for fish developed comparatively recently, an attitudinal slant that has been gradual but inexorable. The ascendancy of supermarkets – combined with a car-driven move away from town centres towards dedicated superstore sites – have effectively killed off the high-street fishmonger, along with numerous other specialist retailers.

Whatever the causes, we are the island nation which

has denied its piscine heritage and which today eschews fish unless it is sanitized in white fillet form or purchased in 'added value' packages. This description is as vile a misnomer as any new marketing speak for, in reality, it means not better value, but worse – with the price loaded disproportionately in return for a little manufactured *mise en place*… a poor scattering of inferior crumb here, a floury coating of suspect sauce there.

Do you have an excellent fishmonger near you and, if you do, do you shop there every week? The answer to both questions is likely to be negative, for if you reply in the affirmative then you are sadly one of a very small minority. People still eat fish and chips, which when good are very, very good; but then they conform perfectly to convenience criteria. Indeed, fish and chips, first introduced around the turn of the century, were the model for all the fast food that has swamped us recently.

A move towards frozen filleted fish has been exacerbated by the dire quality of most supermarket 'wet' fish, which may be up to a week old before it reaches the store. Temperature fluctuation is what speeds decomposition and frozen fish can, in these circumstances, easily be superior to what is laughingly referred to as 'fresh'. The old adage that 'if it smells fishy then it is time for the dustbin' holds true. Really fresh whole fish smells of the sea and is unmistakable; with its bright eyes, deep red gills, gleaming scales and slippery surface sheen.

GRILLING FISH

There is no better means of cooking good fresh fish than grilling – that simplest and most difficult of cooking treatments which, more than any other, reminds us of Mediterranean journeys and holidays by the sea.

So many fish are suitable for grilling: sea bass, red and grey mullet, red snapper and monkfish are all firm – and white-fleshed candidates for the fire. However, barbecuing fish is a challenge for even accomplished cooks, since there is so little control over the heat. Whole fish are tricky anyway, because they come inconveniently in different sizes and different thicknesses. The distribution of bone varies from species to species, while some fish are more oily than others. Fish under 450g/1lb in weight are difficult not to overcook, while fish over 900g/2lb are hard to cook uniformly. If the centre at the bone is done, then the flesh closer to the skin is frequently dry.

The ideal weight for grilling is 450–675g/1-1½lb but, of course, fish as small as sardines or anchovies can be cooked successfully this way, while trained hands and the gift of tin foil can deliver fine results even with something as large as a whole salmon. Very small fish benefit from being wrapped in fresh vine or fig leaves before grilling, to help them stay moist. Cooking in our ideal weight range, a handy piece of kit is one of those fish-shaped metal baskets with a handle, which makes turning easy and avoids damaging the fish by eliminating direct contact with the grill slats.

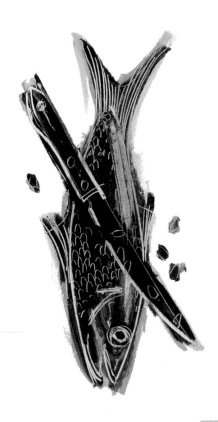

You will need 450g/1lb of whole fish for each person. Leave fish larger than 900g/2lb to the expert and take heart from the fact that the cooking time is the same whether the fish weighs one or two pounds. Scale the fish by holding it by the tail and scraping towards the head with a sharp knife. Snip off the fins and gills with kitchen scissors and, if preparing sea bass, be careful not to get any of the sharp dorsal spikes under your fingernails or skin – they are poisonous and the wound will be very painful. If the body cavity of the fish has any blood in it, rub with salt then rinse under cold running water. Make two incisions deep into the flesh on each side of the body of the fish, cutting down to the bone. This will help it cook evenly. Sprinkle the outside of the fish liberally with sea salt. Do not brush the skin with oil.

An overhead grill is really a very good substitute for a barbecue and is often better. Place your seasoned fish under the grill or over the fire, about 15cm/6in from the heat source, for about 5 minutes. Leave it alone – push it around too soon and you will only damage the skin. Wait until it starts to change colour, while the head and tail lift slightly. If using a grilling frame, turning is easy. Otherwise, carefully slide a spatula or large fork under the fish, working from the tail and pushing along the length of the fish before lifting and turning. If you try to turn it by lifting in the middle the fish may break. Cook the other side for 4 minutes. Remove and check that it is done by pushing a knife tip down and gently lifting the flesh away from the rib bones or spine.

It is fish cooked like this which is winning people back to its culinary potential.

BROILED HALIBUT WITH ONION RELISH

Broiling applies grill heat to both the top and bottom of something at the same time; a technique which, when applied to fish, crisps and cooks the skin from below while the flesh cooks from the grill heat above – so eliminating the need to turn it. This technique also works well with cod or monkfish.

The relish is spicy without being too hot for the delicate and expensive halibut.

INGREDIENTS

4 chicken halibut steaks, each
    weighing 115–170g/
    4–6oz
1 tbsp olive oil
30g/1oz butter
salt and pepper

FOR THE ONION RELISH:
3 heaped tsp cumin seeds
3 heaped tsp coriander seeds
675g/1½lb onions
1 garlic clove
1 small hot chilli, deseeded
2 large ripe tomatoes
1 lime
handful of coriander leaves
3 tbsp sunflower oil
225g/8oz chopped tinned
    tomatoes, drained

PREPARATION

First prepare the onion relish: gently toast the cumin and coriander seeds in a heavy pan over a low flame for a couple of minutes, shaking and stirring. Grind and reserve (a coffee grinder is best for this job).

Peel and slice the onions and garlic. Deseed the chilli and slice into thin strips.

Blanch, skin and dice the fresh tomatoes. Juice the lime. Chop the coriander leaves, leaving some whole for garnish.

COOKING

Preheat the grill to maximum. This applies to a gas grill just as much as to an electric one – despite British Gas home economists' claims to the contrary – but it only takes a couple of minutes to heat up. Cook the relish: sweat the garlic and onions in the sunflower oil until the onions start to soften – but they must not brown!

Add the chilli strips, together with the ground spices, stirring and tossing. Fry together for a minute, add the drained canned tomatoes and bubble over a high heat until amalgamated. Remove from the heat and season to taste.

Over a medium heat warm a heavy frying pan which will fit under the grill. Do not oil it.

Brush the top of the fish steaks with olive oil. Season with salt and pepper. Then lay them in the hot pan for 1 minute. Dot the tops with butter and put the pan under the grill for 3 minutes, by which point the fish should be just cooked and the skin will pull away from the flesh.

While the fish is cooking, finish the relish by returning the pan to the heat. Add the tomatoes and lime juice. Shake and stir. Remove from the heat. Stir in the chopped coriander leaves and keep warm.

SERVING

Arrange a pile of relish on the centre of each plate. Place a halibut steak on top, strew over a few of the reserved coriander leaves and serve at once.

LIBYAN FISH TAGINE

The Libyan provenance is purely academic, for this cumin-flavoured stew of fish and potatoes could be found anywhere from Tunis to Istanbul. Whether it is something the good Colonel Gadafi has enjoyed is unknown. If he has, then it would have been made from small fish like red mullet. However, this redefinition benefits from being cooked with larger fish steaks. You could use sea bass or cod, for example, in which case the steaks should each weigh 150–170g/6–7oz. The key to success is to have the potatoes just cooked when you add the fish. The easiest way to achieve this is to use two pans as described below.

INGREDIENTS

4tsp cumin seeds
1 celery stalk
675g/1½lb potatoes
285g/10oz onions
2 garlic cloves
2 red chillies
5tbsp olive oil
4 kaffir lime leaves (optional)
2tsp paprika
2tsp turmeric
4 cod steaks
4 sets of squid tentacles
    (optional)
575ml/1pt passata
salt and pepper
large handful of coriander
    leaves, to garnish

PREPARATION

Toast the cumin seeds in a dry pan for 2–3 minutes over a low heat. Grind to a powder and reserve.

Trim the celery and dice. Peel the potatoes and cut into 1cm/½in cubes. Peel and slice the onions and cut into thin rings. Peel, smash and chop the garlic. Destalk and deseed the chillies and cut into julienne strips.

COOKING

Put half the olive oil in one large frying pan and half in the other, ideally non-stick and with a lid.

Put the potato dice in the non-stick pan and fry, tossing and turning from time to time.

At the same time in the other pan, fry the onions and celery, stirring occasionally. When the onions begin to soften, add the lime leaves, chillies, garlic, cumin, paprika and turmeric. Cook for a further 2–3 minutes, then season lightly with salt and pepper and turn off the heat. Leave in the pan while the potatoes finish cooking.

As soon as you judge the potatoes are cooked, season the fish steaks with salt and pepper and put them on top of the potatoes. Spoon the onion mixture over and around the steaks and pour over the passata. Bring to a bubble over a medium heat, immediately lower it, put the lid on and cook gently for 3 minutes.

Add the squid tentacles, if using, replace the lid and cook for another 3–4 minutes, when the cod should be just done. Taste and adjust the seasoning if desired.

SERVING

Serve in large warmed bowls, scattered with coriander leaves.

TUNA AU POIVRE

Blue-fin tuna is perhaps the Mediterranean's finest fish. It breeds off the coast of Turkey and is caught in the Straits of Messina and Gibraltar, but within hours of being docked most of the catch is flown to Tokyo's central fish market. There it commands astronomic prices as the connoisseur's tuna for sashimi.

It has always been revered. The Phoenicians followed its migrations and the Romans held it in high esteem, particularly that taken near Byzantium. Tuna preserved in olive oil featured on the Greek menu two thousand years before anybody thought of putting it in tins.

Seared tuna served rare has become a fashionable alternative to fillet steak. If cooked to well done, however, it becomes unpalatably dry and chewy. Buying tuna is not easy as it deteriorates rapidly once butchered. The best place to buy it is from a Japanese fishmonger, who will offer it beautifully prepared in trimmed fillets.

For this recipe you need a 675g/1½lb steak, cut from the middle section of the fish. When trimmed it is cut into four portions about 2.5cm/1in thick and each weighing 115–140g/4–5oz. This is quite large enough, as the flesh is very rich. Cling wrap and use as soon after purchase as possible, refrigerating until a few minutes before you cook it.

INGREDIENTS

4 trimmed tuna steaks from
    the middle section (as
    above)
1 tbsp olive oil
1 tsp salt
2 tsp mignonette (coarse)
    black pepper
55g/2oz butter, chilled
1 lemon
small handful of flat-leaf
    parsley
150ml/¼pt chicken stock or
    beef consommé

PREPARATION

Brush the steaks with olive oil. Mix the salt and pepper together and roll the steaks in it to coat.

Preheat a heavy frying pan over a medium heat. Dice the chilled butter. Juice the lemon. Destalk and chop the parsley.

COOKING

Dry-cook the oiled and seasoned steaks in the pan, giving the first side 2 minutes and the other 1 minute. Transfer to a warmed serving dish and keep warm.

Turn the heat up under the pan and pour in the consommé and lemon juice. Boil rapidly until the liquid become syrupy.

Off the heat, add the parsley and then the butter pieces, swirling in to liaise the sauce.

SERVING

Pour the sauce over the steaks and serve at once.

HAKE WITH SAGE & SPINACH

Hake is the favourite fish of Portugal and adored on the Mediterranean coast of Spain, but not greatly respected here. An Atlantic fish, it is mainly caught by our fishermen to export to those countries… an odd thought, but typical of how we deal with so much of what is taken off these shores.

The best cuts are deemed to be fillets taken from the upper part of the backs of large fish, though steaks cut across from whole smaller hake are also prized. The first cooking method is for steaks cut from a large fish. The second, for cylindrical steaks taken from a smaller whole fish, demands an oven-roasting technique which is also a good way of cooking any small fish on the bone, like the red mullet below.

INGREDIENTS

450g/1lb spinach
8 small sage leaves
4 hake steaks, each weighing about 200–210g/ 7–7$^1/_2$oz
85g/3oz flour
5tbsp light olive oil
$^1/_2$ nutmeg
1 lemon
salt and pepper

PREPARATION

Put a pan of lightly salted water to heat. Pick over and destalk the spinach. Preheat the grill and put over a low heat a heavy non-stick frying pan large enough to hold the fish steaks in one layer.

Blanch the spinach for 30–45 seconds in the fast boiling water, refresh in cold water and drain. Reserve.

Press 2 sage leaves into each steak and dredge with the flour seasoned with 1 teaspoon of salt and $^1/_2$ teaspoon of pepper.

COOKING

Put 2 tablespoons of the oil in the warming heavy pan, turn the heat up to medium and lay the steaks in it. Brown the undersides for 2 minutes. Brush the tops of the steaks with a little more oil and put under the grill to finish for 3 minutes.

Alternatively, if your heavy non-stick frying pan is ovenproof, preheat the oven to 250°C/475°F/gas9 and put the pan of fish into the oven rather than under the grill and roast for 12–15 minutes. The fish will pull easily away from the spinal bone when cooked.

Transfer to a warmed serving plate and wipe out the pan. Add the remaining oil and, when hot, toss the spinach briefly in it. Grate over nutmeg to taste and some pepper. Transfer to the serving plate.

SERVING

Dress with the juice from the lemon and serve at once.

BARBOUNIA WITH FENNEL & ORANGE

Depending on the time of year, as you pass through a Mediterranean open-air market the elderly head-scarved party who lurches towards you with a gap-toothed grimace may well be proffering a handful of partially dried flowering heads of fennel for sale – precisely what you want to perfume this dish of roast red mullet – barbounia in Greek. You are not likely to be so accosted in this country and will have to make do with the feathery leaves or bulb of the plant. These are not eaten, but will deliver enough fennel flavour to make the point and you can always add a little more emphasis with a teaspoon or two of pastis if you are in a particularly aniseedy mood. Ask the fishmonger to clean and scale the mullet. If the idea appeals to you, ask for the livers to be left in; some regard them as a delicacy.

4 red mullet, each weighing
  about 150g/5½oz,
  cleaned and scaled
about 5tbsp olive oil
4 bay leaves
2 flowering heads of fennel or
  2 handfuls of fennel fronds
  or 1 fennel bulb
1 orange
2 lemons
salt and pepper

PREPARATION

About 1 hour before cooking: brush the fish with olive oil and season with salt and pepper. Put a bay leaf in each body cavity.

When ready to cook: preheat the oven to 200°C/400°F/gas6. Chop whichever bit of fennel you have to hand and use it to cover the base of an oiled roasting dish in which the fish will just fit snugly on their sides.

Dribble the fennel with oil and lay the fish on top. Cut the unpeeled orange across into thin slices and put some overlapping on top of each fish. Juice one lemon, pour it over and leave to marinate for about 30 minutes.

COOKING

Slice the second lemon and arrange over the fish, dribble some oil over the slices, sprinkle with 1 tablespoon of water and roast uncovered for 15–20 minutes. The fish are done when the flesh lifts away easily.

SERVING

Transfer the fish to warmed plates and spoon over the pan juices.

RED MULLET IN FILO WITH PESTO

Red mullet is not difficult to fillet, but you have to ensure that all the bones have been removed. Ask your fishmonger to fillet the fish, but still check carefully for any bones that may have been left behind and pull them out with tweezers.

This is a very pretty dish when the crisp brown filo crust is cut open to reveal the moist fillet of red mullet on a bed of potato and pesto. The potatoes are not new potatoes, but small mature potatoes like Belle de Fontenay. The packets can be prepared several hours in advance and kept refrigerated until needed.

INGREDIENTS

4 small potatoes (see
  introduction)
12 sheets of filo pastry
5tbsp Pesto (see page 91)
4 fillets of red mullet,
  carefully boned
30g/1oz butter
salt and pepper
olive oil, for greasing

PREPARATION

Cook the potatoes in their skins in a pan of boiling salted water for 15–20 minutes or until just cooked.

Preheat the oven to 200°C/400°F/gas6.

Peel a potato and slice crosswise into 4. Brush 3 sheets of filo with olive oil and arrange overlapping but at angles to one another. Lay the potato slices in a row across the centre and put a teaspoon of pesto on top of each slice. Put a red mullet fillet on top, skin side up, season with salt and pepper and fold the pastry over, wrapping loosely as if making a parcel.

Put on an oiled baking tray. Make 3 more parcels in the same way, transferring them to the tray when done. Melt the butter and brush them all over with it.

COOKING

Bake for 20 minutes until the filo is puffed up and golden.

SEA BASS WITH OLIVES & ROAST TOMATOES

Throughout the Mediterranean, whole baked fish feature on every seaside restaurant menu. Typically these will be grey mullet, sea bream or sea bass. The following treatment – where the fish is cooked in the oven on a bed of potatoes surrounded with roast tomatoes – can be used for any of them. It is also a good way to cook a large piece of cod fillet, in which case it goes in skin side up.

Your fishmonger should gut and descale the fish and cut out the gills for you. If for some reason you have to do this yourself, use a strong sharp pair of scissors to cut off the back and side fins, being careful of the back spines which are poisonous. A third of the way along the fish from the tail, make an incision in the belly, then cut forward to just behind the head. Pull out and detach the mass of guts where they adhere behind the head. Cut out the gills with scissors. Use a small sharp knife to scrape the scales from the fish, rubbing and scraping from the tail end towards the head.

INGREDIENTS (FOR 6)

12 plum tomatoes
2–3tsp caster sugar
250ml/8fl oz olive oil
675g/1½lb potatoes (peeled weight)
2 slices of baguette
3 garlic cloves
10 basil leaves
1 sea bass, weighing about 900g–1kg/2–2¼lb, or equivalent weight of cod, cut from the thick end of the fillet
20 black olives
1 glass (150ml/¼pt) of dry white wine
1 lemon
salt and pepper
large handful of flat-leaf parsley

PREPARATION

Preheat the oven to 250°C/475°F/gas9.
First prepare the roast tomatoes: cut the tomatoes in half lengthwise. Pack into a gratin dish, cut side up, and season with salt, pepper and 1 teaspoon of caster sugar. Dribble over 2 tablespoons of olive oil.

COOKING

Roast the tomatoes for 40 minutes, moving them around after 20 minutes to ensure even cooking.

While they are roasting, put a large pan of salted water to heat. Peel the potatoes and cut into slices about 1cm/½in thick. Parboil the potato slices for 8–10 minutes. Drain and reserve.

Toast the slices of baguette and process to a fine crumb. Peel, smash and chop the garlic and rub together with the bread.

Remove the tomatoes from the oven when they are cooked and have started to shrink. Leave the oven on.

Brush the bottom of a roasting dish with olive oil. Cover the base with sliced potato in a single layer. Brush with oil, spread the basil leaves along the centre and lay the fish on top, skin side up. Arrange the roast tomatoes around the edges and scatter the olives on top of them.

Pour over the wine and the remaining olive oil. Season the fish and potatoes with salt and pepper. Scatter the garlic breadcrumbs over all but the tomatoes. Moisten with a little more oil.

Put in the oven. After 5 minutes, turn the setting down to 200°C/400°F/gas6 and bake for 15 minutes more. Squeeze over the juice from the lemon and return to the oven for a further 10 minutes.

SERVING

Serve with lots of parsley leaves strewn over.

SALT FISH

The Mediterranean's fish have been depleted and its sea polluted to a point where local catches in many areas have become tragically sparse. It is the same the whole world over, but the Mediterranean is comparatively small, and contained by too many countries hungry for its resources. The result has been devastating. Varieties that have always been associated with the Mediterranean – like tuna, red and grey mullet, John Dory and sardines – are increasingly caught farther afield, with more and more fish coming in from Brazil and the Seychelles. However, for hundreds of years the voracious appetite of Mediterranean countries for fish has been partly satisfied by distant netting grounds, with salt cod the most obvious example.

Drying and salting, either separately or in combination, are – along with smoking – the most ancient forms of food preservation known to man. Wind-drying of meat and fish still features in the Cantonese diet, as it has done for thousands of years. Bombay duck, the small sea fish sun-dried in that Indian city, is still a pungent and traditional accompaniment to curry dishes, though not for the faint-hearted. Bonito, a large mackerel-like game fish, is dried and flaked to make *dashi* broth, an essential ingredient in Japanese cooking. Salt-pickled and dried Mediterranean fish, like anchovies, sturgeon, tuna and swordfish from the Caspian and Black Seas and tuna hearts from Spain and southern Italy, were luxury foods in ancient Rome. Over a thousand years ago, Atlantic and North Sea cod was caught by fishermen from the Mediterranean countries, heavily salted in barrels and taken back to the hotter climes of the south, establishing a culinary tradition which is still evident in the Mediterranean diet in dishes like *brandade de morue* and *bacalao*.

In the age of canning, deep-freezing and *sous-vide*, historic treatments for preservation of perishable foods are today used principally for the unique flavours and textures they impart. Think of smoked salmon and lightly cured kippers. Both are exposed briefly to salt first and then to a relatively cold smoking over oak to cure them. In their original form, they were coarse by comparison. The red herring of popular reference, for example, lent itself to analogy because it was so salty, so smoky and so strong-tasting that it dominated any other flavour and drew attention to itself.

Pretty much any fish can be salted and dried, though when this is done traditionally, as with salt cod, the resulting board-hard flesh needs lengthy rehydration in running water before it is palatable. Three days in cold water would be typical. Salt cod has enjoyed a vogue in chic restaurants in recent times, making its rather heavy presence felt in reworkings of dishes like fish cakes, where little benefit is perceivable over the fresh alternative. And, if cod is not as fresh as it should be, then a winning option is good-quality frozen cod fillet, which continues to beat non-frozen 'fresh' cod in blind tastings.

One way of experiencing the flavour benefits of preserved fish without the aggravation of rehydrating one of those wooden blocks from an Italian delicatessen is to try salting cod yourself.

Before you can eat commercial dried cod it needs to have lengthy soaking in cold water. The best way to do it is by leaving the fillets in a basin with water trickling in from the cold tap for 24 hours. If this is not possible, then change the water as often as you can manage over a 24-hour period. Test for saltiness by cutting a thin slice from the centre of a fillet and chewing it. If it is still too salty then continue soaking, and check every hour until you are happy with the taste. You can now cook it any way you would cook fresh cod – grilling, broiling, sautéing, roasting or in a fish broth or chowder. It is particularly delicious marinated in fresh lemon or lime juice and served raw on a bed of dressed rocket with borlotti beans.

Home-salted Cod Fillets

The kind of salt cod we associate with the Mediterranean is the heavily salted and sun-dried stockfish that hang like wooden boards outside food shops. These are cod prepared as they have been for a thousand years, to produce a basic protein source that keeps in the hottest weather without going off.

While dishes like Provençal *brandade de morue* and Portuguese *bacalao* use it to best advantage, one should not think salt cod is intrinsically superior to fresh. Indeed, it only existed at all because refrigeration and freezing did not. Traditional salted fish is therefore more to be judged for its preservative merits than on its culinary excellence. The limitations are known and should be understood.

However, salting purely to improve succulence, flavour and texture is a splendid technique to embrace enthusiastically at home. Fresh or frozen cod fillets are exposed to salt for between 2 and 24 hours and then the fish is soaked to remove excess salt before use. That something so easy can produce such extraordinary and beneficial changes is difficult to believe until you try it yourself. It does not really work with less than 900g/2lb of cod, and 1.8kg/4lb is better.

For every 450g/1lb of cod fillets you will need 55g/2oz Maldon sea salt. Scatter half the total salt over the base of a metal or glazed pottery dish and lay the fillets on it, flesh side down. Put the rest of the salt on the top, pressing into the skin. If you are doing more than one layer, ensure an even distribution of salt between each layer of fish, taking care that there are no areas without salt, or those parts will go off in a very nasty and smelly fashion. Cover tightly with cling film (foil is not impervious to the pickle), place a weight on top and leave overnight in the refrigerator. Once salted it will keep for a week without deterioration in the refrigerator, but no longer. Home-dried cod needs a maximum of 30 minutes' desalination under a dribble of cold running water before use.

HOME-SALTED COD CROQUETTES

These croquettes can be made using unsalted cod, but a couple of hours' salting in the refrigerator followed by 30 minutes' desalination in running water does wonders for the depth of flavour.

You can either deep- or shallow-fry. The advantages of the former method are speed – they cook at 180°C/350°F in 3–4 minutes – and uniformity of crispness in the finished coating. The latter is marginally less calorific, but takes 10–15 minutes and it is more difficult to turn the cylinders without breaking them and to get an even finish.

You can serve these croquettes as a mezze or with Quick Tomato Sauce (page 60) as a lunch main course, with some green beans or spinach. You can halve the amounts, but it is worth making this much because they freeze well.

INGREDIENTS

450g/1lb desalinated Home-salted Cod Fillets (see page 109) or fresh cod
450g/1lb potatoes
5 eggs
bunch of flat-leaf parsley
575ml/1pt milk
1 bay leaf
1tbsp olive oil
55g/2oz Parmesan cheese (optional)
4 individual (15g/$\frac{1}{2}$oz) bags of plain potato crisps or 55-85g/2-3oz dry breadcrumbs
85g/3oz flour
$\frac{1}{4}$ nutmeg
salt and pepper
sunflower oil, for frying
1 lemon, to serve

PREPARATION

Well ahead of time and ideally the day before: if using fresh cod, salt as described on page 109.

Rinse the salted fish under cold running water for 30 minutes. Cut the fish into pieces.

Peel the potatoes and cut them into chunks. Separate 2 of the eggs. Remove the stalks from the parsley and chop the leaves.

Put the fish in a saucepan with the milk, parsley stalks and bay leaf. Bring to the boil, turn down the heat and simmer for 4 minutes, or until just done. Strain through a sieve, reserving the milk. When the fish is cool enough to handle, remove and discard the skin, bones and bay leaf.

While the fish is cooking and cooling, cook the potatoes in a large pan of rapidly boiling lightly salted water until just tender. Drain and return to the pan.

Ideally using an electric whisk, beat the potatoes with the cod. You can also use a masher or a fork, but do not use a food processor which will turn the mixture into glue.

While whisking or mashing, add 1 whole egg and the whites of the 2 separated eggs. Then dribble in 1–2 tablespoons of the reserved milk and 1 tablespoon of olive oil, until you have a smooth thick purée. You want to achieve a consistency which you can handle and shape, so do not allow the mixture to get too slack. If liked, also grate and add the Parmesan at this stage. Season with grated nutmeg and pepper. If using salted fillets, you are unlikely to need to add salt, but you make that decision when you taste.

Mound into a bowl and refrigerate for at least 2 hours, before attempting to make the croquettes.

When ready to prepare the croquettes: if using the crisps, put them in a tray and crush with a rolling pin. Put the flour seasoned with 1 teaspoon of salt and $\frac{1}{2}$ teaspoon of pepper in a large soup bowl and whisk the egg yolks with the remaining whole eggs and put into a similar dish.

Using a tablespoon, scoop out enough mixture to make a croquette about 5cm/2in long with a diameter of 3cm/1$\frac{1}{4}$in. Drop it into the flour and, using one hand, roll the croquette in it to coat. Then coat it with egg and finally, using your other hand, roll it in the crushed crisps or crumbs. Transfer to a baking tray. Repeat until you have used up all the mixture. If you run out of the egg mixture, just whisk up another whole egg at a time.

If deep-frying, preheat the sunflower oil to 180°C/350°F. If shallow-frying, use 2 large frying pans to avoid crowding. Cook, in batches if necessary, for about 4–5 minutes if deep-frying or 10–15 minutes if shallow-frying, turning once.

After they are done, drain briefly on paper towels before serving. If cooking in batches, keep each batch warm on a pile of paper towels in a low oven with the door open until all are cooked.

SERVING

If serving them on their own, cut a wedge of lemon for each plate.

LLANA-STYLE SALT COD

This essentially Catalan treatment is easy and quick to cook. The Catalans would, understandably, prefer a more complex interpretation. The cod is briefly home-salted (see page 109), which adds to its succulence and texture. The contrasting colours of the grilled pepper strips make the dish look very pretty. It needs nothing with it, apart from some bread to mop up the juices. On reflection, culturally dissonant mashed potatoes would also be nice.

INGREDIENTS

550g/1¼lb Home-salted
    Cod (see page 109, with
    cod cut from the thick end
    of the fillet)
1 large or 2 small red sweet
    pepper(s)
1 large or 2 small yellow
    sweet pepper(s)
2 plum tomatoes
1 hot red chilli
2 spring onions
3 garlic cloves
large handful of flat-leaf
    parsley
4-6tbsp olive oil
½tsp ground cinnamon
small bunch of chives
1 bay leaf
1tsp sugar
1 glass (150ml/¼pt) of
    dry white wine
flour, for dusting
salt and pepper

PREPARATION

Cut the cod into 4 pieces and put in cold running water until desalinated.

Cut the sweet peppers in half lengthwise, remove the seeds and pith and grill on a dry ridged grill pan, turning frequently, until blackened and blistered on the outside. Transfer to a bowl, cover and leave for 15 minutes, then peel and cut into 1cm/½in strips.

Preheat the oven to 190°C/375°F/gas5.

Blanch the tomatoes briefly in boiling water. Refresh in cold water, peel, deseed and dice. Split the chilli, deseed and cut across into thin strips. Trim the spring onions and slice into the finest julienne strips. Peel, smash and chop the garlic. Destalk the parsley and chop half of it. Chop the chives.

Drain the cod and dredge in lightly seasoned flour.

COOKING

Brown the cod lightly on both sides in 3 tablespoons of olive oil in a frying pan. Transfer to a roasting dish in which the pieces will just fit in a single layer. Scatter the pepper strips over. Add the garlic, chilli, cinnamon, chives and bay leaf to the pan. Cook over a moderate heat, stirring, for 2 minutes. Then add the tomatoes, spring onions, sugar and wine. Bubble briskly until it thickens to a sauce-like consistency and pour over the cod. Spoon over the remaining olive oil and the chopped parsley. Bake for 15 minutes.

SERVING

Scatter over the whole parsley leaves and serve immediately.

SOUTHERN SEAFOOD RISOTTO

We think of risotto as being inherently northern Italian — rich and creamy with butter and stock — but when cooked with olive oil and a fish fumet and studded with shellfish it takes on the qualities of an altogether lighter and sunnier dish.

INGREDIENTS

225g/8oz squid
225g/8oz mussels
2 tsp cumin seeds
2 carrots
1 large onion
6 shallots
2 garlic cloves
2 celery stalks
large handful of flat-leaf
    parsley
1/2 bottle (400ml/14fl oz)
    of dry white wine
450g/1lb cooked prawns in
    their shells
sprig of thyme
2 bay leaves
14–16 saffron threads
100ml/3 1/2 fl oz olive oil
350g/12oz Arborio rice
225g/8oz small clams
    (optional)
salt and pepper

PREPARATION

Clean the squid and cut into strips. Scrub and beard the mussels, discarding any which do not close when tapped.

Toast the cumin seeds in a dry pan, grind to a powder and reserve.

Peel and dice the carrots. Peel the onion and cut it into pieces. Do the same with the shallots. Peel, smash and chop the garlic. Coarsely chop the celery. Destalk the parsley and chop the leaves.

COOKING

Put the white wine in a saucepan and bring to the boil. Throw in the mussels, put on a lid and cook for 2 minutes, or until the mussels are cooked and have opened. Remove the mussels with a slotted spoon. Cut the mussel flesh out with a small knife and reserve in a bowl, returning the shells to the wine in the pan.

Dehead and peel the prawns, putting the prawns with the mussels and adding the heads and shells to the stock-pot.

Add the carrots and onions to the pan, together with the celery, thyme, bay, parsley stalks and 1 litre/1 3/4 pt of water. Bring to the boil, lower the heat, skim and then simmer for 30 minutes. Strain through a sieve into another saucepan, season to taste and keep at a bare simmer on the hob.

Ladle a little of the hot stock over the saffron and leave to steep.

In a suitable large heavy saucepan, fry the shallots in 3 tablespoons of the olive oil until translucent. As they soften, add the chopped garlic and cook for a minute. Then add the rice and ground cumin and stir for 2 minutes to coat.

Start to add the fish stock, a ladleful at a time, stirring until the liquid is absorbed before adding the next ladleful. Repeat until the rice is cooked and creamy, which will take about 20 minutes. If you use up all the stock before the rice is done, put the kettle on and finish with ladlefuls of boiling water.

About 5 minutes before the end of cooking, add the saffron and its steeping liquid together with the clams, if using, and stir briefly until they open. Stir in the mussels and prawns, cover the pan with a lid and take off the heat to rest for 5 minutes.

Put the remaining olive oil in a frying pan and quickly stir-fry the squid over a high heat. This will take literally 60–90 seconds. Stir into the risotto. Adjust the seasoning, if neccessary.

SERVING

Serve in warmed soup plates, scattered with the chopped parsley.

SEARED SQUID STEAKS WITH OLIVE OIL MASHED POTATOES

Cleaned squid bodies — white slippery flaccid tubes — look like something familiar and contemporary, but neither of us can think quite what that is. With the exception of this dish, every recipe in the book demands small squid. Here you want as big a squid body as you can find. Two 450g/1lb tubes would be perfect to give four rectangular steaks, 115–140g/4–5oz in weight, with the flesh at least 5mm/¼in thick. You can find frozen cleaned squid bodies which grill well and which weigh about 225g/8oz each. Cut down one side and opened up then trimmed at the pointed (tail) end, these will make one steak each. Once trimmed carefully, cut a diamond cross-hatch into each side, taking care not to cut all the way through.

Squid cooks in seconds, then becomes rubbery — not as tough as octopus, but too resilient to get a blunt table knife through without a struggle. The secret is to use two very hot frying pans and to cook the steaks for no more than 30 seconds a side. When the rectangles hit the pan, they will balloon upwards briefly. Immediately turn them the other way up and within seconds they will roll determinedly into a cylinder.

INGREDIENTS

1 red onion
4tbsp olive oil
2 hot red chillies
2 garlic cloves
4 squid steaks (see above)
salt and pepper
small handful coriander leaves, to finish
extra-virgin olive oil, to serve (optional)

FOR THE OLIVE OIL MASHED POTATOES:
900g/2lb potatoes
5tbsp extra-virgin olive oil
¼ nutmeg

PREPARATION

Peel the potatoes and cut them into chunks. Cook them in a large pan of boiling salted for 20 minutes, or until just tender.

While they are cooking, peel and dice the onion and fry until browned in a little of the olive oil.

Deseed the chillies, cut the flesh into thin strips and add to the onion. Peel, smash and chop the garlic, adding to the pan only as the onions are cooked. Stir to cook briefly and remove from the heat and reserve.

Prepare the squid steaks as described, brush with the remaining oil, season with salt and pepper.

When the potatoes are cooked, drain well and mash them with the extra-virgin olive oil and season with salt, pepper and grated nutmeg. Keep warm.

Destalk and chop the coriander.

COOKING

Heat 2 dry heavy frying pans until very hot. Lay 2 steaks in each, turn with tongs after 30 seconds. Turn and, as they roll up, take the pans off the heat and scatter over the onion mixture.

SERVING

Transfer to warmed individual serving plates and serve at once, with a big spoonful of the mashed potatoes and with the fried onion, garlic and chilli mixture scattered over. Finish with chopped coriander leaves. A little more extra-virgin olive oil may be poured over, if desired.

CHILLI-MARINATED OCTOPUS

Octopus is sold throughout the Mediterranean, but few of our fishmongers buy it from the market. It can be rubbery and impossibly tough, but this is entirely to do with how it is cooked. You must either cook it for ages or eat it almost raw. Cook moderately and you may as well put a steel-belted radial on the plate.

Here only the tentacles are served – and big ones, with a diameter of about 2.5cm/1in, are ideal. If you are lucky enough to have an Oriental fishmonger to hand, then he will almost certainly have regular supplies of octopus. Japanese fishmongers actually offer ready-blanched tentacles, which need no preliminary cleaning or blanching. If you do persuade your local fishmonger to get octopus for you, you may have to take the whole thing; in which case, get him to behead and gut it – an unpleasant chore.

INGREDIENTS (FOR 8)

900g/2lb octopus tentacles
1 kaffir lime leaf (desirable but optional)
1 small hot red chilli
2 lemons
salt
3tbsp extra-virgin olive oil, to dress
few drops of Kikkoman soy sauce, to dress
handful of chives, to garnish

PREPARATION

At least 1¼ hours ahead of serving: put to heat a large pan of heavily salted water (think saline, think sea water).

Clean the tentacles by putting them in a large bowl, coating them liberally with coarse salt and rubbing it in for 5 minutes. It is best to wear rubber gloves for this task. Rinse thoroughly.

When the water is boiling rapidly, holding with tongs, dip a tentacle into it for 20 seconds. Remove, then dunk it back in again for a further 20 seconds. Repeat the process a third time and put it into a pottery or glass dish. The tentacle will curl up during this blanching process. Blanch the other tentacles in the same way and add them to the dish. This three-dip technique is called 'scaring' the octopus and is said to tenderize it more than if you just stuck it in the boiling liquid and left it there for the whole minute.

If using, shred the lime leaf finely. Deseed and finely chop the chilli. Stir these in with the octopus. Juice the lemons and pour this over. Sprinkle with a little salt and leave to marinate for at least 1 hour at room temperature, turning frequently. It will keep, cling wrapped and refrigerated, for up to a week – and indeed benefits from such lengthy marinating.

SERVING

Cut the tentacles at an angle into scalloped 1cm/½in slices, leaving the curled tips intact. Arrange on a serving dish, pour over the marinade and dress with the extra-virgin olive oil.

Pretend a Japanese visitor to the Mediterranean brought some Kikkoman soy sauce along and, out of deference to him, add a few drops to complete the dressing. Finish the presentation with some snipped chives.

POLPO & POTATO HASH

Octopus may be barely cooked or well cooked. In this treatment the octopus is simmered in a lemon-acidulated court-bouillon until tender, then cut into bite-sized pieces and tossed with cubes of spiced potato, onion and garlic – a hash with a difference.

Gnarled Mediterranean fishermen give the creatures a terrible beating on the rocks to tenderize the rubbery brutes prior to taking them to the markets. This is a favourite photograph for food books. Note that wherever the fishermen come from – Greece, Spain, you name it – they are always gnarled. Perhaps there is a modelling agency which specializes in this esoteric area. 'I need a shot of a fisherman battering an octopus on the rocks. He must look archetypal and weather-beaten, sort of craggy-faced. We will supply the loose-knitted navy-blue jumper, but he must be gnarled.' There is a pause as the agent checks availability. 'We have Julio or Spiros, depending on ethnic preference. They are very experienced and have appeared in illustrated food books all over the world. And they are both extensively gnarled.'

INGREDIENTS (FOR 6)

450g / 1lb octopus tentacles
450g / 1lb potatoes
450g / 1lb onions
3 garlic cloves
2 chillies
5 tbsp olive oil
1 tbsp paprika
1 tbsp turmeric
salt and pepper

FOR THE LEMON COURT-BOUILLON:
1 onion
2 celery stalks
bunch of parsley
3 lemons
4 kaffir lime leaves
12 black peppercorns
2 tbsp salt

PREPARATION

The octopus and court-bouillon can be prepared the day before.

Make the court-bouillon: coarsely chop the onion and celery. Destalk the parsley, reserving the stalks, and chop the leaves. Juice the lemons.

Put the onion, celery, parsley stalks, lemon juice and all the other court-bouillon ingredients in 2.25 litres/2qt of cold water. Bring to the boil and simmer for 20 minutes. Strain into another pan.

Bring the strained cooking liquid to a simmer. Put in the tentacles and poach for 90 minutes. Taste a piece: if it is not tender, continue cooking until it is. Turn off the heat and leave to cool in the court-bouillon.

Peel the potatoes and cut into large dice.

COOKING

Parboil the potatoes in a large pan of boiling salted water for 10 minutes, then strain through a colander.

While they are cooling, peel and dice the onions and garlic. Destalk and deseed the chillies and cut into julienne strips.

Fry the onion and garlic in half the olive oil until translucent. Then add the chillies and cook for a minute. Remove and reserve.

Cut the tentacles into bite-sized pieces, pulling away the skin and discarding it.

Put some more oil in the pan, add the potatoes and cook over a medium heat, tossing until they start to brown. Return the onions and garlic to the pan, scatter over the paprika and turmeric and toss and turn for 2–3 minutes.

Add the octopus pieces, season, stir and warm through.

SERVING

Serve scattered with chopped parsley.

SEAFOOD PLATEAU

Seafood salads are too often grim travesties, a dumping ground of overcooked ingredients that are cooked together then allowed to sit around and fester. This is called a plateau to distinguish it from these poor relations, for here the end result is improved by cooking all the elements separately and only mixing them together at the last moment before the dish is dressed and brought to the table. This means the different elements are cooked for precisely the right length of time and their individual flavours and textures are kept sharp and identifiable.

Get your fishmonger to open and clean the scallops for you, but ask for the shells which, when scrubbed, will play an important visual part in the presentation.

INGREDIENTS

12 tiger prawns
2$\frac{1}{2}$ garlic cloves
3 lemons
about 175ml/6fl oz olive oil
24 mussels
1 glass (150ml/$\frac{1}{4}$pt) of
    dry white wine
4 large scallops with shells
1tsp ground coriander seeds
1tsp ground cumin
24 palourde clams
350g/12oz squid bodies or
    tentacles
1 small hot fresh red chilli
4 tomatoes
handful of flat-leaf parsley, to
    garnish
extra-virgin olive oil, to dress
salt and pepper

PREPARATION

Remove the heads of the prawns (if present) and reserve for stock. Using a small, sharp knife, cut through their backs. Remove the digestive tract, then cut carefully all the way through the flesh to the inside of the shell, making sure you do not cut through it. Open and gently press them flat to make a triangular shape, with the two pieces of meat on either side and the uncut shell base underneath. Put the prawns flesh side up on a tray.

Peel the garlic and chop as finely as you can. Juice the lemons. Sprinkle most of the garlic over the prawns, then dribble over about two-thirds of the lemon juice and a couple of tablespoons of the olive oil. Season and leave to marinate for 10 minutes.

COOKING

To cook the prawns: preheat the grill and a heavy frying pan on the hob. Put the prawns in the pan, shell down, and cook for 2 minutes. Pour over the marinade and finish by putting the pan under the grill for 30 seconds. Transfer to a large serving dish and allow to cool.

Debeard, scrape and wash the mussels, discarding those that don't close when tapped. Then steam them briefly with the wine in a tightly lidded saucepan until they open. Drain, reserving the juices. Leave to cool and remove the upper shells.

Clean the scallops and slice each into 2 or 3 discs, as their thickness permits. Mix the ground coriander and cumin with $\frac{1}{2}$ teaspoon each of salt and ground black pepper in 2 tablespoons of olive oil. Gently toss the scallop slices in this mixture to coat.

Heat a heavy dry pan until very hot. Lay the scallop slices in it and sear for 30 seconds, then turn and cook for another 30 seconds. Remove from the pan, allow to cool and put with the prawns.

Cook the palourde clams in a lightly oiled pan over a medium heat until they open. This they usually do one at a time. As they do so, remove and add to the mussels, but do not remove the upper shells. Do not wash the pan as you will use it to finish the dressing.

Cut the squid into bite-sized pieces. Make a seasoned oil as for the scallops, adding the deseeded and finely chopped chilli and the reserved finely chopped garlic clove. Coat the pieces in this oil.

Sauté over a high heat, tossing for 2 minutes. Do not overcrowd the pan: cook in 2 batches if necessary. Remove and allow to cool.

Scald the tomatoes for 30 seconds in a pan of boiling water, refresh briefly in ice-cold water, then peel. Cut in half and deseed with a small spoon, then cut the flesh into small dice.

Put the mussel liquor, the remaining lemon juice, the chopped tomato and the remaining olive oil in the squid pan. Bring to the boil, whisk and remove to cool.

SERVING

Put all the seafood together in the serving dish. Whisk the just warm dressing and pour it over. Toss gently, trying not to dislodge the clams from their shells. Put the scrubbed scallop shells on individual plates and arrange the seafood on them. Serve immediately, scattered with parsley and dressed with a little extra-virgin olive oil.

SEAFOOD & PARSLEY LASAGNE

This is a very special lasagne, using expensive ingredients. Pre-cooked pasta sheets, bought ready to go into the oven, are one of the great labour-saving boons of recent times and, as long as you remember to make your sauce more liquid than you otherwise would, the results are generally excellent. However, if you have a pasta machine and are in the habit of making your own, then you know that rolling out sheets is quick and easy. This recipe invites you to make the dish with an egg-rich home-made lasagne but, of course, it will still be good using the commercial instant variety — you will need one 225g/8oz box. Cooking time in the oven is critical — too long and all those expensive shellfish will go rubbery.

INGREDIENTS (FOR 8)

1 litre/1³/₄pt Quick Tomato
  Sauce (see page 60)
55g/2oz flour
55g/2oz butter
850ml/1¹/₂pt milk
1 bay leaf
1 sherry glass (4tbsp) of dry
  sherry
¹/₂ nutmeg
450g/1lb clams
24 tiger prawns
450g/1lb squid
bunch of flat-leaf parsley
1 kg/2¹/₄lb mussels
about 5tbsp dry white wine
salt and pepper

FOR THE PASTA:
500g/1lb 2oz strong white
  bread flour, plus more for
  dusting
small pinch of salt
5 eggs

PREPARATION

If using your own, first make the pasta dough by sifting the flour with the salt into a food processor. Add the eggs and turn on at full speed, stopping as soon as the dough balls. Transfer to a floured surface and knead as for bread for 8–10 minutes, shaking on a little more flour if it gets too sticky. Wrap in cling film and leave to rest for 1 hour. (You will also need to rest after all that kneading, but can do so without being cling-wrapped.)

Roll out it out into sheets, using a pasta machine setting 2.

Make the tomato sauce as described on page 60.

Make a béchamel sauce: melt the butter in a saucepan over a gentle heat, stir in the flour and cook the roux for a few minutes or so. Whisk in the milk, add the bay leaf and the sherry and simmer for 20 minutes. Season with grated nutmeg, salt and pepper.

While the sauce is simmering, put the clams in the freezer for 15 minutes. They will then open just enough for you to slip a knife in and lever them open. Detach the clams and add to the tomato sauce.

Peel and devein the prawns and add those to the tomato sauce. Clean the squid and cut into bite-sized pieces and add to the sauce.

Chop up 4 tablespoons of parsley and stir this in too.

Debeard, scrape and wash the mussels, discarding those that don't close when tapped. Then steam them briefly with the wine in a tightly lidded saucepan until they open. Drain, reserving the juices. Leave to cool slightly and remove from the shells. Add the shelled mussels and reserved juices to the sauce.

Preheat the oven to 200°C/400°F/gas6. Brush a rectangular 27cm/10³/₄in ovenproof dish with olive oil.

If using fresh pasta, arrange the sheets overlapping the sides as well as covering the base. In any case, start by covering the base first.

Spoon over one-third of the tomato and shellfish sauce. Put 4 tablespoons of béchamel on top. Put on a second layer of pasta and another third of the tomato sauce. Then arrange another pasta layer, followed by the remaining tomato sauce and a final layer of pasta. Pour over the remaining béchamel and grate nutmeg over the top.

COOKING

Put the dish on a baking sheet and bake for 25–30 minutes.

SERVING

Leave to stand for 10 minutes before cutting, but serve piping hot.

TIGER PRAWNS & BEANS

This combination works best with fresh cannellini beans — which are obtainable for a brief period during August — but it is also very good with premium-quality dried, which are always to be found in Italian shops. If none are available, then use haricots. Prawns 'n beanz sounds a slightly odd pairing, but is eaten avidly throughout central and southern Italy.

Tiger prawns are imported frozen in blocks, most often from the estuaries of rivers running into the Bay of Bengal. When sold in fishmongers or markets, they tend to have been defrosted and you will have no idea whether this was done the day before or, even worse, perhaps longer ago than that. It is, therefore, best to buy them frozen and only defrost them 3 hours before you are going to prepare them. This will give you the freshest taste and the best texture. Allow about 40 minutes to prepare the prawns prior to cooking.

INGREDIENTS

20 frozen tiger prawns in the
    shell
450g/1lb fresh cannellini or
    225g/8oz dried haricots
1 bay leaf
2 dried red chillies
2-3 garlic cloves
1 lemon
3tbsp olive oil
1tbsp Gremolata (see page
    92)
salt and pepper

PREPARATION

Three hours before you intend serving the dish: remove the prawns from the freezer and spread them out on a tray at room temperature to defrost. (They are frozen in a water glaze to give the seller more profit and, as they defrost, you can watch the money drain away.)

After preliminary soaking (see pages 48-9 for general comments on cooking dried pulses), fresh cannellini take about 40 minutes to cook and the dried variety about $1\frac{1}{2}$ hours. Bubble them in plenty of lightly salted water together with some black pepper, the bay leaf, chillies and whole garlic cloves for the requisite time. Skim frequently and top up with water as necessary.

Prepare the prawns by cutting carefully through the back and extracting the intestinal thread. Wipe the flesh inside with a damp cloth. Put them in cold salted water for 10–15 minutes, then swirl with your fingers, gently rubbing them. Transfer to a colander or sieve and rinse briefly under cold water. Leave to drain.

When the beans are done, remove the bay leaf, chillies and garlic and leave in the water to keep warm. Juice the lemon.

COOKING

Put a large non-stick frying pan over a low heat to warm thoroughly before turning the heat up to medium. This is the best way to slow down deterioration of the non-stick surface. Put a cold non-stick pan over a high flame and you kiss the surface goodbye.

Put the prawns into a bowl with a spoonful of olive oil and some black pepper and toss to coat.

Throw them all at once into the pan and toss and stir for 2 minutes. The shells will blush and the prawns open along the cut, while the flesh becomes white and opaque. Do not overcook.

Put the prawns into a warmed serving dish, add the lemon juice, gremolata and 2 tablespoons of olive oil. Drain the beans, add to the bowl and toss all together to mix thoroughly.

SERVING

Serve at once, after reminding your guests that the allocation is 5 prawns each to avoid any ugly scenes.

5 POULTRY & GAME

Free-range chickens are among the nicest things we can think of to eat. Before dreaded battery farms came on the scene, chickens were expensive and a real treat. Then they got literally tainted with fish meal and the grotesquely cruel conditions in which they were – and still are – raised. They got cheaper and cheaper, and nastier and nastier. Today we are becoming more aware of the difference in flavour and texture between a free-range chicken – allowed space, some daylight and the opportunity to graze on worms and insects – and one raised on horrible things and denied access to the open air. This is not imagination or emotive and liberal nonsense, but based on objective comparisons by food scientists. You can literally taste the difference; and if you cannot, then perhaps cooking is not really your *métier*. Supermarkets are pretty evasive on the subject of what precisely defines a free-range chicken but, even if what they sell under that name are not quite what a French shop would sell as a *poulet label rouge* or a *poulet de Bresse*, they are not half bad and will provide you with all you need to cook the recipes that follow.

Mediterranean cultures have little dealings with intensive chicken rearing, so fowls still have an honourable place on the table, along with partridge, wild

pigeon, duck and squab – that is, domesticated ring-neck doves. Throughout Arab countries, by the *souks* of the old towns, you will find cafés that specialize in hot-pit barbecuing squab and chicken, which revolve by the dozen on long fast-rotating spits. They are constantly basted by a grill cook who uses a paint brush tied to a long handle to do the job, but it must be hotter than Hades for him just the same. A group of English tourists watch his perform-ance with detached interest before ordering: 'That's four beers and four dove and chips, Mohammed.' Ah, the new army that travels on its stomach…

SPICY GRILLED CHICKEN WINGS

Chicken wings may be cheap, but they can become quite special when marinated and spiced and then grilled until the skin crisps. Supermarkets sell them in large packs, as the near give-away bonus of dismembering birds to sell as breast, drumstick and thigh joints. Looking at the size of some of these wings and extrapolating from them to the stature of the whole chicken can lead to uneasy thoughts about their life-style. You have never seen a chicken that big because, if you had, it would stick in the memory. 'I was driving past Chix-Stix plc the other day when a chicken the size of an ostrich ran across the road.' Perhaps they are raised secretly in giant percheries and fed a diet of anabolic steroids and growth hormones, so better not give them to the children too often unless of course you want them to be professional basketball players.

Because they are high in fat, the wings take a lot longer to get crisp than you might think; even after 20–25 minutes' grilling they will not be overdone. Start cooking about 13–15cm/5–6in away from the grill to avoid burning the outside before they are cooked around the bones. Turn frequently and move them closer to the heat once the wings start to brown properly. If your grill is quite small, you will need to cook them in two batches. Keep the first batch warm while cooking the second then, when they are done, return the first batch to the grill and re-crisp briefly.

INGREDIENTS (FOR 6 AS A FIRST COURSE)

18–24 large chicken wings, depending on size
4tsp coriander seeds
2tsp cumin seeds
4 hot chillies
2 garlic cloves
4tsp Tabasco sauce
2tbsp Zagzoug & Matbouli Middle Eastern Worcestershire sauce (substitute Lea & Perrins if unobtainable)
3 lemons
100ml/3½fl oz olive oil
12–18 spring onions
1tsp salt
½tsp pepper

TO SERVE:
handful of coriander leaves
2 limes or lemons
Harissa (see page 89)
Quick Tomato Sauce (see page 60)

PREPARATION

Cut each chicken wing through the joints into 3 pieces, discarding the tips or freezing them to add to your next stock pot.

Toast the coriander and cumin seeds in a dry pan over a low heat for 2–3 minutes, then grind to a powder and put this into a bowl.

Destalk and deseed the chillies and cut into very tiny dice. Peel, smash and finely chop the garlic. Add to the bowl of spices, together with the diced chilli, the Tabasco and Worcestershire sauces, the juice of the 3 lemons and the oil. Season and stir well.

Put them into a large zip-lock bag (or 2 bags if there are too many for one) and add the marinade. Zip closed and leave for 4 hours, turning and shaking from time to time. Alternatively, marinate at room temperature for 2 hours and refrigerate overnight, removing from the refrigerator 2 hours before grilling.

COOKING

Grill about 15cm/6in away from the flame or electric elements, turning frequently. Baste at intervals with the marinade.

Trim the spring onions and brush them with the marinade and reserve.

Just before you judge the wings are done, preheat a ridged grill pan. When hot, toss the spring onions in it until they are marked with charred stripes and slightly wilted.

SERVING

When the wings are done, put them on a large warmed serving plate. Scatter the onions over and a handful of chopped coriander leaves. Put a quarter of lime or lemon on each plate and put a pot of harissa on the table for brave hearts to help themselves or tone it down a bit by mixing the harissa half and half with cold Quick Tomato Sauce. This makes a terrific spicy dipping sauce. This has to be finger food, so bowls of warm water with lemon juice beside each plate and plenty of paper napkins will be appreciated.

SAFFRON CHICKEN & MUSSELS

Chicken goes surprisingly well with lobster, freshwater crayfish or mussels. In the Mediterranean region it is most famously combined with them in a Spanish paella, while a sauce Nantua of crayfish is a classic French accompaniment to chicken. That American initiative of pairing lobster tail with steak, called so attractively 'surf 'n turf' – which sounds like a skin disease – is an unfortunate emulation of this honourable tradition that alas does not work.

Here the mussels are shelled and the dish is sauced conservatively as a main course to serve with rice. Alternatively, you can serve it with the chicken breasts whole and the mussels in the shell, with a broth rather than a sauce. If following this method, add 575ml/1pt of chicken stock when cooking the mussels. Leave out the yogurt and add two diced peeled plum tomatoes and four tablespoons of olive oil to the final amalgamation.

INGREDIENTS

1kg/2¼lb mussels
14 saffron threads
1 leek
1 carrot
1 garlic clove
handful of flat-leaf parsley
4 chicken breast fillets
300ml/½pt dry white wine
150ml/¼pt chicken stock
1 bay leaf
5tbsp plain yogurt, stabilized
   (see page 125)
about 4tbsp olive oil
salt and pepper

PREPARATION

Beard and scrub the mussels, discarding any that stay open when tapped. Put the saffron to soak in 2 tablespoons of hot water. Trim and wash the leek and carrot. Cut them into julienne strips. Peel, smash and finely chop the garlic. Wash and destalk the parsley.

You will see that the chicken breasts have a small loose piece of flesh on the underside which you can pull away. Do so, season the skin with salt and pepper and reserve.

COOKING

Put the wine, chicken stock, parsley stalks, bay leaf and garlic into a large saucepan with a lid and bring to the boil.

Add the mussels, cover and cook, shaking from time to time, for 2–3 minutes, until the mussels have opened. Strain through a sieve into another pan. Shell and reserve the mussels.

Bring the liquid to the boil and continue to boil hard until reduced by half. Add the stabilized yogurt and stir it in. Lower the heat and leave to simmer gently.

While it simmers, brush a non-stick frying pan with a little olive oil and put over a low heat. When the pan is hot, add the chicken breasts, skin side down, and fry, turning after 10 minutes. Turn once more and cook until the flesh just springs back when pressed, which will take a total of 15–20 minutes.

Transfer to a warmed dish and keep warm. Turn up the heat and rapidly fry the 4 little pieces of breast you detached earlier, turning frequently. This only takes 2–3 minutes. Add to the other breasts.

Put 1 tablespoon of olive oil in the pan and stir-fry the carrot strips until they start to wilt, then add the leeks and cook for a further 2 minutes.

Add to the yogurt sauce the mussels, saffron and soaking liquid and parsley leaves, reserving a few for garnish. Warm through.

SERVING

Cut the breasts across on the bias into slices and arrange in warm soup plates. Spoon over the mussel sauce, scatter over a few parsley leaves and serve with plain boiled long-grain rice.

YOGURT

Yogurt is an ever-present feature in the food of the Eastern Mediterranean and North Africa, where – apart from being thinned to drink – it crops up all over the place in bread-making, sauces, relishes and soups. It is a fermented dairy product that is made naturally by airborne acid-producing bacteria but it is capable of being easily cultured. Around the Mediterranean, it is made most often from goats' or sheep's milk.

To make thick yogurt, drain it through a sieve lined with cheesecloth. Leave it long enough and what is in the sieve will thicken to a basic sour cheese, called *labna* in Arabic. It can be served dribbled with olive oil and with chopped mint as a dip in a *mezze*. How cheese-tasting the *labna* becomes and how thick it is will depend on how long you leave it to drain. It is fun to experiment with. Unsalted and while still of a spoonable consistency, it makes a simple dessert when dribbled with honey.

The trouble with using yogurt in cooking is that it separates the instant you put it into a hot liquid or bring it to the boil. It therefore needs to have a stabilizing agent cooked into it before it is added to a boiling or simmering liquid. The easiest way to do this is to add a level tablespoon of cornflour to every 575ml/1pt of yogurt, first mixing the cornflour to a paste with cold water. Put this with the yogurt in a mixer or processor and whizz briefly, or beat with a whisk until smooth and liquid. Season with a little salt, pour into a saucepan and bring to the boil over a low heat. Then simmer, stirring at regular intervals, for 10–15 minutes until thick and creamy. You can now pour it with impunity into your stew or dessert instead of cream. It is best used immediately and should not be covered, as this seems to have a destabilizing effect.

HOME-MADE YOGURT

Yogurt can be made from whole-fat milk or skimmed milk, by simply adding a tablespoon or two of already cultured natural yogurt and keeping it at the right temperature for the lactic streptococci and lactobacilli to become active. This must not vary more than a couple of degrees, or the bacteria become petulant and uncooperative.

The foolproof way to make yogurt at home is in a yogurt-maker, which is no more than a low-power heater with a thermostat, which keeps the milk at a constant 38–43°C/100–110°F while the culture thickens and sours the milk as it incubates. The yogurt-maker has a number of screw-topped plastic pots which sit in depressions in the heated basè. These are filled with the milk and starter, then usually left overnight or for 12 hours. The night operation is preferable because you are not tempted to peek, a practice that the bacteria object to and that causes them to go on strike.

INGREDIENTS

1 litre/1³/₄pt milk (cows', sheep's or goats', full-fat or skimmed)

2 tbsp plain live yogurt (shop-bought or from a previous home-made batch)

PREPARATION

Bring the milk almost to boiling point, turn off the heat and cool to 43°C/110°F. Add 1 heaped tablespoon of the live yogurt and whisk it in. Pour into the containers and screw on the lids tightly. Put them into the yogurt-maker and leave undisturbed for 8 hours. The keys to success are using absolutely clean, covered containers and maintaining the temperature without fluctuation.

Yogurt was made long before yogurt-makers came on the scene and if you don't have one, try putting the mixture in a vacuum flask. Again, do not touch or move it during incubation because it is temperamental stuff and, if you inadvertently jog it, it will separate out of bacterial spite. An airing cupboard is likely to be too hot, but you might try checking the temperature of an oven with only its pilot light lit.

HARIRA

In its original Moroccan form, harira is a relatively simple chickpea soup that may be made using either lamb or chicken for flavour rather than substance. Here the dish is closer to a liquid stew, with the chicken playing a central role.

Chickpeas, lentils and rice on the same plate may sound daunting, but any heaviness is avoided by deliberately breaking the preparation into separate steps to strike a new and sophisticated note. Care is taken to avoid overcooking the chicken and a main course emerges which manages to be satisfying without being too substantial. The addition of masses of coriander leaves and flat-leaf parsley just before serving makes the dish look ravishing while imparting a delicious freshness.

INGREDIENTS
(FOR 6–8)

200g/7oz dried chickpeas
about 100ml/3¹/₂fl oz olive
   oil
1.35kg/3lb chicken
675g/1¹/₂lb onions
2 garlic cloves
2.5cm/1in piece of root
   ginger
12 saffron threads
900g/2lb ripe plum tomatoes
   or canned chopped tomatoes
2tbsp sunflower oil
1.75 litres/3pt chicken stock
2tbsp white wine vinegar
115g/4oz lentils
115g/4oz basmati rice
large bunch of coriander leaves
bunch of flat-leaf parsley
1 lemon
salt and pepper
extra-virgin olive oil, to serve
6–8 pitta breads, to serve
   (optional)

PREPARATION

The night before: put the chickpeas to soak in plenty of cold water. Next morning: drain the chickpeas, cover with fresh water and bring to the boil. Drain again. Cover with fresh water by a depth of about 2.5cm/1in head and again bring to the boil. Lower the heat, film the surface with olive oil and cook at a bare simmer for 1 hour. Check periodically to make sure the chickpeas are always beneath the surface, adding more water as necessary. Bite into one to see if they are cooked. The pea should have some crunch, but be quite mealy. If still too hard, continue to simmer, tasting every 10 minutes until done to your satisfaction. Drain and reserve.

Dried chickpeas can be rehydrated more quickly by bringing them to a fast boil for 5 minutes in masses of water, then leaving them to stand for 1 hour. However, the overnight soaking delivers better results.

Joint the chicken, discarding wing-tips, parson's nose and excess skin. Peel and chop the onion and garlic. Peel the ginger. Put the saffron to soak in half a cup of hot water. Blanch, peel, deseed and chop the tomatoes, if using fresh.

COOKING

Brown the chicken pieces, skin side down, in a little sunflower oil and reserve.

In a large saucepan, fry the onion in 2 tablespoons of olive oil until translucent. Add the garlic and cook for a further minute.

Add all the chicken pieces save the breasts and pour over the stock, vinegar and 1.1 litres/2pt of water. Bring to the boil, lower the heat to a gentle simmer and skim. Poach the chicken for 10 minutes or until just resilient when pressed. Remove with a slotted spoon and transfer to a chopping board.

Add the lentils and tomatoes to the stock and simmer for 20 minutes, then add the rice and continue to bubble gently until both the lentils and rice are just cooked. Stir in the chickpeas.

Cut the meat from the chicken pieces. Slice each breast into 4 pieces and put all the chicken flesh into the pot together with the saffron and its soaking water. Simmer for 5 minutes. Taste and season with salt and pepper.

Grate the ginger. Destalk and coarsely chop the coriander and parsley leaves. Juice the lemon.

Remove the pan from the heat and stir in the ginger, coriander, parsley, lemon juice and 6 tablespoons of olive oil.

SERVING

Serve in large soup bowls. Put extra-virgin olive oil on the table for people to add more if they wish. Offer warm halved pitta breads from a cloth-lined basket at the table if you wish.

POT-POACHED SPICED CHICKEN

This dish is prepared using the universal and ancient one-pot technique, which is here enlivened by considered spicing and the addition of lightly cooked vegetables at the end of the cooking process. Finally, it is thickened with pitta. All poached meat dishes are improved by cooking in strongly flavoured stock and this is no exception.

It is good practice to make chicken stock on a continuing basis, for it complements any meat and, in some cases, may be also used with fish. When you get into the habit of producing stock beware, for the process is not an end in itself. You make stock as a preliminary ingredient. If this sounds too obvious, consider the case of Gordon Gout, an enthusiastic cook who became obsessed with creating ever more toothsome chicken stocks, which he spent hours clarifying until they glowed like jewels. He grew to love them for themselves, would take visitors to the refrigerator to compare the colour and jelly of different batches, until — under a three-line whip from his wife Brenda — he reluctantly moved on to reducing and freezing his collection in ice trays. While still unwilling to use these broth icons, he is being helped to do so by counselling.

INGREDIENTS

1 free-range chicken, weighing about 1.35kg/3lb
1 litre/1³⁄₄pt chicken stock (optional)
2 kaffir lime leaves
3tsp cumin seeds
4 large ripe plum tomatoes
2.5cm/1in piece of root ginger
4 large garlic cloves (ideally new season's)
2 onions
1 large hot red chilli
handful of coriander leaves
4 stale pitta breads
2tbsp olive oil
salt and pepper
extra-virgin olive oil, to serve

PREPARATION

Put the chicken in a pot which will just hold it snugly, pour over the stock and top up with cold water to cover. (If you have no stock, put the chicken in a larger pot surrounded by some carcasses and bones together with sliced peeled carrots and unpeeled onions, then cover with cold water.) Bring to the boil, lower the heat and skim. Then simmer for 50–60 minutes, until a leg will pull easily away.

Carefully transfer the chicken to a dish. When cool enough to handle, cut and pull off the flesh and reserve. Return the bones to the pot, add the lime leaves and simmer for another 1–2 hours.

Pass the stock through a sieve into a clean saucepan and boil over a high heat to reduce by one-quarter.

Toast the cumin seeds in a dry pan over a low heat for 2–3 minutes. Grind to a powder and reserve.

Blanch, peel and deseed the tomatoes, then dice the flesh. Peel the ginger and garlic and grate. Peel and dice the onions. Split, deseed and mince the chilli. Destalk the coriander leaves, reserve a few for garnish and chop the rest. Cut the pitta into 1cm/¹⁄₂in strips.

COOKING

Put 2 tablespoons of olive oil into a pan large enough to hold all the ingredients and sauté the onion, ginger, garlic and chilli over a moderate heat for 2 minutes, stirring well.

Add the chicken meat, together with the ground toasted cumin seeds and the chopped coriander leaves. Pour over the stock and bring to a simmer. Simmer the mixture gently for 10 minutes.

Add the pitta strips and tomato dice and stir. Taste and season with salt and pepper. Bring back to a simmer, stir again, turn off the heat and cover. Leave to stand for 5 minutes.

SERVING

Transfer to a warmed tureen for serving in large soup bowls. Garnish with the reserved whole coriander leaves and dribble over a little extra-virgin olive oil.

CHICKEN CHILLI SAFFRON PIE

This is a pie which eats as well at room temperature as it does hot from the oven. The onion sauce in which the pieces of poached chicken are smothered is made golden with saffron and fragrant with nutmeg. Tiny shreds of hot red chilli give the pie a tingling spiciness without making it at all fierce. While filo pastry is used here, good quality glazed puff pastry also works very well as a pie crust.

INGREDIENTS (FOR 10)

1 free-range chicken,
    weighing about
    1.35kg/3lb
sprig of tarragon
sprig of thyme
2 bay leaves
2 celery stalks
12 whole black peppercorns
900g/2lb onions
140g/5oz butter
55g/2oz flour
575ml/1pt milk
2 hot red chillies
yolks of 4 eggs
1tsp freshly grated nutmeg
12 strands of saffron
450g/1lb filo pastry
salt and pepper

PREPARATION

Put the chicken in a pot in which it will just fit snugly, cover with cold water and bring to the boil. Skim, lower the heat to simmer and add a tied bouquet garni made of the herb sprigs, bay leaves and celery stalks. Season with a level dessertspoon of salt and add the whole black peppercorns. Cook gently for 50 minutes.

Remove the chicken and transfer to a chopping board. Remove and discard the bouquet garni and increase the heat to bring to the boil. Skim and leave to bubble, while you cut the meat from the carcass, discarding the skin. Reserve the meat and return the bones to the pot and simmer for another 30 minutes.

Peel and slice the onions thinly. Sauté them in 55g/2oz of the butter in a heavy-based saucepan, until they are translucent.

Shake on the flour and stir. Then ladle in 300ml/$\frac{1}{2}$pt of the strained chicken broth, stirring until this starts to thicken. Beat in the milk in a thin stream, bring to a bubble, then reduce to a gentle simmer and cook for about 20 minutes, stirring from time to time. Taste and season with salt and pepper.

Halve the chillies, strip out the seeds and cut across into fine strips. Whisk the egg yolks in a bowl and cut the chicken into bite-sized pieces.

Remove the onion sauce from the heat and stir in the grated nutmeg, the chilli shreds and saffron. Stir the chicken pieces into the sauce.

Preheat the oven to 190°C/375°F/gas5.

Melt the remaining butter in a small pan. Use it to brush the base and sides of large baking dish, measuring about 38x23x8cm/15x 11x3in. Brushing each sheet of filo first with the butter, layer 8 sheets to cover the bottom and sides, with some hanging over the sides.

Pour and spoon the chicken mixture into the baking dish. Cover the top with 8 more sheets of butter-coated filo, folding the side overhangs back on top to finish.

COOKING

Bake the pie for 35–40 minutes, until the top is crisp and golden brown. Leave to cool for 10 minutes or leave to cool to room temperature.

SERVING

Cut into rectangles for serving.

BONED CORIANDER
DOUBLE CHICKEN

Coriander pesto is used to imbue the moist cold chicken with a delicious fragrance. The 'double' in the title comes from the fact that the boned chicken is stuffed with chicken breasts to make a dish designed to be served cold and which, when sliced, makes something as fresh and succulent to eat as it is handsome to look at on the plate. The pancetta used here is the fat bacon sold in Italian delicatessens, cut very thin to eat raw like Parma ham.

The dish is effectively a galantine and is best made the day before. You can even make the pesto up to a week in advance and keep, filmed with oil, in a tightly shut jar in the refrigerator until needed.

INGREDIENTS (FOR 6)

1.35kg/3lb free-range
   chicken, boned (get your
   butcher to do it for you)
2 large chicken breasts
4 thin slices of pancetta
large sprig of tarragon
sprig of lemon thyme
2 garlic cloves
1 glass (150ml/$\frac{1}{4}$pt) of
   dry white wine
1 tbsp olive oil
salt and pepper
coriander and parsley leaves, to
   garnish

TO SERVE:
extra-virgin oil
2 lemons

FOR THE CORIANDER PESTO:
2 large bunches of coriander
   leaves (sufficient to fill the
   bowl of a processor after
   the stems have been
   removed and when loosely
   packed)
1 large bunch of flat-leaf
   parsley
2 large garlic cloves
12 chive stalks
150g/5$\frac{1}{2}$oz Reggiano
   Parmesan cheese
85g/3oz pine nuts
300ml/$\frac{1}{2}$pt extra-virgin
   olive oil

PREPARATION

First make the coriander pesto: destalk the coriander leaves and the parsley. Peel and chop the garlic. Cut up the chives into small pieces. Break the cheese into pieces small enough to push down the feeder tube of the food processor.

Turn on the processor at full speed and work the cheese until it has the texture of coarse breadcrumbs. Do not over-process. Add the garlic and pine nuts and whizz briefly to incorporate. Stop the processor between each ingredient addition. Now add the coriander, chives and parsley and work again briefly until all the ingredients are evenly mixed.

With the processor working continuously now, pour in the olive oil in a thin stream to achieve a thick oily paste. Taste and add salt and pepper as you like. Process again briefly to incorporate the seasoning and taste.

Preheat the oven to 200°C/400°F/gas6.

Spread half of the pesto on the inside of the flattened carcass of the boned bird. Wrap the chicken breasts in 2 of the pancetta slices and place these centrally on the pesto. Now spread the remaining pesto on top of them. Wrap the boned bird around these to make a neat joint.

Put the herbs and unpeeled garlic in a suitable terrine into which the chicken joint will sit snugly, or use a 900g/2lb loaf tin. Pour round the wine, brush the breasts of the bird with the olive oil and season with salt and pepper. Then put the remaining pancetta slices on top and cover loosely with foil.

COOKING

Roast for 1$\frac{1}{2}$ hours, removing the foil and basting after 1 hour. Baste again 20 minutes later.

Remove from the oven and leave to cool in the tin or dish, then refrigerate overnight.

SERVING

Remove from the tin, place on a board and cut across into slices about 2.5cm/1in thick. Drizzle with a little extra-virgin olive oil and scatter the plate with fresh coriander and flat-leaf parsley. Put a wedge of lemon, cut lengthwise, beside each slice.

POACHED CHICKEN WITH AVGOLEMONO SAUCE

What Greek restaurant does not serve kotopoulo soupa avgolemono, chicken soup with egg and lemon? Avgolemono is actually the name of the sauce made from eggs (avgo) and lemons, which is added to soups and stews to thicken and add a sharp lemony taste. Normally the avgolemono soup has no solid meat element, simply being the thickened broth, parhaps with the addition of a little rice. In this recipe the moist poached chicken is the central feature.

INGREDIENTS

1 free-range chicken,
   weighing about
   1.35kg/3lb
1 large carrot
2 onions
2 celery stalks
1 kaffir lime leaf
1 sprig of thyme
$1/2$ tbsp salt
20 black peppercorns
4 eggs
3 lemons
bunch of flat-leaf parsley

FOR THE CARDAMOM RICE:
6 cardamom pods
1 cinnamon stick
225g/8oz Basmati or Patna
   rice

PREPARATION

Cover the chicken with cold water (or better still, chicken stock) and bring to the boil. Lower the heat and skim.

Peel the carrot and onion. Coarsely chop these and the celery. Add these with the lime leaf, thyme, salt and peppercorns. Simmer for 50 minutes, or until a leg will pull away easily. Transfer the chicken to a chopping board.

Joint the chicken, first removing legs and thighs, then the wings. Cut the breasts off whole and carve each into 4 pieces, discarding the skin. Arrange on a warmed serving plate and keep warm.

Return wing and leg tips, ribcage and backbone to the stock and reduce rapidly to about 850ml/1$1/2$pt of well-flavoured broth.

COOKING

First cook the cardamom rice: bring a big pan of salted water with the cardamom pods and cinnamon stick to a fast boil. Pour in the rice and bring back to the boil, then lower to a gentle bubble. Taste a grain after 8 minutes: it should be al dente; if not, continue to cook, tasting at 60 second intervals, until done. Drain, transfer to a warmed serving dish and keep warm. Discard the cinnamon stick.

When the broth is sufficiently reduced, separate the eggs and whisk the yolks in a bowl. Pass the broth through a sieve into a jug. Put 2–3 tablespoons of the hot broth into another bowl then, whisking, add the egg yolks. Then add the juice of the lemons.

Add the remaining broth, a ladle at a time, whisking continuously. Then put into a clean saucepan over a low heat and cook, whisking, until thick. Add a handful of chopped parsley, taste and adjust the seasoning.

SERVING

Spoon the broth over the chicken and serve with rice on the side.

MARINATED ROAST CHICKEN

You can marinate and roast a whole chicken this way, or cook four leg and thigh joints. The marinade has affinities with a tandoori yogurt mixture and gives a similarly moist result. Serve with boiled new potatoes tossed in extra-virgin olive oil and chopped coriander leaves.

INGREDIENTS

1 free-range chicken,
    weighing about
    1.35kg/3lb, or 4 leg and
    thigh joints

FOR THE MARINADE:
4 garlic cloves
2 lemons
large handful of flat-leaf
    parsley
4tbsp Dijon mustard
4tbsp olive oil
1tsp ground fenugreek
1tsp salt
1tsp pepper

PREPARATION

Prepare the marinade: peel and chop the garlic. Juice the lemons. Destalk and chop the parsley. Put with all the other marinade ingredients in a food processor and whizz to a paste. Spoon over the chicken. If cooking a whole bird, working from the neck end, carefully pull the skin up and away from the breast and spoon some of the marinade between it and the breast. Also put some in the cavity. Leave to marinate at room temperature for 4 hours.

Preheat the oven to 220°C/425°F/gas7.

If cooking a whole chicken, remove it from the marinade, reserving the marinade which has not adhered to the chicken. Place it breast down on a rack over a roasting tin and roast for 20 minutes.

Remove from the oven and turn breast side up. Spoon over some of the marinade, turn the oven down to 190°C/375°F/gas5 and roast for a further 40 minutes, spooning over more marinade from time to time. Leave to rest for 15 minutes before carving.

If cooking chicken joints, roast them on a tray, starting skin side down for 10 minutes. Then turn skin side up, with the temperature at 200°C/400°F/gas 6, and cook for a further 25–30 minutes. Spoon over some marinade when you turn the joints. The finish will be very brown, but the flesh will be moist and tender.

PEPPERED SPATCHCOCKED COQUELETS

Coquelet is a nicer word for a baby chicken than poussin. Coquelets are cheap and the implications of this fact need to be taken on board, for there is no such thing as a free-range baby chicken. Even so, you can get a delicious result by marinating them before grilling, which will give you an excellent depth of flavour and a lovely crisp skin. Half a bird per person is sufficient for a first course, while a whole one makes a generous main dish with a salad.

If cooking on a barbecue, be careful not to start too close to the heat or you will burn the skin before the inside is cooked.

INGREDIENTS

4 coquelets (see above)
2 garlic cloves
2 hot red chillies
3 lemons
100ml/3½fl oz olive oil
2tsp dried oregano
1tbsp sea salt
2tbsp coarsely ground pepper

PREPARATION

Cut each bird through either side of the backbone to open it out. Slam down hard with the heel of your hand to flatten the breastbone and put in a large zip-lock bag or bags.

Peel, smash and chop the garlic finely. Destalk and deseed the chillies, then shred. Juice the lemon and pour into the bag(s) together with the garlic, chilli, oil, oregano and salt and pepper. Seal, shake and leave to marinate at room temperature for 2 hours before cooking or refrigerate overnight (but remove 2 hours before cooking).

COOKING

Before grilling, grind some more pepper over the birds.

Grill, turning frequently and basting with the leftover marinade. Finish with the skin side to the heat to give a good crisp finish. Leave to rest for 10–15 minutes before serving.

COCOS WITH SHREDDED CHICKEN & ROCKET

Allan Hall, a former 'Atticus' in the Sunday Times and a noted member of The Société des Gastronomes, in his middle years became very knowledgeable about wine and would frequently attend grand and prestigious tastings. If these happened to be in the West End of a lunch time, he might afterwards stop at The Colony Room Club in Dean Street for some cleansing and restorative draught on his way home. On one such occasion he astonished that club's largely alcoholic denizens by announcing upon his arrival that he had just come from a mineral water tasting where all had been unanimous in voting Badoit 'The Queen of Waters,' an observation which caused considerable hilarity.

Thinking of regal qualities and applying them to pulses, if Badoit is 'The Queen of Waters' then the cocos is 'The King of Beans'. These uniformly oval haricots, about 1cm/^{1}/$_2$in across, are highly prized in Provence and their popularity means that they are invariably eaten fresh from the pod and are rarely dried. Ask your greengrocer if he can get hold of some or bully your supermarket manager on the subject. They will deny all knowledge but, then, whoever said being a cook was an easy option or that shopping was an unalloyed pleasure? Cocos are lovely as a vegetable in their own right, but in this combination they help turn what could be just another bean dish into something special. If rocket is unavailable, substitute spinach or other greens. You could accompany the dish with a glass of Badoit, but most would prefer a glass of wine as well.

INGREDIENTS (FOR 6)

2kg/4^1/$_2$lb cocos in the pod
1 carrot
1 onion
2 garlic cloves
1 hot chilli
1 celery stalk
1 sprig of rosemary
1 bay leaf
2 ripe plum tomatoes
2tbsp sherry vinegar
4tbsp olive oil
225g/8oz rocket
3 chicken breasts
575ml/1pt chicken stock
salt and pepper
large handful of whole celery
　　leaves, to garnish
extra-virgin olive oil, to dress

PREPARATION

Shell the beans straight into a saucepan. You should end up with just under 1kg/2^1/$_4$lb of cocos. Peel the carrot, cut it in 4 lengthwise and push into the beans. Top and tail the onion and put whole and unpeeled in the pot, together with the unpeeled garlic cloves, the whole chilli, the celery stalk broken in half and the herbs.

Blanch and peel the tomatoes and add them whole. Add the vinegar and cover with cold water, film the surface with a little of the olive oil and bring to the boil.

Lower the heat and simmer for 45 minutes. Season with salt and pepper only when the beans are cooked. Premature salting of fresh beans will make their skins tough. Strain through a colander, reserving the cooking liquid. Discard everything except the beans.

Pick over and destalk the rocket. Blanch for 30 seconds in a large pan of rapidly boiling salted water. Refresh in cold water.

Brush the chicken joints with olive oil, season with salt and pepper.

COOKING

Cook the chicken in a non-stick pan over a low heat for 15–20 minutes, turning 2 or 3 times until just resilient when prodded. Allow to rest for 10 minutes.

Bring the chicken stock and 575ml/1pt of the bean cooking liquid to a simmer. Add the beans and warm them through. Stir in the blanched rocket and warm for 1 minute.

SERVING

Ladle the broth and beans into large warmed bowls. Slice the chicken breasts across at an angle. Distribute between the bowls. Gloss with a little extra-virgin olive oil and scatter over some celery leaves.

MUSTARD YOGURT TURKEY ROAST

When Christmas comes around, scores of increasingly desperate people telephone and write to us begging for different things to do with turkey. They are not always amused by the answer. For those who have only ever eaten overcooked turkey, roasted to the consistency of wood chippings, this annual panic is understandable. Nowadays, however, nobody need fear the arrival of the ostrich-sized monster. All they have to do is buy a turkey breast joint on the bone, ignore the instructions on the wrapper and give it this delicate Middle-Eastern treatment, which imparts an appealing flavour reminiscent of tandoori chicken. You can, of course, use this marinade and roasting baste on a whole chicken, chicken leg and thigh joints or with chicken breasts on the bone.

INGREDIENTS

1 turkey breast joint,
 weighing about 1kg/
 2^1/$_4$lb

FOR THE MARINADE:
4tsp cumin seeds
2tsp black peppercorns
4 garlic cloves
2 lemons
handful of flat-leaf parsley
handful of coriander leaves
5tbsp plain yogurt
5tbsp Dijon mustard
3^1/$_2$tbsp olive oil
1tsp salt

FOR THE YOGURT SAUCE:
^{1}/$_2$ onion
2tbsp olive oil
2tbsp Dijon mustard
12-16 saffron strands
575ml/1pt natural plain
 yogurt, stabilized (see page
 125)
^{1}/$_2$ nutmeg
salt and pepper

PREPARATION

First make the marinade: toast the cumin seeds and peppercorns in a dry pan over a low heat and then grind to a powder.

Peel, smash and chop the garlic. Juice the lemons. Chop the the herbs. Put these into a bowl together with the ground spices and all the other marinade ingredients and stir to mix evenly.

Put the turkey joint, breast side down, in an ovenproof casserole dish into which it will just fit snugly and pour the marinade over it. Leave for 4 hours at room temperature, or overnight in the refrigerator (if you do, remember to remove it 2 hours before you start cooking).

Preheat the oven to 200°/400°F/gas6.

COOKING

Turn the joint breast side up, spoon marinade over the top and roast for 45 minutes, basting frequently.

Remove the joint and transfer to a cutting board. Leave to stand for 15 minutes.

Make the sauce: first peel and dice the onion. Fry it in 2 tablespoons of olive oil over a moderate heat until translucent.

Scrape the pan juices into a food processor. Add the onion, mustard and saffron and whizz at full speed. Pour the yogurt in through the feeder tube. Transfer this sauce to a pan and bring to the boil. Lower the temperature and simmer for 5 minutes. Season with grated nutmeg, salt and pepper. It should be ready as the turkey gobbles, 'Carve me!'

SERVING

Cut the breasts off whole, then cut them across at an angle into thick slices. Spoon the sauce over the meat and serve with plain boiled rice scattered with lots of coriander and parsley leaves.

QUAIL SALAD WITH POLENTA, ROCKET & MUSHROOMS

The Mediterranean would not be the Mediterranean without the enthusiastic consumption of small birds. There is a frequently brutal attitude in which the word 'conservation' never raises its head, where song birds are blown from the sky or caught cruelly in nets. The great thing about quail is that, while they have all the requisite qualities of size and delicate flavour, they are farmed and can be regarded pretty much as Lilliputian chickens.

This is a particularly delicious dish, full of interesting contrasts of texture, colour and flavour. As with so many foods of the sun, it has been created to be eaten at room temperature.

INGREDIENTS

4 quail
200g/7oz rocket
4tbsp Gremolata (see page 92)
4 large flat field mushrooms
150ml/¼pt extra-virgin olive oil
salt and pepper

FOR THE MARINADE:
1 garlic clove
2 lemons
4tbsp olive oil

FOR THE POLENTA:
140g/5oz instant polenta
25g/¾oz Parmesan cheese
¼ nutmeg
100ml/3½fl oz double cream
4tbsp olive oil
4tbsp sunflower oil

FOR THE BALSAMIC VINAIGRETTE:
1tbsp balsamic vinegar
4tbsp extra-virgin olive oil

PREPARATION

Spatchcock the quail: first cut out their backbones with poultry shears or strong scissors. Slam the heel of your hand down to break the breastbones and flatten.

Make the marinade: peel and smash the garlic and chop finely. Juice the lemons and mix the juice with the garlic, generous amounts of salt and pepper and the olive oil.

Marinate the quail in this mixture for 2 hours at room temperature or for up to 24 hours in the refrigerator.

Make the polenta, following the packet instructions but using two-thirds of the specified amount of liquid. As it thickens in the pan, grate in the Parmesan and season with salt, pepper and nutmeg. Stir in the cream. Pour into an oiled Swiss roll tin to cool and set.

Pick over, wash and dry the rocket. Peel the mushrooms and detach the stems. Make the gremolata.

Make the balsamic vinaigrette: mix the vinegar and olive oil. Season to taste.

Cut the polenta into triangles (3 per person; some will be left over for another dish).

Preheat the grill and a ridged grilling pan or barbecue.

COOKING

Grill the mushrooms dry, giving them 3 minutes on the white side and 1 minute on the black. Transfer to a dish, sprinkle over 2 tablespoons of the gremolata and dribble over a little of the extra-virgin olive oil.

Over a medium heat, cook the quail on the grilling pan or barbecue, 4 minutes each side. Turn 4 times for quadrillage (see page 151) if using a ridged pan.

Remove and allow to rest in a warm place for 10 minutes.

In a frying pan, sauté the polenta triangles in the olive oil and sunflower oil mix.

SERVING

Toss the rocket in vinaigrette to coat each leaf and mound in the centre of 4 plates. Arrange the polenta around. Slice the mushrooms and scatter them around. Put the quails on top of the rocket. Sprinkle with the remaining gremolata. Dress with a little extra-virgin olive oil. This is partly finger food, so finger bowls would be a good idea.

HERB-BRAISED RABBIT

Wild rabbits which feed on the aromatic rock herbs of Provence are said to be flavoured with them, a handy ante mortem mise en place for the cook. Hopefully, when hunting in that neck of the woods you will not take a rabbit with a fondness for lavender or the result might be reminiscent of an airing cupboard. Most of us will be denied such exotica and will be working with farmed product, for which this recipe is anyway designed. You can give it all the herbal emphasis you want in this dish, where we treat our flopsy friend to a double dose of flavours: the hard edge of bay, rosemary, thyme and sage during marinating and cooking; and the softer touch of parsley, basil, chives, mint and tarragon in the sauce. Unusually in our Mediterranean context, the sauce is finished with cream.

Ask your butcher to cut the rabbit across the saddle to give 2 joints, with the rear legs and shoulders presented separately. You now have 6 pieces of meat on the bone. Unless you want to frighten the children, allow the butcher to keep the head.

INGREDIENTS

2 garlic cloves
1 farmed rabbit (ideally with
    liver and kidneys)
4tbsp olive oil
6 sage leaves
1 sprig of thyme
2 sprigs of rosemary
2 bay leaves
$^{1}/_{2}$ bottle (400ml/14fl oz)
    dry white wine
salt and pepper

FOR THE SAUCE:
10 basil leaves
large handful of flat-leaf
    parsley
small handful of mint leaves
20 tarragon leaves
handful of chive stalks
300ml/$^{1}/_{2}$pt double cream

PREPARATION

Peel, smash and chop the garlic.

Put the rabbit pieces in a roasting dish in which the pieces fit snugly. Brush with olive oil, then chop and scatter over the 'hard' herbs, garlic and salt and pepper, rubbing them in well. Leave for an hour at room temperature to take on the flavours, turning once.

COOKING

Preheat the oven to 180°C/350°F/gas4. Roast the rabbit for 15 minutes. Turn the pieces, pour over the wine and return to the oven for another 15 minutes. Turn again and give it a final 15 minutes. Remove from the roasting dish and keep warm.

Make the sauce: destalk the 'soft' herbs and pack into a processor or liquidizer.

Add a little water to the roasting dish and boil down on the hob, scraping and stirring the sediment with a wooden spoon, until you have about 300ml/$^{1}/_{2}$pt of well-flavoured sauce. Pass this through a sieve into a saucepan, add the cream and bring to the boil, lower the heat and simmer until thick.

Purée the herbs and stir into the sauce.

SERVING

Spoon the sauce over the rabbit on individual plates.

HONEY-GLAZED DUCK & GRAPE PILAF

A honey glaze on a roast duck is a difficult thing to get right, because the sugar easily burns, blackening the skin and making it go bitter. The way to overcome this irritating tendency is to reverse the usual roasting procedure and start at a lower temperature, only increasing it during the last 20 minutes of cooking time – and to cook the bird breast down for most of the time. The high fat content of the breast makes duck a suitable candidate for this treatment.

Pilaf has some similarities with risotto in that the rice is first turned in hot butter before being cooked in stock which the rice absorbs. The consistency, however, is much lighter and a long-grain rice – like Basmati – is used. The best way to make a pilaf is to start the cooking in a pan on the hob, transferring the rice with the flavouring ingredients you use to a rice steamer together with a measured amount of stock to finish the cooking. At around £30, rice steamers are not expensive and have the advantage of freeing up space on the hob. When the rice is done, the steamer automatically switches to keep the contents hot and in perfect condition for several hours.

INGREDIENTS

1 dressed duck, weighing
    about 2.3kg/5lb

FOR THE GLAZE:
5cm/2in piece of root ginger
3tbsp Kikkoman soy sauce
2tbsp honey
2tbsp white wine vinegar
4 cloves

FOR THE GRAPE PILAF:
1 red onion
115g/4oz butter
375g/13oz long-grain rice
30g/1oz slivered almonds
1 litre/1³/₄pt chicken stock
    (if using a rice steamer,
    follow the manufacturer's
    instructions for the amount
    of liquid)
225g/8oz seedless white
    grapes
salt and pepper

PREPARATION

The day before: strip out any excess fat from inside the duck carcass and push a butcher's hook in at the neck end from which to suspend the duck. With a needle, carefully prick the duck skin all over – you want to pierce the skin but not push the point into the meat.
Make the glaze: peel and chop the ginger. Put this and the other glaze ingredients into a pot large enough to hold the duck. Add 850ml/1¹/₂pt of water. Boil and stir to mix and dissolve the honey.

Put the duck in the pot and baste it until it has an even coating. Then hang it up to dry in a cool airy spot overnight. If you are doing this in the summer and it is too hot to leave the bird out overnight, hang it to dry in front of a fan for 1 hour or bribe a child to blow it with a hair-dryer on cold. The skin should be dry and shiny.

COOKING

Preheat the oven to 180°C/350°F/gas4.

Put 300ml/¹/₂pt water in a roasting tin. Sit the duck, breast side down, on a rack over it and cook for 1 hour. Then turn it breast side up and cook for a further 10 minutes. Increase the temperature setting to 230°C/450°F/gas8 and give it 20 minutes more to crisp and brown – a total cooking time of 1¹/₂ hours. If at any time the glaze starts to blacken, cover the bird loosely with foil, removing it for the last 15 minutes.

While the duck is crisping, start making the pilaf: peel and dice the onion and sweat it in 55g/2oz butter until translucent. Add the rice and almonds and turn to coat.

If cooking in a saucepan, boil the stock and pour it over. Stir, add 2 teaspoons of salt and put on a lid. Return to the boil, turn the heat right down and simmer for 25 minutes. Stir in the grapes and remaining butter, turn to mix and heat the grapes through.

If using a steamer, fry the onion, almonds and rice in a pan before transferring to the steamer and adding the manufacturer's recommended amount of liquid. When done, stir in the grapes and butter, put the lid back on and leave for 10 minutes to heat through.

When the duck is ready, transfer to a serving dish and keep warm while resting for 20 minutes before carving.

SERVING

Cut the breasts off the duck, cut off the legs and thighs and reserve the carcass for stock. Transfer the pilaf to a warmed serving dish and fluff with a fork before serving.

6 MEAT

Where meat is concerned, the Mediterranean message is that less is more. Historically, this is an attitude of necessity; not one developed consciously because of any contemporary concerns for less saturated fat in the diet, but simply because the lands that surround much of the Mediterranean are not rich in pasture or suitable for raising cattle. The hotter and drier it gets, the less hospitable for animals. Sheep will eke out a living where cows will not, and goats will survive where neither can find sustenance.

Ergo, if there is a meat which is more Eastern and Mediterranean than any other, then it is goat. In a suitably perverse fashion, you will find no goat meat recipes in this book. That being said, if you are determined to seek out goat for your next dinner party, do not let this omission stop you. Several of the more heavily spiced dishes are as appropriate for young goat as they are for late-season's lamb. Mind you, given that goat is very little eaten in this country, it is advisable not to say in your invitation that you will be eating a kid. In an age where Hannibal Lektor is one of our most popular screen villains, the reference might be misunderstood.

You will find recipes for beef in this section, like our version of Corfu's *pastitsatha*, an appropriate dish for the most lush of all the Greek islands. Pork is not a food of

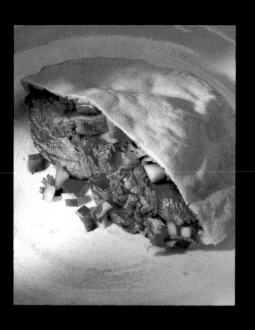

the sun and is abhorred as unclean in both Islamic and Jewish cultures for very much the same reasons – that, while a pig is a naturally clean animal, it is omnivorous and when roaming wild will eat literally anything, including corpses. Lamb, on the other hand, is well represented for it is ideally suited to the emphatically spiced treatments of North Africa, which use cumin, coriander, chilli, nutmeg and saffron to such good effect in dishes like *tagines*, *kofta* and *merguez* sausages.

Lamb is also an ideal meat for grilling, either skewered or in larger pieces. A boned leg marinated in yogurt and lemon juice makes a perfect cut for slow grilling over wood or charcoal. Using a relatively large piece of meat also means you get well-done bits as well as rare, so you can satisfy different preferences. The key to barbecuing a large piece of meat is not to have it too close to the fire. Boning a leg is quite tricky, so ask your butcher to do it for you while you watch. Next time you can have a go yourself, though you will need a boning knife for the job – far and away the most dangerous knife in any kitchen and one that is particularly difficult to keep razor-sharp. When blunt, they are lethal… you have been warned.

WINE-ROAST SADDLE OF LAMB

A saddle of new-season's lamb — that is, the rib section of the young animal on the bone including the kidneys — makes a great roasting joint. It should weigh no more than 2.3kg/5lb and will serve 6 people. This simple treatment is unsuitable for older lamb, where the saddle will weigh as much as 5kg/11lb and taste strongly of old sheep. The small saddle is slow-cooked and is meant to be well done. Serve it with roast potatoes and the Runner Bean Salad with Chilli and Garlic (page 76).

INGREDIENTS (FOR 6)

2tsp coriander seeds
2tsp cumin seeds
1tsp fennel seeds
1tbsp black pepper
1tbsp sea salt
1tsp oregano
1 saddle of lamb (see above)
5tbsp olive oil
1 bottle (750ml/27fl oz) of
   dry white wine
handful of fresh rosemary
   leaves
handful of flat-leaf parsley, to
   garnish

FOR THE SAUCE:
1 small hot red or green chilli
3 red sweet peppers
350ml/12fl oz chicken stock
10 basil leaves

PREPARATION

Three or four hours before eating: toast the dry spices, pepper and salt in a dry heavy pan over a low flame for 2 minutes, when a strong pungent aroma will be released. Grind to a coarse powder, stir in the oregano and reserve.

Trim the lamb of all excess fat, but leaving the kidneys attached. Brush with olive oil, then rub the spice mixture all over, inside and out. Skewer the flaps on either side to make a compact joint and put, back upwards, into an ovenproof dish in which it will just fit. Leave for 1–2 hours at room temperature.

Preheat the oven to 250°C/475°F/gas9

COOKING

Put the lamb to roast for 10 minutes. Remove and turn the joint so that its back is downwards and return to the oven for another 10 minutes.

Pour over half the wine, lower the temperature setting to 150°C/300°F/gas 2 and cook for 30 minutes. Remove and turn the joint back upwards again, scatter over the rosemary and pour over the remaining wine. Continue to roast for another 1 hour, basting every 10 minutes for the last 30 minutes. It will have had a total of 1 hour 50 minutes in the oven.

While the lamb is roasting, start preparing the sauce: deseed the chilli and cut it into fine strips. Roast the sweet peppers over an open flame (see pages 62-3). Peel and deseed them and cut into 1cm/½in dice.

When the lamb is fully roasted, remove it from the oven and allow to rest in a warm place for 20 minutes.

Put the roasting dish over a medium heat. Pour in the chicken stock and add the diced peppers and chilli strips. Boil vigorously, stirring and scraping up the sediment, for 3–5 minutes. Put into a food processor or liquidizer and whizz to a smooth sauce.

SERVING

Carve the saddle into portion-sized chunks on the bone and arrange on a hot serving plate. It won't look neat. Cut the kidneys into 6 pieces and scatter them around the meat. Garnish with parsley. Cut the basil leaves into strips, add to the sauce and pour it over.

LAMB, PEPPER & ARTICHOKE SAUTÉ

In an ideal world you would make this dish with fresh young artichokes, but it is still very good using premium-quality tinned artichokes, carciofi alla Romana (for how to prepare fresh baby artichokes, see page 68). The best kind of olives to use are the Greek ones you buy salted and partly dried in jars. The polenta croûtes are made here with rocket, but you could substitute spinach.

INGREDIENTS

2 red sweet peppers
2 yellow sweet peppers
4tbsp olive oil, plus more for
   greasing and frying
24 stoned black olives
8 cooked fresh or tinned baby
   artichokes
12 mint leaves
$^1/_2$ lemon
675g/1$^1/_2$lb lamb neck fillet
salt and pepper

FOR THE POLENTA CROUTES:
225g/8oz rocket
$^1/_2$ packet (225g/8oz) of
   instant polenta
30g/1oz butter
$^1/_2$ nutmeg

FOR THE GRAVY:
1 onion
1 carrot
1tbsp olive oil
about 450g/1lb bones from
   neck of the lamb, plus other
   lamb bones from your
   butcher, chopped into
   5cm/2in pieces
2tbsp white wine vinegar
2tsp sugar
250ml/8fl oz dry white wine
250ml/8fl oz passata

PREPARATION

First make the polenta croûtes: blanch the rocket for 30 seconds in a large pan of boiling salted water and refresh in cold water. Drain, squeeze out residual water and reserve.

Make the polenta according to the packet instructions, adding the butter, salt, pepper and grated nutmeg at the end. Chop the rocket and stir it in. Pour and spoon into an oiled Swiss roll tin.

Grill the sweet peppers, turning until charred and blistered. Put into a bowl and cover. Leave for 5 minutes, remove and peel. Cut in halves and deseed, then cut into 2.5cm/1in squares. Put into a bowl and toss with 2 tablespoons of the olive oil. Stir in the olives.

Drain the artichokes, rinse under cold running water, cut in half lengthwise and add to the peppers and olives. Shred the mint and add this.

Cut the lamb across into 16 medallions. Toss in a bowl with 2 tablespoons of the olive oil, the juice from the lemon half and salt and pepper. Marinate at room temperature for 1 hour.

Preheat the oven to 230°C/450°F/gas8.

Prepare the gravy: peel and coarsely chop the onion and carrot. In a roasting tin, brown them in the olive oil over a high heat. Trim any excess fat off the bones, add to the tin and roast for 20 minutes.

Put the bones and vegetables into a saucepan. Deglaze the roasting tin with 2 tablespoons of wine vinegar and scrape into the saucepan. Add the sugar and sauté over a high heat to caramelize.

Pour over the wine and passata and add cold water to cover. Bring to a boil, skim, then continue boiling and reduce to about 575ml/1pt. Strain through a sieve and reserve.

COOKING

In a large frying pan over a medium heat, brown the lamb thoroughly, giving the medallions 4 minutes on each side. Transfer to a hot serving dish and put in a low oven to keep warm.

Using a 5cm/2in pastry cutter, cut out rounds from the polenta and fry them for a few minutes on each side to brown adding a little oil, if necessary. Put in the oven with the lamb.

Turn up the heat under the frying pan, add a few tablespoons of gravy and deglaze the pan. Then add the rest of the gravy and boil to reduce by half. Add the peppers, artichokes, olives and the mint. Lower the heat and simmer for 2 minutes.

SERVING

Put a polenta croûte in the middle of each plate and arrange 4 medallions around it. Pour around the gravy.

BONED STUFFED LEG OF LAMB

Pine nuts are very expensive, but you do not need many of them to make an impression on a dish. Indeed, if you use too many they can impose a slightly odd chemical taste rather like too much saffron. They are used throughout the Mediterranean in both savoury and sweet dishes, perhaps most famously with basil and Parmesan in pesto. Here they provide an exotic addition to a sweet stuffing which balances the lamb nicely.

INGREDIENTS

1 leg of lamb, weighing
    2.5–2.7kg/5^1/$_2$–6lb
    (boned weight about
    1.8kg/4lb – have the
    butcher chop up the bones)
1 onion
3 tbsp sunflower oil
3–4 sprigs of rosemary
1 glass (150ml/^{1}/$_4$pt) of dry
    white wine
2 lemons
4 tbsp olive oil
salt and pepper

FOR THE STUFFING:
55g/2oz instant couscous
2 tsp cumin seeds
2 tsp coriander seeds
1 tsp ground cinnamon
55g/2oz slivered almonds
55g/2oz pine nuts
2 onions
4 tbsp olive oil
2 garlic cloves
55g/2oz sultanas
1 tsp oregano
bunch of coriander leaves

PREPARATION

First prepare the stuffing: in a large bowl, plump the couscous with 150ml/^{1}/$_4$pt of boiling water, stir and leave to stand.

Roast the cumin and coriander seeds with the cinnamon in a dry heavy pan for 2–3 minutes over a low heat. Grind to a powder.

Roast the almonds and pine nuts in the same way, stirring until lightly browned. Remove and reserve.

Peel and finely chop the onions. Put the olive oil into the pan and fry the onions until translucent. Peel, smash and chop the garlic and stir in. Add the spices and fry, stirring, for 2 minutes. Stir in the couscous, pine kernels, almonds, sultanas and oregano. Remove from the heat. Chop enough of the coriander leaves to produce 4 tablespoons and stir that in. Reserve.

Prepare the lamb: put 5 pieces of string in parallel lines on your work surface. Put the boned lamb, skin side down, across them and rub lots of salt and pepper into the meat.

Spoon the stuffing on the meat. If possible, tuck its outer flaps over, roll the meat into a sausage shape and tie the string tightly to make a neat package. This is a job for two people.

Preheat the oven to 250°C/475°F/gas9.

COOKING

Put the lamb bones with the whole unpeeled onion and the sunflower oil in a roasting tin and roast for 15 minutes to brown.

Put the rosemary sprigs into a roasting tin into which the joint will just fit. Put the lamb on top of the rosemary. Pour the wine and juice from the lemons around it and spoon the olive oil over the meat. Season the top with salt and pepper and put to roast.

After 15 minutes, turn the temperature setting down to 200°C/400°F/gas6 and cook for 30 minutes, basting occasionally.

If you have an oven grill, switch to it and decrease the oven to 220°C/425°F/gas7 for 25 minutes. Remove the lamb and leave it to stand in a warm place for 15 minutes. The meat should be pink.

Make a gravy by adding 575ml/1pt of water to the bones and onion, together with the juices from the lamb and boil over a high heat, stirring and scraping to reduce to about 200ml/7fl oz.

SERVING

Slice the meat and arrange on a warmed serving plate. Any stuffing that falls out, spoon down the middle. Pass the gravy in a sauce-boat. Serve with plain boiled long-grain rice.

AEGEAN LAMB CASSEROLE WITH PASTA

This is a variation on a theme as old as time, lamb simmered slowly in the oven to perfection with a mixture of tastes and textures that announces the Mediterranean. Shoulder of lamb is the best cut for this dish, because it has the perfect mix of meat to fat and provides the bones to enrich the sauce. This is flavoured with rosemary and sweetened with tomato pulp and slow-cooked onions, with just-cooked ditali pasta stirred in before serving. Shoulder is an awkward thing to bone, so ask your butcher to do it for you and have him chop the bones which you then add to the dish during cooking and remove before serving.

INGREDIENTS

1 shoulder of lamb, about 2.3kg/5lb unboned weight, boned but with the bones reserved and chopped (see above)
1/2 bottle (400ml/14fl oz) of dry white wine
675g/1 1/2lb onions
2 garlic cloves
4tbsp olive oil
2 celery stalks
2 bay leaves
2 sprigs of thyme
2 sprigs of rosemary
900g/2lb chopped tinned tomatoes
225g/8oz ditaloni pasta
salt and pepper

FOR THE GARNISH:
handful of flat-leaf parsley
handful of mint leaves
55g/2oz Parmesan cheese

PREPARATION

Cut the lamb into 6 pieces and marinate in the wine at room temperature for 1 hour.

Preheat the oven to 200°C/400°F/gas6 and put the bones to roast until browned, about 30 minutes. Remove and reserve.

Peel and slice the onions and garlic. Toss them in the olive oil to coat and put half of them in a casserole dish. Add a tied bouquet garni of the celery, bay, thyme and rosemary.

COOKING

Brown the lamb in a frying pan over a high heat, then arrange together with the bones on top of the onion and the bouquet garni. Cover with the remaining onions and garlic. Pour over the wine marinade and the tomatoes with their liquid. Season with plenty of salt and pepper.

Cover with a piece of greaseproof paper and a lid. Put in the oven, lower the temperature setting to 150°C/300°F/gas2 and bake for 1 1/2 hours.

Take out of the oven and test to see if the lamb is done. It should be very tender, but not breaking up. Cook a little longer if necessary, perhaps another 20–30 minutes.

While the lamb is cooking, cook the pasta in a large pan of boiling salted water for 7 minutes, drain and refresh in cold water.

At the end of the 1 1/2 hours' cooking time, remove the bones and bouquet garni from the casserole with a pair of tongs and discard.

Stir in the drained pasta and simmer on top of the stove for 2 minutes.
Prepare the garnish: destalk the parsley and mint and chop the leaves. Grate the Parmesan.

SERVING

Ladle into deep soup plates and sprinkle over the garnish.

STAMNA-BAKED LAMB WITH AUBERGINES

Meat and vegetable dishes that are slow-cooked in earthenware pots are common throughout the Eastern Mediterranean region and across North Africa. The techniques are basic, eschewing preliminary frying. The pots, which are usually glazed inside but unglazed without, have different names – stamna in Greece, tagine in Morocco, and so on. We all have a tendency to fall into a sort of automatic pilot when we cook a certain type of dish we know well. Thus, when making a stew we start by frying the onions and garlic in oil, season, flour and brown the meat and add similar bouquet garnis as a standard procedure. There is a lot to be said for making a conscious decision to break these patterns on occasions, and this simple lamb and aubergine dish is a good place to start.

INGREDIENTS (FOR 6)

900g/2lb lamb neck fillet
2 hot red chillies
675g/1¹/₂lb onions
4 garlic cloves
5cm/2 in piece of root ginger
1 tbsp dried oregano
10 rosemary leaves
1 bay leaf
150ml/5fl oz olive oil
3 red sweet peppers
225g/8oz potatoes
450g/1lb small aubergines
450g/1lb tinned chopped
   tomatoes
salt and pepper

FOR THE GARNISH:
handful of coriander leaves
handful of flat-leaf parsley

PREPARATION

At least 5 or 6 hours before serving: cut the lamb into 5cm/2in cubes and put into a bowl. Deseed the chillies, cut the flesh into thin strips and scatter them over the lamb. Peel and thinly slice the onions. Peel the garlic and cut into paper-thin slices. Peel the ginger and cut it into julienne strips. Sprinkle all these over, together with the oregano, rosemary leaves and crumbled bay leaf. Grind about 1 teaspoon of black pepper over all. Pour over the olive oil and turn to coat and mix. Cover the bowl with cling film and leave to marinate at room temperature for 3 hours.

Holding point – you can prepare the dish to this point and refrigerate it for up to 24 hours but, if you do, remember to bring it to room temperature at least 2 hours before cooking because the olive oil will set in the refrigerator and not work as an effective marinade.

When ready to cook: preheat the oven to 200°C/400°F/gas6. Char the peppers over an open flame until blistered, then put in a covered bowl for the skins to steam loose. Peel, deseed and cut the flesh into strips. Add to the meat.

Peel and cut the potatoes into 2.5cm/1in cubes. Cut the aubergines into cubes the same size. Stir the potato and aubergine cubes into the meat, together with the chopped tomatoes with their liquid. Season with salt. Transfer to a casserole into which all the ingredients will just fit and cover with the lid.

COOKING

Bake for 30 minutes, then lower the temperature to 160°C/325°F/gas3 and continue to cook for a further 1¹/₂ hours, checking from time to time that it is not drying out. If it does, add a ladleful of water, but this should not be necessary.

Remove from the oven and try a piece of the meat; it should be meltingly tender and moist. If necessary, cook a little longer and add more salt if you think it needs it.

SERVING

Serve in bowls, scattered with whole coriander and parsley leaves.

YEMENI-STYLE LAMB CHOPS

This is an excellent way of serving lamb in the early autumn, the strong flavours overriding the rather strident taste of the older meat. It is also an excellent way of cooking mutton chops, if you can find them, or even goat.

INGREDIENTS

8 lamb chops from the shoulder
1 tbsp cumin seeds
2 tsp coriander seeds
2 tsp turmeric
3 cloves
$^{1}/_{4}$ nutmeg
450g/1lb onions
6 garlic cloves
3 tbsp sunflower oil
1 tbsp olive oil
2 tbsp tomato paste
450g/1lb tinned chopped tomatoes
150ml/$^{1}/_{4}$pt chicken stock or water
large handful of coriander leaves
handful of flat-leaf parsley, to garnish

PREPARATION

Trim any excess fat from the chops.

Roast the spices gently over a low heat in a dry heavy pan for 3 minutes, stirring. Grind them to a powder.

Peel the onions and slice them. Peel, smash and chop the garlic.

COOKING

Fry the onions slowly in the oils until golden. This will take about 20 minutes. Stir in the garlic, then the spice mix and tomato paste.

Preheat the oven to 180°C/350°F/gas4.

Rub salt and pepper into the chops, then brown them on both sides in a dry heavy casserole dish.

Remove the lamb, put one-third of the onions on the bottom of the casserole and arrange the chops back on top. Cover with the remaining onions, pour over the can of tomatoes and the chicken stock or water.

Bake for 30 minutes. Remove from the oven, turn the chops and return to the oven for a further 30 minutes. Remove and stir in the coriander leaves.

SERVING

Serve with couscous or plain boiled rice and sprinkle with plenty of parsley leaves.

SPICED LAMB CUTLETS WITH ONION & BLACK BEAN RELISH

Lamb is the most revered meat in the Middle East, but then they don't have a lot of choice. After all, the Aberdeen Angus is unlikely to feature. A whole lamb makes a magnificent centrepiece at a grand summer barbecue but — given the difficulty of achieving a succulent result — this is, perhaps, an exercise best left to partying sheep-farmers. In Arab countries, the number of whole lambs served at a party denotes the importance of the occasion and the honour paid to the guests. Grilled on a spit over charcoal while constantly basted with oil and lemon, the meat is scented by the rosemary brushes used to apply the baste.

The amount served is, in reality, the least important element in the equation and here we make the most of very small pieces of meat. The cutlets are first marinated in lemon juice, balsamic vinegar and cumin and are then seared on a ridged grill pan before being served on a bed of black beans and spicy sautéed onions.

INGREDIENTS

12 lamb cutlets
1 tbsp cumin seeds
2 lemons
1 tbsp balsamic vinegar
extra-virgin olive oil, to dress
small handful of coriander
    leaves, to garnish

FOR THE BLACK BEAN AND
ONION RELISH:
450g/1lb black beans
1 bay leaf
1 tsp dried oregano
5 tbsp olive oil
2 tsp coriander seeds
2 garlic cloves
900g/2lb onions
$^1/_2$ sweet red pepper
4 tbsp chicken stock
salt and pepper

PREPARATION

The night before: in a large saucepan, put the beans to soak overnight in plenty of cold water.

The next day: bring the pan of beans to the boil, then discard this water. Cover again with fresh water, with a 1cm/$^1/_2$ in head, and return to a high heat. Add a bay leaf and the oregano. Bring to the boil, then bubble rapidly for 10 minutes. Lower the heat, add 2 teaspoons of salt and simmer until the beans are just cooked. This will take 10–20 minutes. Strain the beans through a colander and rinse in cold water.

Discard the bay leaf and put the beans in a bowl, add 2 tablespoons of the olive oil and turn with a spoon to coat.

Holding point – the beans can now be kept for up to 3 days in a covered container in the refrigerator.

About 4 hours before you are ready to do the final cooking: remove the lamb from the refrigerator.

Toast the cumin seeds in a small dry heavy pan over a very low heat, stirring, for 3 minutes. Put into a coffee grinder and whizz to a powder.

Juice the lemons and mix to a thin paste with the cumin and the vinegar. Brush this liberally on the cutlets, pour over any remaining mixture and put to marinate at room temperature, turning the meat from time to time.

Toast the coriander seeds like the cumin, whizz to a powder in a grinder and reserve.

About 20 minutes before you want to eat: remove the beans from the refrigerator.

Peel, smash and chop the garlic. Peel and thinly slice the onions. Chop the red pepper.

Fry the onions over a medium heat in the remaining olive oil, stirring at regular intervals, for 10 minutes.

Lower the heat and add the coriander powder, the chopped sweet red pepper and 1 teaspoon of salt and 1 teaspoon of black pepper. Stir for 1 minute.

Add the black beans, the garlic and chicken stock. Continue to warm, stirring from time to time, and allow the flavours to develop until ready to serve.

Preheat the dry ridged grill pan over a high heat for 5 minutes. The pan should be smoking hot when the meat goes in.

Cook the cutlets on the pan for 2 minutes on each side. You want them seared with a neat cross-hatch on the outside, giving a slightly charred crust and very pink in the middle. To achieve the cross-hatch – or quadrillage – lay the cutlets at an angle of 45 degrees across the ridges, all pointing in the same direction. After 60 seconds, turn the cutlets and lay them in the same direction to sear the other side for another 60 seconds. Now turn them again to give the first side its second searing, laying them so that they face across the ridges at 45 degrees in the opposite direction. After 60 seconds turn and finish the other side, laying the cutlets at precisely the same angle. After another 60 seconds, both sides have now been exposed twice to the searing heat for a total of 2 minutes each side.

If you are worried that this will be too rare, cook for a total time of 3 minutes each side, that is 90 seconds each searing. If your pan is not large enough to take all the cutlets in one go, then cook in 2 batches, keeping the first batch warm in a very low oven while you cook the second batch.

SERVING

Serve as soon as all are cooked, mounding the black bean and onion relish on the plates and arranging 3 cutlets on top, with the bones upwards. Pour over a little extra-virgin olive oil and garnish with whole coriander leaves.

LAMB SHANK SOFRITO

Sofrito is a slow cooking technique in which meat on the bone is partly roast and partly stewed on top of the stove in a tightly covered pot, to which only a small amount of liquid is added. Americans would call it pot-roasting, but sofrito sounds like a lot more fun.

Lamb shank used to be sold very cheaply by our butchers, until the cut became fashionable and, at the time of writing, popularity has made them harder to come by. It is an appealing individual joint which cooks well and presents nicely on the plate.

INGREDIENTS

4 lamb shanks
about 150ml/¼pt olive oil
2 lemons
1tbsp turmeric
salt and pepper

PREPARATION

Scrape the bones and trim the individual joints neatly at the point where the bone joins the meat. Rub them all over with salt and pepper.

In a frying pan, brown the shanks in 3 tablespoons of the olive oil, turning them with tongs.

Arrange the shanks, bones pointing upwards, in a casserole dish into which the shanks will just fit and which has a tight-fitting lid. Dribble the shanks with 3 or 4 tablespoons of fresh oil. Juice the lemons and mix the juice with the turmeric and 100ml/3½fl oz of water. Pour this over the lamb.

COOKING

Cover the pan and bring to a bubble over a medium heat. Then lower the temperature and cook at the lowest possible heat for about 1½ hours. Check from time to time and add 1 or 2 spoonfuls of water if it shows signs of drying out.

SERVING

Serve with Olive Oil Mashed Potatoes (see page 113)... sort of Aegean soul food.

CAPER BERRY LAMB

Caper berries are the fruit of the caper bush and an expensive speciality of Andalusia, where they are most often lightly pickled in sherry vinegar and brine. The caper bush grows wild in arid volcanic soil or, as often happens, in crumbling walls — having the same ability to grow in the most inhospitable habitats as the ubiquitous buddleia. The berry is the false fruit in which the seeds, its true fruits, are contained. The caper — as opposed to the caper berry — is the unopened bud of the caper flower. These were apparently eaten fresh in Greek and Roman times, but are now either first salt-packed or brined. The salt-packing treatment produces capers of better flavour and quality than brining, but is more expensive.

The best way to eat caper berries is uncooked and straight from the brine, as a nibble with a glass of chilled fino — a delicious combination. Come to think of it, they don't go amiss with a large glass of neat vodka. Just don't eat the stalks, however much you drink. Caper berries are also very good with lamb, but are added to the sauce only at the last moment to warm through and are not actually cooked as this would rather defeat their purpose.

Serve plain couscous with the lamb or make polenta croûtes as served with the Quail Salad on page 136.

INGREDIENTS

12 lamb cutlets
40 caper berries
1 onion
55g/2oz butter
55g/2oz flour
300ml/^{1}/$_2$pt chicken stock
300ml/^{1}/$_2$pt milk
1 bay leaf
^{1}/$_4$ nutmeg
handful of flat-leaf parsley
salt and pepper
couscous or polenta croûtes, to
    serve

PREPARATION

Trim the lamb cutlets. Detach the caper berries from their stems and reserve. Peel and chop the onion.

COOKING

Make an onion velouté sauce: melt the butter in a saucepan and cook the onion in this gently until translucent. Stir in the flour and cook gently for a minute or so. Beat in the stock and milk. Add the bay leaf, season with salt, pepper and grated nutmeg and simmer gently for 20 minutes, whisking from time to time.

Preheat a ridged grilling pan over a high heat, then grill the lamb cutlets for 3 minutes each side, turning three times and at opposite angles to achieve a neat cross-hatch pattern or quadrillage on each side (see page 151).

SERVING

Pile the couscous or polenta on a warmed serving plate and arrange the lamb around or beside them. Scatter parsley over all.

Remove the bay leaf from the sauce, add the caper berries and stir for 1 minutes. Then spoon into a sauce-boat to offer at the table.

TAGINES

For *tagine*, substitute the word 'stew'. If you are a romantic, leave it where it is. *Tagines* are the meat dishes which sit closest to the heart of Morocco, rich and aromatic without being fancy or contrived. It is also the name for the earthenware casseroles with conical lids like witches' hats in which the meat is simmered. *Tagines* are everyday food in the same sense as a Lancashire hot-pot, or a shin of beef stew with caramelized carrots. The difference is purely environmental and perhaps a tad psychological. Consider... our stews are warming; we eat them in autumn and winter, while pointedly eschewing them when the calendar tell us we have entered summer. The instant the temperature soars into the low sixties, Britons eat salads of toad-skin lettuce soused with malt vinegar to cool their heated blood – perhaps fearful that a pot of stew might make them explode. Yet *tagines* are eaten in Morocco when you can fry an egg on the pavement, hot food in a hot country. It is only we of the north who provide such a pointedly calorific time-frame. Other lands are not so costive. Think of curries. You don't have to see frost patterning the windows before you enjoy a burst of chilli on the tongue which, come to think of it, is just as well for the people of Madras and Bombay.

Tagines are most often of lamb, but they can just as easily be made with beef. Fruit is not a constant, but its inclusion is typical. Here we propose a lamb *tagine* with apricots or beef with prunes. You could use prunes with the lamb and apricots with the beef if you felt so inclined, or the same weight of fresh dates or plums. We use chicken stock instead of lamb stock, which would mask the flavour of the apricots too much. Serve *tagines* with plain boiled rice or couscous.

LAMB TAGINE WITH APRICOTS

INGREDIENTS (FOR 6)

225g/8oz dried apricots
5cm/2in piece of root ginger
450g/1lb red onions (or
   Spanish if unavailable)
2 red chillies
handful of flat-leaf parsley
handful of coriander leaves
4tsp cumin seeds
1.35kg/3lb lamb neck fillet
4tbsp olive oil
1tbsp paprika
1 cinnamon stick
4 kaffir lime leaves
1.75 litres/3pt chicken stock
300ml/½pt yogurt,
   stabilized (see page 125)
salt and pepper

PREPARATION

Pour boiling water over the apricots and leave to soak for 2 hours or preferably overnight.

Peel and julienne the ginger. Peel and slice the onion. Destalk, deseed and finely chop the chillies. Destalk and chop the parsley and coriander leaves.

Toast the cumin seeds in a dry heavy pan over a low heat. Grind to a powder.

Preheat a ridged grill pan until very hot.

Butterfly the lamb neck fillet: cut from the side down the length of the fillet and almost all the way through, so it folds open. Cut it into rectangles about the size of a postcard. Brush with oil. Season with salt and pepper.

COOKING

Sear the pieces of lamb on both sides twice to seal and make a neat quadrillage (see page 151). Reserve.

Fry the onions in the oil in a heavy casserole until translucent.

Stir in the chillies, paprika and cumin. Fry for 2 minutes, then add the lamb, apricots, cinnamon stick and lime leaves. Season with salt and pepper.

Pour over the stock and bring to the boil. Lower to a bare simmer, cover and cook for about 1 hour until the lamb is tender.

Remove the cinnamon stick and lime leaves and discard. Stir in the stabilized yogurt, and all but a little of the parsley and coriander leaves for garnish. Taste and adjust the seasoning.

SERVING

Serve on soup plates or in large bowls, with a mound of couscous or rice and the reserved parsley and coriander leaves scattered over.

BEEF TAGINE WITH PRUNES

Wine is absent from the traditional cooking of countries where religious observance forbids its consumption. Vinegars have, however, been used since ancient times and make an excellent substitute in dishes like these. Their use must be judicious, for vinegar behaves differently from wine in that its impact intensifies during cooking, so it can only be added in small quantities. Balsamic vinegar is suggested here because its aromatic and sweet properties work particularly well with the prunes, but any good wine vinegar will do.

INGREDIENTS (FOR 6)

450g/1lb prunes
1tbsp coriander seeds
1.35kg/3lb boneless shin of
　beef
450g/1lb onions
2 celery stalks
4 garlic cloves
large handful of flat-leaf
　parsley
20 spring onions
85g/3oz flour
5tbsp olive oil
2tsp allspice
2tsp chilli powder
2tbsp balsamic or white wine
　vinegar
2 bay leaves
1.75 litres/3pt beef or
　chicken stock or water
300ml/$\frac{1}{2}$pt yogurt,
　stabilized (see page 124)
salt and pepper

PREPARATION

Pour boiling water over the prunes and leave for 2 hours or preferably overnight. Stone the soaked prunes and reserve.

Toast the coriander seeds, grind to a powder and reserve.

Cut the beef shin into postcard-sized slices about 2.5cm/1in thick.

Peel and slice the onions and celery. Peel, smash and chop the garlic. Destalk and chop the parsley. Trim the spring onions.

COOKING

Dredge the pieces of beef in the flour seasoned with 1 teaspoon of salt and $\frac{1}{2}$ teaspoon of pepper. Seal in 3 tablespoons of the oil in a frying pan. Transfer to a tagine or casserole.

Add the onions and garlic to the frying pan with a little more oil. Sauté until translucent. Add the chopped garlic and fry for a minute, stirring, then add the ground coriander, allspice and chilli powder. Cook for 2 minutes, then stir in the vinegar and bubble gently for a minute or so.

Add the contents of the pan to the meat, together with the prunes and bay leaves. Season with salt and pepper. Pour over the stock and bring to the boil. Lower to a bare simmer and cover.

Cook gently on the hob for 1$\frac{1}{2}$ hours, stirring from time to time and adding a little water if it starts to dry out. Taste to see if the meat is done. If not, continue cooking until it is tender, but do not take it too far: overcooking will dry and flake the meat and cause it to fall apart.

When done, the tagine can be left to cool and kept to reheat gently the next day. This actually improves the flavour.

After warming through, and about 5 minutes before serving, remove the bay leaves and stir in

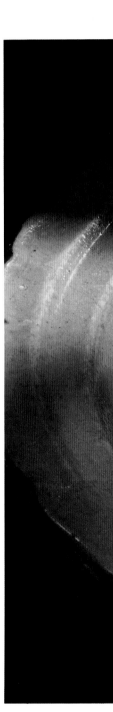

2 tablespoons of the chopped parsley. Taste and adjust the seasoning, if necessary.

Warm the yogurt gently in a small pan and wilt the spring onions briefly in a dry pan.

SERVING

At the last minute, pour over the warmed yogurt and garnish with the wilted spring onions and remaining parsley. Serve with plain boiled rice, couscous or Olive Oil Mashed Potatoes (see page 113).

SPICED PASTITSATHA BEEF STEW

This stew — with its almost Indian spicing and use of beef rather than lamb — is not what we think of as being typically Mediterranean, but it is based on a Corfiot dish. The island of Corfu has been much influenced by its proximity to Italy, hence the inclusion of noodles. Rolled brisket is used in the original dish, but since the meat is sliced only to be returned to the sauce there seems little logic or culinary gain from working with a whole piece of beef. Use shin instead, as this delivers a more moist and tender result. Serve it with home-made thick-cut noodles, like pappardelle.

INGREDIENTS (FOR 6)

6 beef flank steaks, each
    weighing about 225g/8oz,
    or 1 shin of beef, weighing
    about 1.35kg/3lb
85g/3oz flour
450g/1lb pickling onions
1 red onion
4 garlic cloves
3tsp cumin seeds
4 cloves
2tsp black peppercorns
5tbsp olive oil
3tbsp red wine vinegar
1 cinnamon stick
1 bay leaf
3tsp oregano
450g/1lb tinned chopped
    tomatoes
850ml/1 1/2 pt chicken or beef
    stock
45g/1 1/2 oz butter
handful of coriander leaves
small handful of flat-leaf
    parsley
salt and pepper

PREPARATION

If using shin, cut it into 6 steaks. Dredge these or the flank steaks in the flour seasoned with 1 teaspoon of salt and 1/2 teaspoon of pepper.

Peel the pickling onions and reserve in a bowl of salted water. Peel and dice the red onions. Peel the garlic and cut it into paper-thin slices.

Toast the cumin, cloves and peppercorns in a small dry frying pan over a low heat for 2 minutes. Then grind to a powder.

COOKING

In a heavy flameproof casserole dish over a medium heat, brown the beef in 3 tablespoons of the olive oil. Transfer to a tray and reserve.

Fry the red onions in the casserole until translucent, adding a little more oil if needed. Stir in the garlic and the powdered spices. Fry for 1 minute, stirring, then add the vinegar and bubble gently for a minute or so.

Add the meat and turn to coat. Put in the cinnamon stick, bay leaf and oregano. Pour over the tomatoes with their liquid and the stock. Season with salt, bring to the boil and immediately lower the heat to a bare simmer. Cook uncovered for 1 1/2 hours, adding a little water from time to time if needed, then taste the meat to see if it is done. Continue to cook until it is to your liking, checking every 10 minutes until it is. Adjust the seasoning.

Rinse the pickling onions and fry in the butter and 1 tablespoon of olive oil until just done. Stir into the stew, together with a handful of coriander leaves.

SERVING

Scatter over the parsley leaves before bringing to the table.

BEEF SHIN GARDIENNE

We are most familiar with shin of beef when it has been cut into portion- or bite-sized pieces and stewed. Here a whole section is cut across the shin and tied into a joint with the bone left in the middle and then braised in white wine, a sort of giant osso buco. It is flavoured with dried tangerine peel and the sauce is glossed and deepened with soy, then finished with a black olive tapenade. You can buy the peel in Oriental markets. Soy sauce? Oriental markets? Absolutely. Serve with boiled new potatoes and caramelized baby turnips or Olive Oil Mashed Potatoes (see page 113). Ask your butcher to saw up some marrow bones for you to enrich the sauce further and give it even more flavour.

INGREDIENTS

1 beef shin joint, weighing
    about 1.35kg/3lb, tied on
    the round
1.8kg/4lb marrow bones, cut
    into 7.5cm/3in pieces
900g/2lb onions
2 garlic cloves
2 celery stalks
1 sprig of thyme
2 bay leaves
handful of parsley stalks
225g/8oz carrots
2 tbsp olive oil
2 pieces of dried tangerine peel
150ml/¼pt Kikkoman soy
    sauce
1 bottle (750ml/27fl oz) of
    dry white wine
3 tbsp Tapenade (see page 91)
salt and pepper

PREPARATION

Preheat the oven to 250°C/475°F/gas9. Roast the bones until well browned, about 20 minutes. Remove and reserve.

Peel and dice the onions and garlic. Prepare a tied bouquet garni of the celery, thyme, bay and parsley stalks. Peel and dice the carrot.

Spoon the oil into a flameproof casserole dish in which the joint will fit with the bones around it.

COOKING

Sweat the onions, garlic and diced carrots gently in the oil in the casserole until softened.

Put the bouquet and peel on top, then arrange the beef centrally. Arrange the bones around to make a tight fit, add the soy sauce and pour the wine over barely to cover. Bring to a boil and put on the lid.

Immediately put to bake in the oven, turning the temperature setting down to 150°C/300°F/gas2 as soon as you close the door. Cook for 3 hours, when the meat should be fork-tender but still moist.

Transfer the joint to a cutting board, sliding a spatula under and lifting carefully because it can easily fall apart at this stage. Return to the switched-off oven with the door open to keep warm while you finish the sauce.

Take out the bones, scraping back into the dish any marrow adhering to them. Remove the bouquet garni and tangerine peel and discard. Add the tapenade and finish the sauce by bubbling gently, stirring, for 5 minutes. Taste and season with pepper. You may not need to add salt as the tapenade is already very salty.

SERVING

Cut the shin into thick slices and arrange overlapping on a warmed serving plate. Spoon over the sauce.

HERBED KOFTA & SPICED TOMATO SAUCE

Kofta have an exotic ring, while meatballs sound dull. They can, however, be excellent fare if made meltingly tender, aromatic and juicy. Because it is a way of making inexpensive cuts of meat delicate, you find variations on the theme throughout the countries of the Eastern Mediterranean. The main characteristic shared by the many meatball recipes you will come across is the texture of the meat, which is actually ground to a paste rather than minced. Traditionally, this is achieved with a pestle and mortar and, if you felt so inclined, you could crouch outside — dressed for authenticity in a dish-dash — and pound and smash to your heart's content. Frankly, however, a food processor does the job effortlessly in a couple of minutes and there is nothing to stop you wearing a dish-dash while you press the switch.

This recipe uses beef but you could experiment with lamb or pork, though you will not find the last featuring much on *Arab* or *Israeli* menus. The tomato sauce with which they are served is a slightly modified version of our Quick Tomato Sauce.

INGREDIENTS

4tsp cumin seeds
1 onion
1 garlic clove
1 hot chilli
small handful of flat-leaf
    parsley
1 egg
450g/1lb lean minced beef
2tbsp olive oil
salt and pepper

FOR THE SPICED TOMATO SAUCE:
2 hot chillies
small handful of coriander
    leaves
about 575ml/1pt Quick
    Tomato Sauce (see
    page 60)
1tbsp balsamic vinegar
1tbsp paprika

PREPARATION

Toast the cumin seeds in a dry heavy pan over a low heat and grind them to a fine powder.

Peel and dice the onion and garlic. Destalk and deseed the chilli and slice into fine strips. Destalk the parsley and chop the leaves.

Put the onion, garlic and chilli into a food processor and whizz briefly to a mush. Add the egg, cumin, parsley and 1 teaspoon each of salt and pepper. Pulse to incorporate.

Now add the meat and grind all together into a paste. Make the mixture into balls the size of small new potatoes, then roll these into cylinders.

Make the spiced tomato sauce: chop and deseed the chillies. Destalk and chop the coriander leaves. Add these with the vinegar and paprika to the quick tomato sauce. Put to warm in a saucepan.

COOKING

Fry the meatballs in olive oil over a medium heat until well browned all over. Add to the tomato sauce and bubble gently for 5 minutes to finish. Serve with plain boiled rice.

MERGUEZ CRÉPINETTES

Merguez are the thin Mediterranean sausages that smell and taste of hotter lands. They are the air that blows from the south, hot with chilli and pungent with North African spices. Made mostly from lamb and reddened with paprika, they are the sausages of Marseilles and Belleville (the Arab quarter of Paris), where they are eaten in the bars and cheap cafés that cater for expatriates. They are part of un film noir, of slouched hats and Belmondo as the gangster, the image slightly grainy, perhaps black and white. The drink in the shadowed bar is pastis. Outside the sun burns, and the light is white enough to hurt the eyes.

Because merguez originate from Muslim countries, they should be made in sheep casings rather than hog skins, but these are difficult to find. If you do not have a sausage-maker and have no objection to introducing pork into the dish, then make merguez crépinettes, patties wrapped in caul fat.

INGREDIENTS (TO MAKE ABOUT 20)

900g/2lb lamb neck fillet
450g/1lb beef (any cut but not too fatty)
about 20 sheep or hog casings or 450g/1lb caul fat
4tsp cumin seeds
2tsp fennel seeds
2tsp black peppercorns
2 cloves
$1/2$ nutmeg
small bunch of coriander leaves
10 mint leaves
6 garlic cloves
1tbsp Harissa (see page 89) or 6 small hot red chillies
2tbsp paprika

PREPARATION

At least three or four days before you want to cook the merguez: ask your butcher to mince the lamb and beef coarsely or do it yourself.

Put your casings or the caul to soak either in cold water overnight or in running water for 2 hours.

Toast the cumin, fennel, peppercorns, cloves and nutmeg in a heavy pan over a low heat for 2–3 minutes, then grind to a powder.

Destalk and chop the coriander leaves. Chop the mint. Peel, smash and chop the garlic. Destalk, deseed and finely chop the chillies, if using.

In a large bowl put the meat, garlic, paprika, ground spices, salt and chopped herbs. Spoon in the harissa or chopped chillies and mix thoroughly by hand, squeezing and turning to get even distribution of all the elements. Fry a spoonful of the mixture and taste. Adjust the seasoning as you like.

Fill the casings or spread out a piece of caul and cut it into 7.5cm/3in squares. Put a ball of the merguez mixture in the centre and wrap the lacy mesentery around it. If there are any holes or gaps, wrap in another square. Press to flatten slightly and arrange on a tray. Refrigerate for a minimum of 3 days and up to a week to mature before cooking.

COOKING

You can fry merguez in a pan, but they are best roasted for 15 minutes on a rack in an oven preheated to 200°C/400°F/gas6. They are good on their own in a mezze, or as a main course with chips.

PEPPERED BAVETTE SANDWICHES WITH CHIVE YOGURT RELISH

Bavette — skirt or flank steak — makes terrific pocket-bread sandwiches; great picnic food which can be made entirely on the barbecue. Mustard and Worcestershire sauce are not very Mediterranean, but they make a fine marinade for beef or lamb. Bavette needs very little cooking for, if well done, it becomes unpalatably tough. If you don't feel like making the bread, use shop-bought pitta. This is something well worth always having to hand in the freezer — where it keeps perfectly for a month or more before starting to dry out. Alternatively, you could use shop-bought tortillas.

Instead of beef, lamb neck fillet can be butterflied to make steaks which can be marinated and grilled in exactly the same way and which take about the same time. When you buy neck fillets they will have been trimmed into roughly cylindrical shapes. Cut from the side down the length of the fillet and almost all the way through, so it folds open into a postcard-sized rectangle. Trim the outside seam and proceed as for bavette.

INGREDIENTS

2 lemons
1 tbsp Worcestershire sauce
2 tsp mustard powder
4 skirt or flank steaks, each weighing about 150g/5$\frac{1}{2}$oz
450g/1lb basic Olive Oil Bread dough (see page 42)
1 small cucumber
4 tomatoes
1 red onion
bunch of coriander leaves
2 tbsp olive oil
salt and coarsely ground black pepper

FOR THE CHIVE YOGURT RELISH:
handful of chives
1 garlic clove
250ml/8fl oz thick plain yogurt
$\frac{1}{2}$ tsp salt
$\frac{1}{2}$ tsp pepper
cayenne pepper

PREPARATION

The day before: make a marinade with the juice of one of the lemons, the Worcestershire sauce and the mustard. Brush the steaks with this paste, put into a zip-lock bag with the remaining marinade and refrigerate for at least 8 hours, or preferably overnight. If you can, turn and shake the bag a couple of times during that time, but don't bother getting up in the middle of the night to do so.

Next day, about 1$\frac{1}{2}$ hours before you plan to start cooking: make the dough and divide it into 4 balls. Dust with flour, cover and leave to rise. Knock down and roll out 2 pieces (the other 2 pieces will keep in the refrigerator for 3 or 4 days in a zip-lock bag, or may be frozen) very thinly. Alternatively you can also roll the dough through a pasta machine. Cut each into a 18cm/7in round. Put to rest on a floured surface, covered with a cloth, at room temperature for 1 hour.

Remove the steaks from the refrigerator, take them out of the bag and put them on a tray to allow to come back to room temperature.

About 30 minutes before serving: dice the cucumber and tomatoes, peel and chop the onion, and chop the coriander leaves. Make a salad with the diced cucumber, tomatoes, onion and coriander leaves. Season lightly with salt and pepper and dress with a little olive oil and the juice of half the remaining lemon.

Make the yogurt relish: finely chop the chives and garlic. Fold these in to the yogurt with the salt and pepper. Dust the top with a little cayenne pepper.

Heavily pepper the steaks with mignonette (coarse) pepper and sprinkle with salt.

COOKING

Preheat a heavy frying pan and a ridged grill pan (or use a barbecue).

Cook the breads by laying them in the hot dry pan and pressing them down with a spatula to encourage them to balloon. Cook for about 1 minute on each side. Wrap in a cloth and keep warm.

Grill the steaks on the ridged grilling pan for 3–4 minutes on each side. Cut into strips.

SERVING

Cut the breads in half, open out the pockets and fill them with meat and salad. Offer the chive yogurt at the table for people to spoon into the sandwiches if desired.

CASSOULET

Beyond doubt the ultimate bean dish, there are three main variations on the cassoulet theme which are said to be based on the Languedoc towns of Carcassonne, Castelnaudry and Toulouse. In reality, there are certain ingredients without which it would be improper to describe the dish as a cassoulet – dried white beans, confit of goose or duck and pork sausage. You can buy ready-made confit and goose fat in tins; if making your own, however, substitute lard as the French do. The confit is best made days in advance and kept in the refrigerator.

This is a substantial dish, so no first course is needed and just a sharpish salad to follow, such as dandelion or rocket with a peppery vinaigrette.

If you are wondering why a dish so closely associated with South-western France should be included in a book of Mediterranean food, consider its key meat elements – notably corn-fed farmed duck, animal fat and pork. None of them are typical of the food of the sun. It is also a dish suited to a cool day. The logic escapes you? Well, think about it. (Answer at foot of the opposite page.)

INGREDIENTS (FOR 8)

3 garlic cloves
2–3tbsp fresh white
    breadcrumbs (optional)
900g/2lb pure pork sausages
    (i.e. 8 Toulouse-style
    sausages – I Camisa's pork
    sausages are perfect)
salt and pepper
flat-leaf parsley or celery
    leaves, to garnish

FOR THE CONFIT:
4 large duck leg and thigh
    joints or 8 legs
2tsp dried mixed herbs
coarse salt
450g/1lb goose fat or lard

FOR THE BEAN STEW:
450g/1lb haricot beans
1 pig's trotter (optional)
170g/6oz fresh pork rind
450g/1lb green streaky bacon
    in a piece
2 carrots
2 onions
4 garlic cloves
2 sprigs of thyme
1 bay leaf
2 celery stalks

PREPARATION & INITIAL COOKING

A few days ahead: joint the duck for the confit and sprinkle the pieces with dried herbs and salt and leave in the refrigerator overnight.
Next day: rinse off the salt and put the duck into a pan, add 4 tablespoons of water and the lard and bring to gentle bubble. Simmer for about 3 hours, when it should be done. Check by pushing a skewer into the largest piece to check for tenderness. Transfer the duck to a tray and reserve. Pour the fat into a bowl and keep for roasting potatoes or to make confit again.
The day before serving: cover the haricot beans for the beans stew with cold water and leave overnight to soak.
At least 6 hours before serving: prepare the bean stew: if using, cover the trotter with cold water and bring to the boil. Boil for 5 minutes. Drain and refresh in cold water. Check its toenails are clean and, if they look unsavoury, give them a swift pedicure.

Roll up the pork rind and tie with string.

Bring the beans to the boil and boil fast for 10 minutes. Drain. This cuts down on flatulence at the table.

Put the beans into a large pot and add the trotter, bacon and pork rind. Peel and dice the carrots, onions and garlic cloves and add to the pot with a bouquet garni of the thyme, bay and celery tied with string. Cover with cold water by about 2.5cm/1in and bring to the boil. Then turn down to a bare simmer.

After 30 minutes, remove the bacon and reserve. Continue to cook the beans with the trotter and rind until the beans are tender. This usually takes about 1½ hours. Taste the cooking liquid and season as needed. Discard the bouquet garni, take out the pork rind and trotter and reserve. Drain the beans, reserving the liquid.

While the beans are cooking, prepare the lamb stew: peel the onions and carrots, trim the celery and chop all of them coarsely. Fry the vegetables in goose fat in a heavy frying pan until lightly browned. Transfer to the pan in which you will cook the stew.

Cut the lamb fillets across into 5cm/2in chunks and salt them. Turn up the heat and brown the lamb in the remaining fat. Then sprinkle with flour, add the wine, crushed garlic and herbs. Transfer to the stew pot, making sure you scrape in all the bits that will have

FOR THE LAMB STEW:

2 onions

2 carrots

2 celery stalks

900g/2lb lamb neck fillet

2 tbsp flour

½ bottle (400ml/14fl oz)
   dry white wine

4 garlic cloves

2 bay leaves

2 tsp dried oregano

450g/1lb tinned chopped
   tomatoes

stuck to the frying pan. Add the tomatoes with their liquid and the trotter, ladle over some of the cooking liquid from the beans and bring to the boil. Skim to remove excess fat and then turn down to bare simmer and cook uncovered till the lamb is tender. This will take about 1½ hours, but check after 1 hour as you do not want to overcook it.

ASSEMBLY

Smash the 3 garlic cloves into a large, fairly deep ovenproof dish (traditionally earthenware, because you serve from it). Untie the pork rind, cut into squares about the size of postage stamps and lay them in the bottom. Then add about one-third of the beans.

Split the trotter, which by now will be a ragged-looking thing and falling apart. Remove the main bones and cut each half into three or four pieces. Arrange with the lamb to make an even layer.

Cover with a further one-third of the beans. Cut the bacon into bite-sized chunks. Arrange on the beans, cover with the remaining beans and ladle over broth and vegetables from the stew until it reaches the surface. If there is not enough liquid, then top up with bean liquor. (You didn't throw it away, did you?)

Now we come to the vital question: a crumb crust or not? This is the sort of debate where adherents to the breadcrumbs get very indignant and ask you outside to fight if you say it is better without them. If you do decide that you are a gratin kind of person, then now is the time to dust the surface with the crumbs and spoon over 3 or 4 tablespoons of melted duck fat. If the cholesterol aspect freaks you, consider the longevity of the people of the Languedoc. Anyway, it is the fat which differentiates the dish more than anything else, so don't be mean with it. Preheat the oven 220°C/425°F/gas7.

FINAL COOKING

The assembled cassoulet is now placed in a hot oven until bubbles begin to break through the surface, about 20 minutes.

At the same time, roast the sausages in a separate tin for that 20 minutes, remove them from the oven and reserve. At the same time, scrape excess fat off the duck and warm through in dry frying pan, skin side down, until crisp and brown.

Lower the oven to 150°C/300°F/gas2 and continue cooking for about 1½ to 2 hours. If you are following the traditional gratin route, then stir in the crust which forms at least three times during the final cooking, adding more crumbs and basting each time with bean liquor to keep the dish moist. Whatever you do, don't let it become dry or you will end up with something to choke a brown dog.

Return the sausages and duck to the oven for 5 minutes to warm through.

SERVING

Serve the cassoulet straight from the dish, accompanied by the sausages and duck and scattered with parsley or celery leaves.

Answer to the conundrum: although belonging strictly to South-west France, cassoulet may be enjoyed in Provence – and elsewhere – in the winter... culinary liberation rather than restrictive cartography.

PENNE MONTE E MARE

Once upon a time there was a suggestion that this book be called The Mountains and The Sea, because topographically the food of the Mediterranean is, in the main, the produce of highlands or the coastal plain and the sea. However, it was felt that this was perhaps a little Hemingwayesque and abstruse, and the idea was discarded. This really is a dish which deserves the title, because it combines the spiced meat of upland pigs with mussels and pasta. The sausages should be those Italian ones that are spiked with chilli or pepper and paprika and may additionally be underpinned with a little fennel. Search out an Italian shop used by Italians, where you will almost certainly find them.

INGREDIENTS

450g/1lb mussels
2 red sweet peppers
8 spicy Italian sausages, weighing about 900g/2lb in total
1 onion
1 garlic clove
1 glass (150ml/¼pt) of dry white wine
2 tbsp olive oil
450g/1lb tinned chopped tomatoes
450g/1lb penne rigate
salt and pepper
large handful of flat-leaf parsley, to garnish

PREPARATION

Scrub and beard the mussels, discarding any open ones that don't close when they are tapped.

Preheat the oven to 220°C/425°F/gas7.

Grill the peppers over a flame until blistered and blackened. Cover for 10 minutes, then peel, deseed and cut into 2.5cm/1in squares.

Part-cook the sausages on a rack in the oven for 10 minutes. Remove and, when cool enough to handle, cut them into bite-sized pieces.

Peel and slice the onion. Peel, smash and chop the garlic. Destalk the parsley for garnish and chop the leaves.

Put the wine into a pan with a tight-fitting lid. Bring to the boil and cook the mussels with the lid on, shaking from time to time, until they are open. Pass through a sieve and reserve both the liquid and the mussels separately.

Put a large pan of salted water to heat.

COOKING

In a large heavy pan, sweat the onion and garlic in the olive oil.

Add the chopped tomatoes with their liquid and the reserved mussel liquor. Boil rapidly to reduce by about two-thirds, stirring vigorously.

Stir in the chopped sausages and peppers. Lower the heat and simmer gently for 15 minutes.

After 5 minutes put the pasta to cook in the pan of rapidly boiling water. Boil for 8–10 minutes, or until al dente. Drain the cooked pasta.

Add the mussels to the tomato and sausage sauce for 2 minutes. Stir in the drained pasta and toss.

SERVING

Serve immediately, scattered with parsley.

MELI-MELO OF ORGANS

In Greece, Turkey and Arab countries, butchers are rather more open about the relationship between what they sell and the animals which provide it. Lungs on hooks, mounds of organs – and the intestines most of us prefer to forget – await the unwary foreign shopper, trained by supermarkets to think that meat comes neatly cling-wrapped on polystyrene trays. Greece has a sort of transplant feast called *enthostia lathorigani*, which includes intestines, sweetbreads, spleen, heart and kidneys. This is pretty unattractive and grey, with everything cut into bits and cooked in the oven in a rather basic fashion.

Having first checked with your guests that they are of the adventurous sort, who will not be squeamish about viscera on the plate, try this organ special. It is really quite a conversation-piece and will be particularly appropriate when you are having a surgeon to dinner. The key to getting the dish right is cooking every element separately to the right degree of doneness and only amalgamating them immediately prior to serving.

INGREDIENTS (FOR 6)

3 lambs' hearts
4tbsp malt vinegar
1 bay leaf
$^1/_2$ bottle (400ml/14fl oz) of
    red wine
1.1 litres/2pt chicken stock
3 lambs' kidneys
1 lemon
450g/1lb lambs' liver
900g/2lb onions
6tbsp olive oil
2 garlic cloves
handful of flat-leaf parsley
85g/3oz flour
salt and pepper

FOR THE BEURRE MANIÉ:
30g/1oz butter
30g/1oz flour

PREPARATION

Cut open the lambs' hearts, rinse under running water and put to soak for 2 hours in water you have acidulated with the malt vinegar.

Drain the hearts, put in a pan with the bay leaf and cover with the red wine and chicken stock. Bring to the boil, skim, lower the heat and simmer gently for $1^1/_2$–2 hours until tender. Remove the hearts and reserve.

Turn up the heat and boil the broth rapidly to reduce by two-thirds.

While the hearts are cooking, skin the kidneys and cut them in half lengthwise. Cut out the fatty core and any tubes. Put to marinate in the juice from the lemon for about 30 minutes, stirring from time to time. Cut the liver into thin slices.

Peel and slice the onions and fry in 4 tablespoons of olive oil until brown. Transfer to a roasting tin and keep warm. Peel, smash and chop the garlic. Destalk the parsley and chop the leaves.

Cut the cooked hearts into bite-size pieces, giving tubes to the borzoi.

Make the beurre manié by kneading the butter and flour together to make a paste and reserve.

Drain the marinated kidneys and pat dry.

Preheat a hot grill and heat 2 large frying pans on the hob.

Brush the kidneys with oil, sprinkle with salt and pepper and put to grill. Dip the slices of liver in the flour seasoned with 1 teaspoon of salt and $1/2$ teaspoon of pepper to coat.

Put a spoonful of oil into each of the pans. When smoking hot, add the garlic to one of them and immediately lay the liver in it.

Put the onions and heart pieces into the other pan, stir and toss. Lower the heat.

Cook the liver for 2 minutes and turn.

Turn the kidneys under the grill.

Cook the liver for a further minute and transfer to a warmed serving dish, arranging the slices overlapping at one end.

Remove the kidneys after 3 minutes and arrange at the other end of the dish. (Both kidneys and liver should be pink in the middle.)

Whisk small pieces of beurre manié into the reduced broth to thicken. Taste and season if needed.

SERVING

Mound the onions and heart in the centre of the serving dish. Pour the sauce over the kidneys and liver. Scatter parsley over all. Serve hot with crusty bread.

COCIDA

You can dress cocida up or down, throw together a simple peasantry of sausages and beans or promenade it as a grande dame of cassoulet complexity. Make of it what you will, for it works either way. The consistency, too, can be solid or soupy. This version of the classic Spanish dish is a stew which you can serve in restrained quantities as a first course or like this, with more of everything, as a substantial dish for a single-course meal. The quality of the sausages determines whether this experience is extraordinary or unremarkable. The ones that will make your heart beat faster are the peppered fresh pork sausages made by I Camisa in Soho's Old Compton Street, which are hand-made and tied with string. They are in natural hog casings, stuffed plump with coarse chopped pork, fired up with rough cracked peppercorns and studded with something delicious that might just be diced prosciutto. If, alas, you live too far away to acquire these sublime sausages, then seek out your nearest Italian delicatessen and buy the best spicy links it has to offer, but make a note to stop by for the real things next time you are in London.

Cocida is not food of the sun, but even Mediterranean countries get cold. It is perfect for a dark misted evening somewhere on the cusp of autumn and winter, the right food with a bottle of Rioja or Barolo to imbue you with contentment after you return hungry from your pre-prandial romp with the gaze hound. He can lie beside the kitchen table while you eat, legs twitching as he chases rabbits up the frosty mountain of his dreams.

INGREDIENTS (FOR 8)

225g/8oz chickpeas
4tsp cumin seeds
170g/6oz pancetta in a piece
5tbsp olive oil
2 onions
1 carrot
3 garlic cloves
2 celery stalks
2 dried hot red chillies
450g/1lb tinned chopped
    tomatoes
2 bay leaves
1kg/2¼lb potatoes
1 raw chorizo sausage
900g/2lb (about 8) spiced
    pork sausages (see above)
225g/8oz black pudding
    (optional)
450g/1lb French beans
handful of flat-leaf parsley
salt and pepper
extra-virgin olive oil, for
    serving

PREPARATION

Put the chickpeas in cold water to cover generously and leave to soak overnight or bring to the boil, boil for 5 minutes and leave to stand for 1 hour.

Toast the cumin seeds in a dry heavy pan over a low heat for 2–3 minutes, then grind to a powder and reserve.

Cut the pancetta into match-stick strips.

COOKING

In a large heavy saucepan, fry the pancetta in half the olive oil over a medium heat.

While they are sizzling, peel and dice the onions, carrot and garlic, slice the celery and destalk and deseed the chillies. Throw them all into the pan, stir and continue to cook for 5 minutes, but do not let the onion colour.

Stir in the cumin, cook for 1 minute, then add the tomatoes with their liquid and the bay leaves. Add the chickpeas, season with salt and pepper and cover with water. Bring to the boil, lower the heat and simmer for 1 hour.

Preheat the oven to 220°C/425°F/gas7. Peel the potatoes and cut them into large chunks.

Add the chorizo to the cocida and cook for 10 minutes more. Then add the potatoes. Cook for 20 minutes, or until the potatoes are just tender.

Brush the sausages and black pudding with oil and roast in the oven for 15 minutes, turning once.

Bring a pan of salted water to the boil. Top and tail the French beans and blanch them in the boiling water for 5 minutes. Refresh in cold water and cut into 2.5cm/1in pieces.

Leave the cooked sausages to rest for 5–10 minutes, then cut into bite-sized pieces. Remove the chorizo from the cocida and do the same with it.

With a ladle, scoop out about 20 per cent of the potatoes and chickpeas and purée them in a blender or food processor. Return to the pan, together with the sausages and French beans. Simmer for a final 5 minutes. Adjust seasoning, if necessary.

SERVING

Ladle into large bowls, gloss with extra-virgin olive oil and scatter parsley over. There may be some left over for the hound(s).

7 DESSERTS

Mediterranean desserts are often very sticky and frequently sweet beyond sweetness, as are the soft drinks which sometimes accompany them. Very sweet drinks feature heavily in those countries where alcohol is little consumed or – as is the case in Saudi Arabia – not consumed at all, unless you are so desperate you will risk a bloody flogging for the sake of a snort.

People in Islamic countries drink sweet tea, sweet coffee and syrup seemingly at any time of the day or night, so the occasional glass of cold salt yogurt or a mineral water comes as a welcome relief to the visitor not steeped in disaccharides from birth. Desserts most frequently feature honey, nuts and syrup, with a sticky filo pastry, *baklava* winning the prize for most common sweetmeat in a sweep round from Morocco to Turkey. Our selection of puddings therefore draws inspiration from some of the most popular Mediterranean dessert forms, but seriously tones down the sugar content or cuts it with astringent citrus. These are desserts where East meets West in happy combinations and each has a slightly new angle to explore.

On days when preparing a dessert seems like just too much trouble – or just plain inappropriate because of the serious nature of the preceding courses – look no further than fruit. Fruit is the ideal ending to any Mediterranean meal and what could be nicer than a large plate or bowl of pristine seasonal fruits? It is something that is rarely offered in this country, which is a great shame. Fruit sorbets are also lovely desserts that take only minutes to make in an ice-cream churn, while fruit salad is also a great way to close any type of meal, simple or grand.

Quite a few of the recipes in this chapter call for the inclusion of orange and lemon rind. You are advised to use organic uncoated fruit or clean them carefully (see our comments on citrus rind on page 92).

ZEPOLLI DI SAN GIUSEPPE

These elegant egg doughnuts are traditionally eaten during the Festival of Fools, which is celebrated in Naples on 19 March. Since there are usually plenty of fools about all year round, do not allow this date to restrict when you cook and eat zepolli. They swell during cooking to emerge golden brown and light as air. Though authentically they are fried in rings, you can simply scrape spoonfuls of dough into the oil, cutting them open after they are cooked and slathering crème pâtissière and cherry jam in the middle. Finish the presentation with a dusting of icing sugar. The amounts given here can be halved.

INGREDIENTS (MAKES 16 DOUGHNUTS)

55g/2oz butter
1tbsp caster sugar
pinch of salt
300g/10$\frac{1}{2}$oz light plain flour
6 size-2 eggs
about 5tbsp black cherry jam
sunflower oil, for deep-frying
icing sugar, to dust

FOR THE LEMON CREME PATISSIERE:
3 size-2 eggs
100g/3$\frac{1}{2}$oz caster sugar
45g/1$\frac{1}{2}$oz plain flour
500ml/16fl oz full-cream milk
1 lemon

PREPARATION

First make the crème pâtissière by whisking the eggs and sugar to a ribbon consistency. Whisk in the flour and milk, transfer to a pan and add the zest grated from the lemon. Cook over a low heat, stirring constantly, until it thickens. Pass through a sieve into a bowl and cool.

To make the doughnuts, weigh the flour then put it in a measuring jug. Note the volume and transfer to a container. Pour in cold water to the same volume, then put this in a pan and bring to the boil.

Add the butter, sugar and salt and turn down to a simmer. Throw in the flour in one go and whisk until mixed smoothly. Take off the heat and add the eggs, one at a time, whisking furiously. It is easiest to use an electric whisk for this job. Even then it sets tenaciously, gripping the whisk like an octopus.

In a deep-frier with basket, or wok or large heavy pan, heat the oil to 190°C/375°F.

COOKING

Using 2 spoons, scoop a tablespoon of batter at a time into the oil. They will look great whatever shape they go in.

Fry about 4 at a time, depending on the size of your deep-frier or pan. As they start to brown underneath, turn them over. Repeat every minute or so. They will swell and turn golden and take 8–10 minutes to cook.

Remove with a slotted spoon and drain on paper towels.

Fill a piping bag with the crème pâtissière. Pipe the cream into the middle of each of the zepolli, and spoon in a little of the cherry jam.

SERVING

Dust the tops with icing sugar and serve while still fresh.

CASSATA SICILIANA

Cassata in its original form is a cake, not an ice-cream, and is based on pan di Spagna, a sponge characterized by a high proportion of eggs to flour and a cooking technique which seems odd when compared to, say, making a Victoria sponge. But then, to most of the world making a Victoria sponge is even odder, so quid pro quo. Non-stick spring-form cake tins work best for the job but, if you don't have one, grease your sticking tin lightly with butter.

Sicily has a tradition of cake decoration which is very much in the sugar-skulls and bleeding-hearts department, usually linked to religious festivals. Cassata is surrounded with a band of pasta reale (pistachio-green marzipan) and topped with crystallized fruit; as Arab a presentation as you could ever meet and — depending on your class antecedents and cultural affiliations — glorious or gross.

While the recipe for the pasta reale is given below, we know there are people who loathe the stuff. The crystallized fruits traditionally used to finish the cake are also an unnecessary addition. Instead fill and top the cake with candied ricotta cream, finishing with curls of bitter chocolate.

INGREDIENTS
(FOR 6-8)

FOR THE *PASTA REALE* MARZIPAN
(OPTIONAL):
285g/10oz blanched whole
   almonds
450g/1lb caster sugar
3–4 drops of green food
   colouring

FOR THE SPONGE:
55g/2oz butter
1/2 lemon
8 eggs
170g/6oz caster sugar
170g/6oz plain flour

FOR THE FILLING:
900g/2lb ricotta cheese
85g/3oz caster sugar
55g/2oz chopped candied
   lemon peel

FOR *ASSEMBLY AND
DECORATION:*
5tbsp dark rum or brandy
100g/3 1/2 oz bitter chocolate

PREPARATION

Day 1... Make the marzipan, if using: whizz the nuts in a food processor until crumbed and, while continuing to run at full speed, pour in the sugar through the feeder tube until evenly mixed.

Add 3 tablespoons of water and the food colouring. Work briefly until it forms a ball (if it doesn't, dribble in a very little more water until it does), then transfer to a cold work surface and knead to a smooth, elastic consistency. Form into a brick, clingwrap and refrigerate. This is a lot more marzipan than you need for the cake, but it is one of those things which seems easier to make in larger quantities and it keeps for ages in the refrigerator or indefinitely in the freezer. After a year, if you have not felt compelled to eat it, you can take it out and feed it to the birds.

Start preparing the ricotta cream: put the ricotta in a sieve over a bowl and put in the refrigerator to drain overnight.

Day 2... Make the sponge cake: preheat the oven to 180°C/350°F/gas4. Melt the butter in a pan, grate in the zest from the lemon and reserve. In a bowl set over hot water, whisk the eggs and caster sugar for about 4 minutes until just warm. Remove from the heat and beat vigorously until trebled in volume and ribbons form. An electric whisk makes this job easier, but it will still take about 15 minutes.

Sift in the flour, then fold in the butter. Pour and scrape this batter into a deep 23cm/9in diameter round spring-form cake tin.

COOKING

Bake for 20–25 minutes, depending on how efficient your oven is. Check it is done by pushing a knife or skewer into the centre; it should come out clean and warm to the tongue. Transfer to a cake rack, leave for 5 minutes and then turn it out on the rack to cool.

Make the filling: put the drained ricotta and sugar into a bowl and whisk until smooth. Fold in the candied peel.

ASSEMBLY

Clean, dry and oil the spring-form tin in which you baked the sponge and line it with cling film, allowing it to hang over the sides.

If using the marzipan, cut slices 1.5cm/$\frac{1}{2}$in thick lengthwise off the brick and roll them out in strips about 5mm/$\frac{1}{4}$in thick. Line the sides of the pan with them, pressing to form a continuous lining.

Cut the cake in half laterally, then into narrow triangular slices and arrange these to fill the bottom half of the tin. You may need to trim them to get them to fit.

Dribble over half the liquor, then spoon over three-quarters of the candied ricotta cream and arrange the other half of the sponge wedges on top. Dribble the rest of the liquor over, then smooth on the remaining cream with a palette knife.

Make chocolate curls by scraping a block of chocolate with a potato peeler and scatter over the top. Refrigerate overnight.

SERVING

Day 3... Unmould, lose the clingwrap and eat accompanied, perhaps, by a glass of Vin Santo or a Marsala.

DIPLOMATICO FREDDO

You will not find a recipe for tiramisu in this book, thank you very much. Wait a few years for it to become as common as muck, and then we have one lurking on the hard disc to rush out along with Black Forest gâteau. Diplomatico Freddo has some similarities with That Pudding but is actually frozen, so it comes out somewhere between an ice-cream and a chilled cake.

Use seriously good chocolate for a superior result. The assembly of the cake is similar to that of the Sicilian cassata, though the result is very different.

INGREDIENTS (FOR 6-8)

450g/1lb premium-quality bitter chocolate
4 eggs
250g/8$\frac{1}{2}$oz caster sugar
500ml/16fl oz double cream
575ml/1pt espresso or strong coffee (or half and half)
5tbsp whisky or rum
400–450g/14–16oz sponge fingers
icing sugar, to dust

PREPARATION

The day before or at least 4 hours ahead: melt the chocolate in a bowl set over hot water.

Separate the eggs, then whisk the yolks and half the sugar with an electric whisk until pale and stiff.

In another bowl, whisk the cream until it forms soft peaks, being careful not to take it too far. Beat the melted chocolate into the egg yolks. When cool, fold in the cream and refrigerate.

Make the coffee and, while it is hot, dissolve the remaining sugar in it. Then add the whisky or rum.

When cool, dip the sponge fingers in it briefly to moisten and arrange half to line the base of a 24cm/9$\frac{1}{2}$in spring-form tin.

Spoon over the chocolate cream and top with the remaining moistened sponge fingers. Freeze for at least 3 hours or overnight.

About 20 minutes before serving: remove from the freezer.

SERVING

Dust the top with icing sugar and unclip the tin.

PISTACHIO ICE-CREAM

Pistachios are the most elegant of nuts and, for some reason, the nut that even those who dislike the breed as a generality seem to enjoy. Salted lightly roasted pistachios are the perfect nibble with an aperitif and there is an enjoyable ritual in prising the partly opened shells apart to deliver the sweet and tender kernels, one at a time, pale and creamy inside, tinged green without.

The enchanting pale green of the young nut is used as a description of that colour in a wider context than the purely culinary and here, raw and unsalted, it tints our ice-cream with the promise of its unique flavour. While the majority of the nuts are puréed to a uniform paste, some are reserved to be coarsely chopped and added towards the end of churning, flecking the finished ice-cream and adding a satisfying crunch to every bite. The golden syrup is added at the same time as the nuts to give a rippled effect. Unusually, it contains no eggs.

While it is possible to make most ice-creams without a churn, this is one ice which really does need to have an electric 'beat and freeze' system to get the desired consistency and to distribute the nuts and syrup evenly.

When buying your pistachios, they will have a better flavour if you shell them yourself, though vacuum-packed shelled nuts save time. Whichever you choose, make sure that they are raw and unsalted or you will end up with a rather odd-tasting dessert.

INGREDIENTS
(FOR 6-8)

1 lemon
30g/1oz caster sugar
850ml/1¹/₂pt full-cream
    milk
300ml/¹/₂pt double cream
225g/8oz shelled raw
    pistachios
5tbsp golden syrup

PREPARATION

Pare off the rind from the lemon in strips. Put with the sugar, milk and cream into a saucepan and bring slowly to a simmer.

While it is heating, purée 170g/6oz of the nuts in a food processor. As soon as the milk mixture comes to the boil, remove the lemon rind and, with the processor working at full speed, pour the milk mixture through the feeder tube.

Leave to cool to hand-hot and pour into the ice-cream maker. There is no need to wait for it to get completely cold. Churn for about 15 minutes and add the remaining nuts, coarsely chopped, and the golden syrup. These final additions should be made as the ice-cream starts to firm up. With some machines this will be after 15 minutes, while with others it will take 20 or even 25 minutes. You can usually tell by listening to the sound of the motor, which changes pitch as it starts to work harder against the solidifying mixture.

Transfer to a suitable container and freeze for at least 1 hour.

SERVING

Remove from the freezer about 15 minutes before serving, to allow it to soften to a scooping consistency. To enjoy this ice-cream at its best, do not freeze it for more than 24 hours.

KATAIF PANCAKES

Kataif – deep-fried stuffed yeast pancakes – can be cloyingly sweet and horrifyingly calorific. It is all very well if you are wearing a loose-fitting dish-dash, but for most of us a modified version – that eliminates the second frying and the heavy syrup with which they are traditionally drenched – produces a lighter and more appealing dessert. The filling of whipped orange or lemon cream means this will never be a mean cuisine option, but it is very good and one does not need a large portion. (Just larger trousers—Ed.)

INGREDIENTS
(FOR 6)

¹/₂ packet (1¹/₂ tsp) of instant
   yeast
30g/1oz caster sugar
pinch of salt
500ml/16fl oz hand-warm
   water
2 tbsp olive oil
1 egg
450g/1lb plain flour
2–3 tbsp clear honey
sunflower oil, to grease
icing sugar, to dust

FOR THE FILLING:
500ml/16fl oz double or
   whipping cream
55g/2oz caster sugar
zest of 1 orange or lemon

PREPARATION

Make the pancake batter in a large bowl by dissolving the yeast, sugar and salt in the warm water. Add the olive oil and beat in the egg. Then gradually whisk in the flour until you have a smooth batter.

Cover the top loosely with cling film and leave to stand in a warm place for an hour to allow the yeast to work, when the batter will have lifted and bubbled. Stir briefly and put ready with a small ladle by the hob.

COOKING

Put some honey to warm in a small saucepan.

Whip the cream with the sugar until it is thick. Fold in the citrus zest.

Heat the pan over a medium heat. When hot but not smoking, turn the heat down slightly. Wipe the cooking surface with a little sunflower oil, pour in a ladleful of batter and cook until the top is lifted and bubbling. Turn the pancake over and cook for 1 minute more. With a spatula, transfer to a warmed plate and keep warm in the oven while you cook another 17 pancakes.

SERVING

Place a pancake on each plate, spread with a layer of cream and put another pancake on top. Top this with more cream and finish with a third pancake. Spoon over a little warmed honey, dust with icing sugar and serve immediately.

HONEY

People get awfully buzzed up about honey. Cool people put it in herbal teas, because it is so natural. It might also just be nice enough to make them palatable, but it is doubtful. A few million years before Tate & Lyle came on the scene, bees brought sweetness to the table as honey – as much a gift today as it was 14,000 years ago, when the earliest painters recorded their industry on cave walls in Spain and Africa. In ages past, when people craved sugar as an antidote to the prevalence of salt, the very word honey became synonymous with generosity, abundance and honesty.

This seems a little extreme today, but Biblical writers could not trumpet its cause too loudly. Moses famously promises the Israelites '… a land flowing with milk and honey', while, of Immanuel, Isaiah says: 'Butter and honey shall he eat, that he may know to refuse the evil, and choose the good.' In Samuel, Jonathan '… dipped (the rod) in an honeycomb and put his hand to his mouth, and his eyes were enlightened.' Funny, that doesn't seem to happen when you crack open a pot of Tesco's best. Honey certainly seized the ancients' imagination and featured symbolically in various touching ceremonies from birth through marriage to death. Honey and beeswax, for example, were used in Egyptian embalming. Honey's sweetness inevitably has sexual undertones. Falstaff's much-fancied pub landlady is 'a most sweet wench… As the honey of Hybla' while, to this day, those just married go on a honeymoon.

Salt was always precious for its preservative properties, but honey was adored principally for its taste, though it too played a preservative role for keeping fruit, a precursor to jam. Throughout recorded history, honey has played an important part in cooking, where it featured in savoury dishes as well as puddings until – with the advent of first sugar cane and later sugar refined from beet – towards the end of the sixteenth century sweetness became identified for the first time with the end of a meal. Honey has not, however, been excluded from contemporary savoury dishes – think of honey glazes for hams and duck.

Egyptian, Greek and Roman civilizations equated sweetness with privilege, as did European culture in the Middle Ages. From earliest times, honey was also an important element in alcoholic drinks like metheglin or mead and was mixed with wine – *oenomelites* or *hydromel* – while honey beers are still brewed in Belgium and Germany. Vikings drank honey-fermented *mjöd* to make them berserk and, having met a triumphant death in battle, they then lounged about drinking it in Valhalla for eternity.

From earliest times man marvelled at the industry of bees, their remarkably organized social structure, the precision of the wax comb and the miracle of transforming the minute quantities of nectar from flowers into honey, for it takes 10,000 individual bee visits to flowers to produce a single drop of honey. After such extraordinary diligence, the principal constituents of honey are fructose, glucose and water – prosaic disaccharides that belie the complex flavours of the end product. The past 20 years have seen a growing popularity for royal jelly and pollen, with extravagant claims made for their medical benefits and longevity-inducing properties. Sadly, these claims do not stand up to scientific investigation, but have been a good way of boosting the income of beekeepers and health-food shops.

Anyway, honey is not about healthy eating but taste, and this always depends on the flowers from which the nectar has been taken. By moving hives, bee-keepers are able to produce the honey of a single flower, allowing a particular fragrance to come through in the taste. This is not achieved by sending the bees to training school, where they learn to be selective. Instead, the keeper fools the bees by transporting the hives to allow them to buzz about in an area during the time a particular blossom holds sway; a practice that carries inevitable costs and accordingly makes single-blossom honeys more expensive. To our palate, these single-source honeys – like lavender, rosemary, thyme, lime, acacia and heather – are overly perfumed, making them ill-suited to most cooking, though they work well enough in ice-cream. The EC regulates honey production and polices claims of organic provenance. Since a bee ranges over an area of several miles, proximity to inorganic fertilization of flowering plants and trees or industrial pollution has to be take into account when labelling pots and jars.

The flavour of honey goes particularly well with nuts and with spices like ginger and cinnamon. It also has an affinity with lemon. In these combinations it is to be found throughout the Mediterranean. *Baklava*, the ubiquitous filo, honey and nut pastries of the Eastern Mediterranean, are perhaps the best-known in this category, though honey's distinctive flavour also makes *halvah* and nougat. Honey can also play a fermenting role, acting rather like a yeast to lift and lighten. French *pain d'épices au miel* is an ancient example; as is English gingerbread, whose sticky texture came originally from honey and later molasses, making it a perennial childhood favourite. Chaucer referred to 'royal spicerie and gyngebreed' and it was one of the sweet treats made into fanciful shapes for children, often gilded to make it look even more special.

Honey today is sold in a clear liquid state, in thick pregranulated form and in pieces of boxed honeycomb. Individual preference is the only key determinant though for obvious reasons clear honey is the form most suitable for cooking. For many of us it is still most delightful for breakfast or tea, on good toasted bread with a little unsalted butter.

PEACH PUDDING WITH GRAPPA CREAM

Fresh peaches are nicer, but tinned will still deliver a good result in this pudding which is served with a sweet grappa-flavoured whipped cream. Grappa can be rough enough to strip paint, but there are some really rather sophisticated single-grape varieties that are not at all harsh. The preferred grappa is made from sweet Chardonnay grapes, but a little brandy can be substituted if you happen to have run out.

INGREDIENTS
(FOR 8-10)

45g/1½ oz unsalted butter
225g/8oz brioche
4 large ripe peaches or 8 canned peach halves
6 eggs
115g/4oz vanilla sugar, or 115g/4oz caster sugar plus 1tsp vanilla essence
575ml/1pt full-cream milk
300ml/½pt single cream
½tsp ground cinnamon

FOR THE GRAPPA CREAM:
575ml/1pt double cream
30g/1oz icing sugar
2tsp grappa

PREPARATION

Melt the butter in a small pan over a very low heat and reserve.
Preheat the oven to 180°C/350°F/gas4.
Cut the crusts off the brioche, cut it into slices about 2.5cm/1in thick and then cut these into cubes.
Toss the brioche cubes in the melted butter to coat, then spread them on baking sheets.

COOKING

Put the brioche cubes in the oven and bake for about 10 minutes, or until lightly browned. Check after 5 minutes as they burn easily. Remove from the oven and set aside to cool. Reduce the oven setting to 160°C/320°F/gas3.
In a large bowl, whisk the eggs with the vanilla sugar.
Bring the milk and single cream to the boil, then beat it into the egg mixture. Add the toasted brioche cubes, stir and leave to amalgamate for at least 15 minutes or up to an hour (if so, turn the oven off and then preheat it in time for baking the pudding).
If using fresh peaches, peel, stone and slice them. If using canned, drain them well. Arrange in a buttered gratin dish and pour over the custard mixture.
Put into a bain-marie with hot water poured to come halfway up the sides of the dish and bake for 40 minutes, or until just set and golden on top.
Take out, dust with cinnamon and leave to cool.
Make the grappa cream: beat the cream with the icing sugar and the grappa until it holds soft peaks.

SERVING

Serve straight from the dish while still warm, with dollops of the cream on the side.

ARROZ CON LECHE PLANCHADO

This is a Spanish rice pudding made with Italian rice and a French toffee topping, a dessert suitable for serving in the EC headquarters commissary in Brussels.

The jeweller's type of personal blow-torch you need to finish this dish can now be found in larger DIY stores. The least expensive to run and maintain are those that run on butane and are refillable, like cigarette lighters.

INGREDIENTS (FOR 6-8)

200g/7oz risotto rice, such
    as Arborio
pinch of salt
1 litre/1³/₄pt milk
75g/2¹/₂oz butter
1 lemon
225g/8oz caster sugar
1 cinnamon stick
3tbsp brandy
yolks of 2 eggs
2tbsp brown sugar

PREPARATION

Put the rice in a pan, barely cover with cold water and add the pinch of salt. Cook over a low heat until all the water has been absorbed.

Reserve 300ml/¹/₂pt milk and bring the rest to the boil. Pour over the rice. Add the butter, grated zest from the lemon, caster sugar and cinnamon stick and cook over a low heat for 20 minutes, stirring at regular intervals otherwise it will stick and burn.

Remove the cinnamon stick and stir in the brandy, together with the reserved milk and the egg yolks and continue to cook for a further 10 minutes. Pour and spoon into a serving dish and leave to cool and set, then refrigerate to chill.

When quite cold, sprinkle the top with a thin layer of brown sugar and caramelize with a blow-torch. If you have run out of butane, brûlée under a preheated hot grill.

SERVING

Serve straight from the dish. You can, of course make this pudding in individual ramekins.

A BIT OF A GREEK TART

This creamy egg custard and semolina dessert nods towards both Greece and Provence. Semolina sounds suspicious, but gives a bit of depth without making it heavy.

INGREDIENTS (FOR 8)

1 lemon and almond pastry
    shell (see page 184)

FOR THE CUSTARD:
850ml/1¹/₂pt full-cream
    milk
1 cinnamon stick
55g/4oz semolina
30g/1oz butter
6 eggs
55g/2oz caster sugar
about ¹/₂tsp grated nutmeg

PREPARATION

First make the pastry shell, blind-bake and allow to cool as described.

COOKING

Make the custard: bring the milk slowly to the boil with a cinnamon stick in it. Take off the heat, remove the cinnamon and whisk in the semolina. Then return to a low heat and cook, stirring, for 5–6 minutes until it thickens. Take off the heat, whisk in the butter and leave to cool for 5 minutes.

While the mixture is cooling, beat the eggs and caster sugar until pale and light. Then stir this gradually into the warm milk mixture. Return the pan to a low heat and cook, stirring, for 4–5 minutes.

Allow to cool briefly, then pour and scrape into the cooked pastry shell. Dust the top with grated nutmeg and leave to firm slightly.

SERVING

Ideally serve while the filling is still warm.

FIG & FRANGIPANE TART

The flavours of this tart combine elements that are very Eastern Mediterranean but which are treated here as a French dessert would be. Frangipane is the pretty French word for almond paste familiar to generations here in Bakewell tart. The precise number of figs you need will depend on their size. They should be ripe but still firm. Tinned figs also taste good cooked this way, but remember to drain them carefully before halving and pushing into the frangipane. The lengthy blind-baking is needed if the pastry is to be a deep nut-brown when the tart finally emerges from the oven. At the risk of offending Mr Kipling, an anaemic appearance is to be avoided at all costs.

INGREDIENTS (FOR 8)

450g/1lb ripe figs (or
   drained tinned)
2–3tbsp Hymettus, or other
   fine clear non-floral honey,
   to glaze
Greek yogurt, whipped cream
   or crème fraîche, to serve

FOR THE LEMON AND ALMOND
PASTRY SHELL:
100g/3$^{1}/_{2}$oz butter
1 lemon
125g/4$^{1}/_{2}$oz caster sugar
55g/2oz ground almonds
125g/4$^{1}/_{2}$oz fine plain flour
1 size-2 egg, plus 1 extra yolk
1tsp Pernod or Pastis
pinch of salt

FOR THE FRANGIPANE:
55g/2oz butter
55g/2oz sugar
55g/2oz ground almonds
55g/2oz fresh white
   breadcrumbs
1 size-2 egg
3 drops of almond essence

PREPARATION

For the lemon and almond pastry shell: dice the butter in small cubes and grate the zest from the lemon. Put the sugar, almonds and flour into a food processor and turn it on at full speed for a few seconds. Add the diced butter and work again until just blended in. The mixture will resemble fine breadcrumbs.

Add the egg and the extra yolk, 2 teaspoons of the lemon zest, the anise and a tiny pinch of salt and work again until the pastry balls.

Scrape this out on a sheet of cling film and form into a cylinder with a diameter of about 5cm/2in. Chill for at least 2 hours.

Because of the high butter content this pastry can be kept in the fridge for a week and freezes well. It is very rich and you will need to flour the surface heavily to prevent it sticking; it is not easy to roll. If it defeats you, cut thin discs off the end of the cylinder and press these into the bottom and sides of a 24cm/9$^{1}/_{2}$in loose-bottomed metal tart tin to make as even a pastry shell as possible. Give a double thickness round the edges and push it right up to the top, as it will shrink as it bakes. Be careful to press into the bottom edges to eliminate air between the tin and the pastry. Freeze until needed.

For the frangipane: put the butter, sugar, almonds and breadcrumbs in a food processor and work briefly to mix. On full speed, add the egg and almond essence until combined to a smooth paste.

Preheat the oven to 190°C/375°F/gas5.

Take the pastry shell from the freezer and put it on a baking tray. Prick the base all over with a fork and line the shell with foil. Fill with beans and bake blind for 25–30 minutes, removing the foil and beans for the last 10 minutes.

Remove the cooked shell from the oven and leave to cool slightly before filling with the almond paste. Scrape the surface smooth and level.

Cut the figs in half, make shallow slashes into the skins with a razor blade (if using tinned figs, do not slash) and press into the paste, cut side up, in concentric circles slightly overlapping .

Bake for 45–60 minutes, when the figs will have crumpled a little and the frangipane will have risen around them. The cooking time is slowed by the liquid exuding from the figs and the amount will depend on how ripe they are. It is therefore impossible to be precise about cooking times. Check periodically by pressing the centre with a finger to gauge whether the frangipane is set firm. Remove from the oven.

Put the honey into a pan and heat gently to liquefy. Brush the top of the figs with it.

SERVING

Serve the tart warm, with spoonfuls of Greek yogurt, whipped cream or crème fraîche.

APRICOT COMPOTE TARTE FINE

Dried apricots are never really that dry when you buy them in plastic packets and do not require lengthy rehydration. However, you do need to make the soaking liquid quite sweet or risk the natural sugars in the fruit being leached out.

This is one of those rare occasions when it is suggested you make your puff pastry. In fact a more accurate description is flaky, for it is butter-rich, light and crisp. It also rises nicely, if not quite as spectacularly as classic puff. It takes time — mainly because of the need to refrigerate between rollings — and a bit of effort, but the result justifies both. If pressed for time, though, do not hesitate to use ready-made.

INGREDIENTS (FOR 8)

115g/4oz caster sugar
1tbsp jasmine tea
450g/1lb apricots
1 glass (150ml/¼pt) sweet
    white wine
yolk of 1 egg
1–2tsp cinnamon
3tbsp apricot jam
crème fraîche, double cream,
    clotted cream or vanilla
    ice-cream, to serve

FOR THE ROUGH PUFF PASTRY:
225g/8oz unsalted butter,
    chilled, plus more for
    greasing
450g/1lb plain flour, plus
    more for dusting
pinch of salt

PREPARATION

The day before: make 1.1 litres/2pt of sweet jasmine tea by putting the sugar and tea in a jug and pouring over boiling water. Stir to dissolve the sugar, leave to stand for 5 minutes and then pour through a sieve over the apricots in a bowl. Leave to soak for a minimum of 4 hours or preferably overnight.

Add the sweet white wine to the soaking apricots, put in a saucepan and bring to a boil. Lower the heat and simmer for 30 minutes. Strain through a sieve and leave the apricots to cool.

Transfer 140g/5oz of the butter from the refrigerator to the freezer and chill for 20 minutes. Then dice.

Sift the flour into a food processor. Add the butter dice and the pinch of salt and whizz briefly to a crumb texture. With the motor running, add 1–2 tablespoons of cold water through the feeder tube until the pastry balls. It is important to use the minimum amount of water. Clingwrap and put to rest in the refrigerator for 30 minutes.

Transfer to a floured surface and roll out into a rectangular strip roughly 2½ times longer than its width.

Cut the remaining butter into small dice and dot two-thirds of the rectangle, leaving a 2.5cm/1in strip clear around the edge with half of it. Fold one end to the middle and then the other end over that. Roll out to the same shape, fold as before, cling-wrap and refrigerate for 1 hour. Transfer to a floured surface and repeat the whole rolling, dotting and folding process, this time starting the rolling at right angles to the previous direction. If the butter starts to come through the surface, sprinkle with flour. Fold, wrap and refrigerate overnight.

About 40 minutes before you plan to serve: preheat the oven to 200°C/400°F/gas6. Lightly butter a non-stick Swiss roll tin. Roll the pastry to a rectangle about 1.5cm/½in thick and lay it in the tin.

Arrange the apricots down the centre, slightly overlapping and leaving a border of 2.5cm/1in. Brush the pastry border with beaten egg yolk and dust the apricots with cinnamon.

COOKING

Bake the tart for 20 minutes. In good time, melt the jam and brush the apricots with this as soon as the tart comes from the oven.

SERVING

Serve warm with crème fraîche, double cream or vanilla ice-cream. If you can get hold of clotted cream then this is arguably the nicest of all accompaniments.

LEMON SYRUP MACADAMIA BAKLAVA

Is it possible to visit the Middle East, even in one's head, and not taste baklava? If ever a sweetmeat deserved the description ubiquitous, this is it. Thin syrup-soaked pastries loaded with nuts pursue you from Morocco through Tunisia and Libya, smile coyly at you in Egypt, peer from behind a yashmak in Saudi Arabia and dance attendance upon your thick black coffee in Turkey. Eat enough of them and you will have a belly to rock and roll with a vengeance. That which is inevitable embrace, so succumb to sweet temptation with these lemony variants on the classic theme, which are filled with chopped macadamia nuts and brandy-soaked sultanas before being bathed in butter and baked until golden crisp. The Imam could not faint over them for reasons of religious observance but, if tempted, should console himself with the thought that the alcohol cooks out in the baking. Supermarkets sell frozen strudel dough, which is specified here in preference to the more usual filo. The redefinition is marginal, but enough to make a difference. The amount of lemon juice and zest in the syrup moderates the sweetness.

INGREDIENTS (MAKES ABOUT 40 PIECES)

225g/8oz sultanas
about 150ml/¼pt brandy
225g/8oz macadamia nuts
2tsp allspice
140g/5oz unsalted butter
4 sheets of strudel pastry

FOR THE LEMON SYRUP:
zest and juice of 2 lemons
350g/12oz caster sugar
1 cinnamon stick

PREPARATION

The day before: put the sultanas in a bowl, just cover with brandy and leave to soak for as long as you can. Ideally make this well ahead.

After the sultanas have soaked for at least 1 hour, put the nuts and allspice in a food processor and chop coarsely. Put in a bowl with the brandy-soaked sultanas and mix together with a spoon. Melt the butter over a low heat. Preheat the oven to 190°C/375°F/gas5. Brush whatever tin you are using with butter. You can lay the baklava rolls in parallel lines in a roasting pan or cut them in half to fit on a Swiss roll tin.

The strudel sheets are large rectangles. Cut one in half lengthwise and brush one half with butter. Spoon one-eighth of the mixture down the centre, leaving a 5cm/2in margin along the sides. Fold the margins over partly to cover the middle, then roll up from one side into a neat sausage. Lay this on the baking tray and brush with butter. Repeat with the other 7 half-sheets, packing them in tightly. If there is any butter left, pour it over. Make shallow cuts with a sharp knife to delineate 4cm/1½in portions.

COOKING

Bake for 50–60 minutes, until crisp and golden.

About 15 minutes into the cooking time, make the syrup: put all the ingredients in a small heavy pan with 300ml/½pt water. Bring to the boil, then simmer over the lowest possible heat for 30–40 minutes. Turn off and leave in the pan until the baklava are cooked.

Remove the baklava from the oven and immediately pour the syrup over them through a sieve. Leave to stand overnight at room temperature and do not cut until just before serving. Cut down through the existing portion marks.

SERVING

Serve as petits fours after dinner or mid-morning with coffee.

SAFFRON SULTANA CAKE

The glowing gold of the saffron makes this sponge visually appealing, while the brandy-plumped sultanas give a sophisticated flavour. The sponge is baked as a shallow cake, from which fingers are cut to serve with a fresh fruit salad of seedless grapes, oranges and grapefruit. It is also excellent for tea and can be baked as one would a Victoria sponge. If so, increase cooking time to 20–25 minutes.

INGREDIENTS

55g/2oz unsalted butter, chilled

125g/4$\frac{1}{2}$oz plain flour, plus more for dusting

pinch of salt

2tsp saffron powder

55g/2oz brandy-marinated sultanas (see page 187)

4 eggs

125g/4oz caster sugar

PREPARATION

Dice the chilled butter. Do not return to the refrigerator. Sift the flour with the pinch of salt and the saffron powder.

Put some water in saucepan of a size that will allow a large heatproof mixing bowl to sit on top of it. Bring to the boil, then lower to a simmer.

Drain the sultanas and toss in plain flour to coat evenly and reserve.

Preheat the oven to 180°C/350°F/gas4. Line a 30x20x5cm/ 12x8x2in Swiss roll tin with non-stick baking paper.

Using an electric hand-held beater, whisk the eggs and sugar in the mixing bowl. Then place this over the saucepan of barely simmering water and continue to whisk for 10 minutes, until the mixture is thick and drops from the whisk in ribbons.

Add about one-third of the flour and fold in with a spatula. Then fold in one-third of the diced butter. Repeat this two-stage process three times, alternating flour then butter, stirring and folding until you have a smooth mass with the butter completely incorporated.

Finally fold in the sultanas and pour the batter into the lined Swiss roll tin.

COOKING

Bake for 6–8 minutes. Remove from the oven, put the tin on a wire cake rack and leave to cool for a few minutes. Then turn the sponge out on the rack. Pull off the baking paper and do not cut the sponge until completely cold.

SERVING

Serve as fingers, with the fruit salad of your choice.